American Book Company

The Standards Experts

Y0-ARU-302

Dear Educator,

Thank you for your interest in American Book Company's state-specific test preparation resources. Enclosed you will find the preview book and/or demonstration disk that you requested. We commend you for your interest in pursuing your students' success. Feel free to contact us with any questions about our books, software, or the ordering process.

Our Products Feature	**Your Students Will Improve**
Multiple-choice diagnostic tests	Confidence and mastery of subjects
Step-by-step instruction	Concept development
Frequent practice exercises	Critical thinking
Chapter reviews	Test-taking skills
Multiple-choice practice tests	Problem-solving skills

About American Book Company

American Book Company's writers and curriculum specialists have **over 100 years of combined teaching experience**, working with students from kindergarten through middle, high school, and adult education.

Our company specializes in **test preparation books and software** for high school graduation tests and exit exams. We currently offer test preparation materials for Alabama, Arizona, California, Florida, Georgia, Indiana, Louisiana, Maine, Maryland, Minnesota, Mississippi, Nevada, New Jersey, North Carolina, Ohio, Oklahoma, South Carolina, Tennessee, and Texas.

We also offer books and software for **middle school review and high school remediation**. The materials in the Basics Made Easy Series are aligned with the standards for the Iowa Test of Basic Skills and the Stanford 9 Achievement Test.

While some other book publishers offer general test preparation materials, our student workbooks and software are **specifically designed** to meet the unique requirements of **each state's exit exam** or graduation test. Whether the subject is language arts, math, reading, science, social studies, or writing, our books and software are designed to meet the standards published by the state agency responsible for the graduation test or exit exam. Our materials provide **no tricks or secret solutions** to passing standardized tests, just engaging instruction and practical exercises to help students master the concepts and skills they need.

While we cannot <u>guarantee</u> success, our products are designed to provide students with the concept and skill development they need for the graduation test or exit exam in their own state. We look forward to hearing from you soon.

Sincerely,

Joe Wood
Curriculum Specialist

PO Box 2638 ★ Woodstock, GA 30188-1383 ★ Phone: 1-888-264-5877 ★ Fax: 1-866-827-3240
Web Site: www.americanbookcompany.com ★ E-mail: contact@americanbookcompany.com

Maryland Government Standards Chart

Passing the Maryland High School Assessment in Government	
Chart of Standards	

The following chart correlates each question on the Diagnostic Test, Practice Test 1, and Practice Test 2 to the Government competency goals *standards and benchmarks published by the Maryland Department of Education*. These test questions are also correlated with chapters in *Passing the Maryland High School Assessment in Government*.

Chapter Number	Diagnostic Test Questions	Practice Test 1 Questions	Practice Test 2 Questions
Goal 1 Political Systems **The student will demonstrate an understanding of the historical development and current status of principles, institutions and processes of political systems.**			
Expectation 1.1 The student will demonstrate understanding of the structure and functions of government and politics in the United States.			
Indicator 1.1.1 The student will analyze historic documents to determine the basic principles of United States government and apply them to real world situations.			
1	1, 11, 29, 41	1, 15, 32, 40	
Indicator 1.1.2 The student will evaluate how the principles of government assist or impede the functioning of government.			
1, 2	4, 12, 24, 38, 44, 49, 52	6, 22, 45, 52	
Indicator1.1. 3 The student will evaluate roles and policies the government has assumed regarding public issues.			
3	13, 26, 39	24, 34, 41, 47	
Indicator1.1. 4 The student will explain roles and analyze strategies individuals or groups may use to initiate change in governmental policy and institutions.			
4	14, 15, 58	4, 17, 56	

Standards Chart

Chapter Number	Diagnostic Test Questions		Practice Test 1 Questions	Practice Test 2 Questions
Expectation 2 The student will evaluate how the United States government has maintained a balance between protecting rights and maintaining order.				
Indicator 1.2.1 The student will analyze the impact of landmark Supreme Court decisions on governmental powers, rights and responsibilities of citizens in our changing society.				
5	7, 21, 57		18	
Indicator 1.2.2 The student will analyze legislation designed to protect the rights of individuals and groups and to promote equity in American society.				
3	5, 6, 56		8, 54	
Indicator 1.2.3 The student will evaluate the impact of governmental decisions and actions that have affected the rights of individuals and groups in American society and/or have affected maintaining order and/or safety.				
5	34, 35		33, 37, 44, 58	
Indicator 1.2.4 The student will evaluate the principle of due process.				
6	22, 30, 46		5, 42, 53	
Indicator 1.2.5 The student will analyze elements, proceedings and decisions related to criminal and civil law.				
6	25, 54		25	

Maryland Government

Chapter Number	Diagnostic Test Questions	Practice Test 1 Questions	Practice Test 2 Questions
Goal 2 Peoples of the Nation and World The student will demonstrate an understanding of the history, diversity and commonality of the peoples of the nation and world, the reality of human interdependence and the need for global cooperation, through a perspective that is both historical and multicultural.			
Expectation 2.1 The student will evaluate the interdependent relationship of United States politics and government to world affairs.			
Indicator 2.1.1 The student will analyze economic, political, social issues and their effect on foreign policies of the United States.			
7	23, 43, 48	38, 51, 55	
Indicator 2.1.2 The student will evaluate the effectiveness of international alliances and organizations from the perspective of the United States.			
7	33	10, 29, 30, 31	
Expectation 2.2 The student will compare and evaluate the effectiveness of the United States system of government and various other political systems.			
Indicator 2.2.1 The student will analyze advantages and disadvantages of various types of governments throughout the world.			
	9, 27, 28	3, 16, 19	

Standards Chart

Chapter Number	Diagnostic Test Questions	Practice Test 1 Questions	Practice Test 2 Questions
Goal 3 Geography **The student will demonstrate an understanding of geographic concepts and processes to examine the role of culture, technology and the environment in the location and distribution of human activities throughout history.**			
Expectation 3.1 The student will demonstrate an understanding of the relationship of cultural and physical geographic factors in the development of government policy.			
Indicator 3.1.1 The student will evaluate demographic factors related to political participation, public policy and government policies.			
8	10, 18, 20, 47, 50	11, 12, 13, 49, 50	
Indicator 3.1.2 The student will evaluate the role of government in addressing land use and other environmental issues.			
8	2, 42	26, 48	
Indicator 3.1.3 The student will analyze the roles and relationships of regions on the formation and implementation of government policy.			
8	8, 31, 40	9, 14, 35, 43, 57	

Maryland Government

Chapter Number	Diagnostic Test Questions	Practice Test 1 Questions	Practice Test 2 Questions
Goal 4 Economics **The student will demonstrate an understanding of the historical development and current status of economic principles, institutions and processes needed to be effective citizens, consumers and workers.**			
Expectation 4.1 The student will demonstrate an understanding of economic principles, institutions and processes required to formulate government policy.			
Indicator 4.1.1 The student will evaluate how governments affect the answers to the basic economic questions of what to produce, how to produce and for whom to produce.			
9	3, 32	7, 23	
Indicator 4.1.2 The student will utilize the principles of economic costs and benefits and opportunity cost to analyze the effectiveness of government policy in achieving socio-economic goals.			
9	16, 53, 55	20, 21, 46	
Indicator 4.1.3 The student will examine regulatory agencies and their social, economic and political impact on the country, a region or on/within a state.			
9	19, 36, 51	28, 39	
Indicator 4.1.4 The student will evaluate the effectiveness of current monetary and fiscal policy on promoting full employment, price stability and economic performance.			
9	17, 37, 45	2, 27, 36	

Standards Chart

PASSING THE

MARYLAND HIGH SCHOOL ASSESSMENT

IN GOVERNMENT

DEVELOPED TO THE CORE LEARNING GOALS

Kindred Howard
Linda Rosencrance
Lisa Bryde
Laura Schaefer

American Book Company
PO Box 2638
Woodstock, GA 30188-1383
Toll Free: 1 (888) 264-5877   Phone: (770) 928-2834
Fax: (770) 928-7483   Toll Free Fax: 1 (866) 827-3240
www.americanbookcompany.com

Acknowledgements

The authors would like to gratefully acknowledge the formatting and technical contributions of Marsha Torrens.

Original graphics and cartoons are the expertise of the very talented Mary Stoddard.

This product/publication includes images from CorelDRAW 9 and 11 which are protected by the copyright laws of the United States, Canada, and elsewhere. Used under license.

Maryland High School Assessment in Government
Preface

Passing the Maryland High School Assessment in Government will help students who are learning or reviewing standards for the Government sections of the **Maryland High School Assessment Test in Government**. The materials in this book are based on the CORE Learning Goals as published by the Maryland Department of Education.

This book contains several sections:

    1) General information about the book itself

    2) A diagnostic test

    3) An evaluation chart

    4) Ten chapters that teach the concepts and skills needed for test readiness

    5) Two practice tests

Standards are posted at the beginning of each chapter, in the diagnostic and practice tests as well as in a chart included in the answer manual.

We welcome comments and suggestions about this book. Please contact the authors at

American Book Company
PO Box 2638
Woodstock, GA 30188-1383

Call Toll Free: (888) 264-5877
Phone: (770) 928-2834
Toll Free Fax: 1 (866) 827-3240

Visit us online at
www.americanbookcompany.com

Preface

About the Authors:

Lead Author:

Kindred Howard is a 1991 alumnus of the University of North Carolina at Chapel Hill, where he graduated with a B.S in Criminal Justice and national honors in Political Science. In addition to two years as a probation and parole officer in North Carolina, Mr. Howard has served for over twelve years as a teacher and writer in the fields of religion and social studies. His experience includes teaching students at both the college and high school level, as well as speaking at numerous seminars. He is the author of several books on US History and American Government and is currently completing both a M.A. in History from Georgia State University and a M.A. in Biblical Studies from Asbury Theological Seminary. Mr. Howard currently works as the Social Studies Coordinator for American Book Company and lives in Kennesaw, Georgia, with his wife and three children.

Contributing Authors:

Linda Rosencrance is the published author of several books as well as a respected journalist for nearly twenty years. In addition to various smaller publications, she has written for the *Boston Globe* and the *Boston Herald*. Ms. Rosencrance has written numerous articles and/or books on the topics of politics, crime, education and environment issues. She has a bachelor's degree from the University of Massachusetts, Boston, and is currently working as a reporter for a computer and technology newspaper in Framingham, Massachusetts.

Lisa Bryde is a 1986 graduate of Georgia State University where she graduated with a B.S. in Secondary English Education. She completed her M.A. in Curriculum Development and Design at the University of Georgia, where she is currently completing her Doctorate in Curriculum Development as well. In addition to fourteen years as a Language Arts teacher and writer in various fields of curriculum, Ms Bryde is also an advocate and speaker for Brain Based Learning. She currently serves as Director of Curriculum for one of the largest distance learning companies in the United States and lives in Lawrenceville, Georgia, with her husband, daughter and four dogs.

Laura Schaefer is a graduate of the University of Wisconsin and is the author of numerous articles and a contributing author to several educational publications. Her works include the book, *Man with Farm Seeks Woman with Tractor*. Ms. Schaefer currently lives in Madison, Wisconsin.

Maryland High School Assessment in Government
Diagnostic Test

The purpose of this diagnostic test is to measure your knowledge of Maryland government. This diagnostic test is based on the Standards for School Improvement in Maryland using the Core Learning Goals and adheres to the sample question format provided by the Maryland Department of Education.

General Directions:

1 Read all directions carefully.

2 Read each question or sample. Then choose the best answer

3 Choose only one answer for each question. If you change an answer, be sure to erase your original answer completely.

4 Certain questions are labeled "BCR." These are "Brief Constructed Response" questions and will require a written response of just a few sentences.

5 Certain questions are labeled "ECR." These are "Extended Constructed Response" questions and will require a longer, more deetailed written response.

6 After taking the test, you or your instructor should score it using the evaluation chart following the test. This will enable you to determine your strengths and weaknesses.

Session

1   **If the governor of Maryland vetoes a bill, how can it still pass?**   1.1.1

  A   It cannot pass without the governor's signature.

  B   Three-fourths of the house and Senate must vote to override the governor's veto.

  C   Three-fifths of the house and Senate must vote to override the governor's veto.

  D   The bill can go to the voters of Maryland in the form of a referendum where a simple majority of the voters can make the bill pass.

2   **A national supermarket chain wants to build a new store in a relatively undeveloped portion of a Maryland county. Some of the county's residents and political leaders are excited about the idea because it will create new jobs and contribute to the area's economic growth. However, others are upset and protest the proposal because they believe such construction will damage the environment and ruin the serenity of nearby residential neighborhoods. What question does this scenario present for the county's government?**   3.1.2

  F   how to best address reapportionment

  G   how to enforce Maryland's Clean Air Act

  H   how to settle disputes about land use

  J   how to promote equity

3   **An economic system in which the government owns the property and determines what and how much is produced is called a**   4.1.1

  A   market economy.

  B   command economy.

  C   traditional economy.

  D   mixed economy.

4   **Read the following quotation:**   1.1.2

> "Government is not the solution to the problem; government is the problem."
>
> – President Ronald Reagan

Reagan's statement was most likely made in support of

  F   limited government.

  G   popular sovereignty.

  H   federalism.

  J   confederation.

Use the following table to answer questions 5 and 6.

Civil Rights Act (1964)	prohibits segregation in public accommodations
Higher Education Act (1972)	guarantees equality between men and women in federally funded schools
Equal Pay Act (1963)	makes it illegal for employers to pay female employees less money than male employees who do "equal work" requiring "equal skill" under similar circumstances
Americans with Disabilities Act (1990)	guarantees equal opportunity for people with disabilities in public accommodations, employment, transportation, government services and telecommunications
Indian Education Act (1972)	addresses the educational needs of Native American students
Maryland Antidiscrimination Act	prohibits discrimination based on sexual orientation in employment, housing and/or public accommodations

5 Miriam is one of the top graduates from her high school and a star soccer player. Fortunately, because the colleges she is interested in attending all offer admittance to girls as well as boys and have intercollegiate women's soccer programs, Miriam has a number of choices. Which of the above laws is Miriam **most** benefiting from?   1.2.2

A   Civil Rights Act of 1964
B   Higher Education Act of 1972
C   Maryland Antidiscrimination Act
D   Indian Education Act of 1972

6 Which of the above laws **most** directly ensures the protection of African-American and Latino rights?   1.2.2

F   Equal Pay Act of 1963
G   Higher Education act of 1972
H   Civil Rights Act of 1964
J   Americans with Disabilities Act of 1990

GO ON

7 The Court's ruling in *Miranda v. Arizona* served to guarantee what right?   1.2.1

A   right to bear arms
B   right to eminent domain
C   right to an attorney
D   right to confession

8 Leaders in Baltimore are disturbed that the city's population has been declining.   3.1.3

BCR

- What actions can the city and/or state take to try to reverse this trend?
- Include details and examples to support your answer.

9 A confederation is <u>best</u> described as   2.2.1

A   a strong national government exercising authority over the states

B   a government in which individual states retain a great deal of sovereignty while being loosely unified as a nation

C   small countries allied with one another and prepared to defend one another against threats from other parts of the world.

D   a government which allows certain regions to practice some autonomy while remaining under the watchful eye of the central government.

10 Which of the following factors would be of <u>least</u> concern to a candidate for president?   3.1.1

F   past voting patterns
G   minority concerns
H   demographic factors
J   zoning ordinances

11 Which of the following statements offers evidence that the US government is a representative democracy?   1.1.1

A   The president is head of the executive branch.

B   Both men and women are eligible to run for public office.

C   Citizens directly elect congressmen and senators to be their voice in Washington, DC.

D   The Declaration of Independence states that all human beings are born with certain inalienable rights.

12 You are a representative of the United States visiting another country. While there, you are asked to deliver a speech to the nation's national assembly. They have asked you to explain to them what principle of government is most crucial to the United States' success: federalism, separation of powers, checks and balances or popular sovereignty.   1.1.2

ECR

- Choose one of these principles to present as the most important.
- Explain why it is the most important principle to US government.
- Include details and examples to support your answer.

13 Social Security is meant to provide which of the following?   1.1.3

A   educational benefits for minorities
B   job training for immigrants
C   retirement income for senior citizens
D   a clean environment

GO ON

Use the following cartoon to answer question number 14.

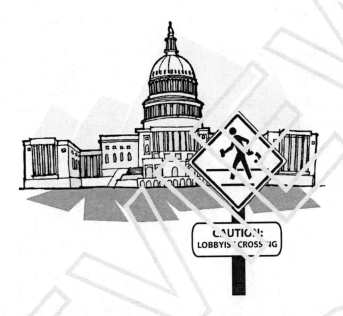

CAUTION:
LOBBYIST CROSSING

14 **What is the message of the cartoon?** 1.1.4

    F   Power is shared by two houses of Congress

    G   The importance of Federalism

    H   Congress is greatly influenced by interest groups.

    J   Lobbyists are banned from Congress.

15 **The citizens of a small Maryland town** 1.1.4
want the county to impose stricter
zoning guidelines. What would be the best
course of action for these citizens to take?

    A   recall state officials

    B   write letters to the EPA

    C   start a local petition to present to local leaders

    D   hire lobbyists to fight for their cause

GO ON

Congress Votes to Increase Social Security Tax

16 The above headline is addressing which of the following?   4.1.2

 F a decision to value economic security more than economic freedom

 G a decision to cut Social Security

 H a policy that will likely upset baby boomers

 J opportunity cost of retirement

17 The manner in which the government manages the economy by controlling the money supply is specifically called what?   4.1.4

 A fiscal policy

 B tax policy

 C monetary policy

 D socioeconomic policy

18 Which of the following <u>best</u> describes the Maryland General Assembly?   3.1.1

 F The General Assembly is comprised of 141 delegates, three from each voting district in Maryland.

 G The General Assembly is bicameral, having 47 senators and 141 delegates. Each voting district in Maryland elects one senator and three delegates.

 H The General Assembly is comprised of nineteen executive department heads who advise the governor and write new laws.

 J The General Assembly consists of a Senate led by the Senate president appointed by the governor and a House of Delegates led by the majority leader of the House.

19 A company wants to market a new kind of candy that it claims tastes great while containing only one-fourth the calories and sugar of other candies. What government agency will have to approve this product?   4.1.3

 A Occupational Safety and Health Administration (OSHA)

 B Environmental Protection Agency (EPA)

 C Food and Drug Administration (FDA)

 D Federal Communications Commission (FCC)

GO ON

20 **In the years following WWII, The US** 3.1.1
experienced a drastic population
BCR increase known as the "baby boom." Today,
these "baby boomers" are reaching the age
of retirement and growing older as average
US life spans increase.

- Describe how the nation's Social Security
  system and healthcare systems will be
  impacted by the "baby boom" generation.
- What solutions would you offer to these
  problems?
- Include details and examples to support your
  answers.

21 **Which court case overturned *Plessy v.*** 1.1.1
Ferguson?

A   *Brown v. Board of Education*

B   *Miranda v. Arizona*

C   *Alexander v. Holmes County*

D   *Gidean v. Wainwright*

22 ***Due process means that*** 1.2.4

F   a defendant cannot be denied legal
counsel.

G   a defendant's confession can never be
used against him/her in court.

H   a defendant cannot be jailed until
he/she has been convicted of a crime.

J   a search of a defendant's home cannot
be conducted unless the defendant is
present.

23 **During his first term, President** 2.1.1
Richard Nixon shocked most
Americans with his willingness to
acknowledge communist China and engage
in talks with both the Chinese and the Soviet
Union. Nixon's actions represented

A   diplomacy.

B   sanctions.

C   embargoes.

D   free trade.

24 **Which of the following is the best** 1.1.2
description of how the president is
elected?

F   Whichever candidate gets the most
popular votes is elected president.

G   Whichever candidate wins the majority
vote in the most states is elected president.

H   Whichever candidate wins the most
votes in the House of Representatives
is elected president.

J   Whichever candidate wins the majority
vote in the Electoral College is elected
president.

GO ON

Jury Acquits Murphy

Raleigh, NC — A jury acquitted James G. Murphy of murder charges on Tuesday after deliberating for two days. Upon interview, several of the jurors stated that the prosecution failed to show that Murphy was the only one with motive who could have committed the crime...

25 **The news article suggests that the jury found Murphy "not guilty" because the prosecution failed to**

   1.2.5

  A   prove its case beyond a reasonable doubt.

  B   show that its case was supported by a preponderance of evidence.

  C   observe due process

  D   suggest a motive for the crime.

26 **Which of these programs would the state government be most involved in?**

   1.1.3

  F   Medicare

  G   Medicaid

  E   Social Security

  I   EPA

GO ON

Use the following diagram to answer questions 27 and 28.

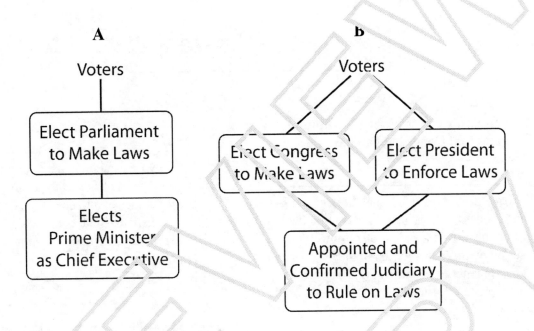

27 Which of the following statements is **true?** 2.2.1

A Diagram A depicts a model of government dominated by the legislature.

B Diagram A depicts a model of government in which the people directly elect their chief executive.

C Diagram A features a separation of powers in government.

D Diagram B is not based on popular sovereignty.

28 Which of the following is **true?** 2.2.1

F Diagram B features a democracy, while Diagram A features an authoritarian government.

G Diagram B is a parliamentary form of democracy.

H Diagram A is a parliamentary form of democracy.

J Diagram A is a federation, while diagram B is a confederation.

9

Session 2

29 The elastic clause of the Constitution states that Congress shall have the power —

1.1.1

> "To make all laws which shall be necessary and proper for carrying into execution the foregoing powers, and all other powers vested by this Constitution in the government of the United States, or in any department or officer thereof."

This clause gives Congress the right to

A override the president's decisions.

B overrule decisions of the Supreme Court when they conflict with the duties of Congress.

C assume powers not specifically stated in the Constitution if they are necessary for effectively carrying out Congress' stated responsibilities.

D make all laws regarding taxation.

30 Which of the following do defendants in both a criminal case and a civil case have in common?

1.2.4

F right to an attorney

G right to due process

H right to jury trial

J right to writ of habeas corpus

31

3.1.3

> "...No state shall make or enforce any law which shall abridge the privileges or immunities of citizens of the United States; nor shall any state deprive any person of life, liberty, or property, without due process of law . . ."
>
> the Fourteenth Amendment

The Fourteenth Amendment has which of the following effects?

A gives all people living in the US the right to vote

B strengthens segregation

C increases the power of state governments

D extends the Bill of Rights to the states

32 An economic system in which producers and consumers are free to produce and purchase what they want, property is privately owned and price is determined by demand is called a

4.1.1

F market economy.

G command economy.

H traditional economy.

J mixed economy.

10

GO ON

33 US reasons for wanting to help "developing nations" would include which of the following?   2.1.2

A the desire for political instability

B the continuing decline in economic globalization

C long-run increase in global economic and political stability

D the fact that the US is also a "developing country"

Use the following sample of a news story to answer questions 34 and 35.

Meredith Becomes First Black Admitted to Ole Miss After President Acts

Oxford, Miss — James Meredith finally took his place as the first Negro admitted to the University of Mississippi, but not until after President Kennedy authorized federal marshals to ensure that the Supreme Court's order to integrate the university was carried out...

34 The above news story shows that   1.2.3

F the president is responsible for enforcing federal laws.

G the Supreme Court has the power to enforce laws.

H the executive branch is responsible for universities.

J decisions of the Court require presidential approval before they become law.

35 Based on the news story, it is clear that   1.2.3

A states rarely abide by federal decisions without the president having to use force.

B the president and the Supreme Court rarely disagree.

C the Supreme Court must first make a law before the president enforces it.

D the Supreme Court is not responsible for enforcing federal law.

36 Which one of the following would most immediately concern the Environmental Protection Agency (EPA)?   4.1.3

F toxic waste

G bird flu

H trade restrictions

J unhealthy additives in foods

37 Which of the following best describes the government's fiscal policy?   4.1.4

A policies on taxing and spending

B policies on lending and producing

C policies that regulate the money supply

D policies regulating safety and health

38 The principle that some powers are delegated to the national government while others are reserved for the states is known as   1.1.2

J popular sovereignty.

G federalism.

H representative democracy.

J separation of powers.

GO ON

Use the following political cartoon to answer question number 39

39 What point is the above cartoon making about the US healthcare system? `1.1.3`

   A   Healthcare in the US is no good.

   B   US healthcare should cover animals.

   C   Healthcare is too expensive for many US citizens.

   D   People should buy insurance.

40 Since Maryland, Pennsylvania and New York all benefit from the Susquehanna River, each state is concerned with making sure the river remains clean and safe. `3.1.3`

   • Describe two or three ways these states can work together to address this regional interest.

   • Include details and examples to support your answer.

41 Which of the following principles is <u>not</u> mentioned in the Declaration of Independence? `1.1.1`

   A   egalitarianism

   B   federalism

   C   natural rights

   D   liberty

42 Which of the following likely concerns Maryland's government the least? `3.1.2`

   F   local decisions regarding land use

   G   economic development near and around the Chesapeake Bay

   H   enforcement of the Critical Areas Act

   J   contents of environmental impact statements in the Sun Belt

GO ON

43 The US has maintained an embargo against Cuba for over four decades because it is ruled by an anti-American, communist leader named Fidel Castro. Such an embargo is an example of what? 2.1.1

A diplomacy
B tariffs
C military action
D economic sanctions

Welfare Reform Bill Shot Down by President

44 The above article is an example of 1.1.2

F federalism at work.
G judicial review serving its intended purpose.
H executive orders.
J inefficiency sometimes caused by checks and balances.

45 The Maryland court system consists of four levels. Which of the following lists the courts in order from lowest to highest? 4.1.4

A District Court of Maryland, circuit court, court of special appeals, court of appeals
B circuit court, District Court of Maryland, court of appeals, court of special appeals
C circuit court, court of appeals, District Court of Maryland, court of special appeals
D District Court of Maryland, circuit court, court of appeals, court of special appeals

46 The Fourteenth Amendment establishes that 1.2.4

F due process guaranteed under the Constitution must be guaranteed by states.
G some powers are reserved for the states rather than the federal government.
H the president has the right to issue executive orders.
J states are not obligated to use grand juries.

47 As more and more citizens migrate to the South and West, these regions gain influence in 3.1.1

A the House of Representatives.
B the US Senate.
C the House of Delegates.
D the judicial branch of government.

48 Taxes placed on imports to help protect domestic markets are called 2.1.1

F free trade.   H subsidies.
G foreign trade.   J tariffs.

GO ON

49 Once appointed by the president, federal judges serve for life, until they retire or until they have to be removed for some wrongdoing.   1.1.2

ECR

- Discuss why federal judges are appointed rather than elected.

- Discuss how/if the people have any say in who serve as judges, whether directly or indirectly.

- Describe why you agree or disagree with judges being appointed rather than elected.

- Include details and examples to support your answers.

50 Which region of Maryland probably gets the greatest amount of funding for public services from the General Assembly?   3.1.1

F Eastern Shore
G Piedmont Plateau
H Mining Region
J Baltimore

51 A large factory is accused of failing to provide a safe working environment for its workers. What federal agency will investigate this case?   4.1.3

A Environmental Protection Agency (EPA)
B Food and Drug Administration (FDA)
C United States Department of Agriculture (USDA)
D Occupational Safety and Health Administration (OHSHA)

52 A Maryland county government decides to reorganize as a charter government. What are the next two required steps for the county to form a charter?   1.1.2

F A charter board in the county must draft a charter and have it approved by the county's voters.

G The state legislature must approve the county board's request to form a charter by a simple majority vote and then the county government must form a committee.

H The state Supreme Court issues an order on request of the county's district attorney mandating a charter reorganization for the county, then the state draws up the guidelines the county must follow.

J The governor issues an executive order formally requesting a county's reorganization as a charter government, then a charter committee appointed by the governor drafts the charter document.

53 The city government of Back River must decide how to spend the final $100,000 of its annual budget. After debate, the council votes to spend the money on new police equipment instead of renovations to the library or relandscaping the park. Which of the following represents the council's opportunity costs?   4.12

A the money spent on police equipment
B other areas in which the council spent money
C the fact that the city has no park
D the enjoyment citizens could have gotten from a renovated library

GO ON

54 If someone breaks a legal agreement, he/she could be sued for   1.2.5

   F   negligence.

   G   breach of contract.

   H   arbitration.

   J   a misdemeanor.

55 The lack of resources to obtain all of one's wants and/or needs is called   4.1.2

   A   economics.

   B   inequity.

   C   scarcity.

   D   opportunity cost.

56 Stricter immigration laws would <u>most likely</u> cause   1.2.2

   F   a sharp increase in the Latino population.

   G   an increase in political activism within the Latino community.

   H   unity amongst citizens on the immigration issue.

   J   an end to illegal immigration.

57 The exclusionary rule states which of the following?   1.2.1

   A   A defendant must be excluded from testifying against him/herself.

   B   Those who have been the victim of a violent crime are excluded from juries.

   C   Evidence seized illegally may not be used against a defendant at trial.

   D   Confessions made to law enforcement may not be used at trial.

58 At times in US history, third parties and/or independent candidates have been able to impact US politics to a certain degree; however, it is only the Republican and Democratic parties that traditionally dominate Congress and dominate candidates who win the presidency   1.1.4

BCR

- Describe why the US political system is dominated by two major parties.

- Describe some of the reasons third parties and independents have trouble overcoming the major parties in elections.

- Include details and examples to support your answers.

EVALUATION CHART FOR MARYLAND GOVERNMENT DIAGNOSTIC TEST

Directions: On the following chart, circle the question numbers that you answered incorrectly, and evaluate the results. These questions are based on the *Maryland Core Learning Goals and Indicators for Government*. Then turn to the appropriate chapters, read the explanations, and complete the exercises. Review other chapters as needed. Finally, complete the Post Test(s) to assess your progress and further prepare you for the **Maryland High School Assessment in Government**.

Note: Some question numbers will appear under multiple chapters because those questions require demonstration of multiple skills.

Chapter	Diagnostic Test Question(s)
Chapter 1: The United States Government	4, 11, 12, 24, 29, 38, 41, 44, 49
Chapter 2: Maryland State and Local Governments	1, 18, 45, 52
Chapter 3: The Government and Public Issues	5, 6, 13, 26, 36, 39, 56
Chapter 4: The Citizen's Role in Government	14, 15, 19
Chapter 5: Government Action and Civil Rights	21, 34, 35, 57
Chapter 6: Criminal and Civil Law	22, 25, 30, 46, 54
Chapter 7: The United States and World Affairs	7, 9, 23, 27, 28, 33, 43, 48
Chapter 8: Geography and Government	2, 3, 10, 20, 31, 40, 42, 47, 50
Chapter 9: Government and Economics	3, 16, 17, 32, 37, 51, 53, 55, 56
Chapter 10: Answering BCR and ECR Questions	8, 12, 20, 40, 49, 53

GOVERNMENT

Chapter 1
The United States Government

This chapter addresses the following expectation(s) from **Core Learning Goal 1 Political Systems**

Expectation 1.1	The student will demonstrate understanding of the structure and functions of government and politics in the United States. *Indicators 1.1.1 and 1.1.2*

1.1 HISTORICAL INFLUENCES ON US GOVERNMENT

In 1788, the United States ratified the US Constitution and established its new government. Long before that, however, earlier governments laid a foundation for the Founding Fathers to build on. The ancient Greeks practiced **democracy**, a form of government where the people rule collectively by voting and voicing their opinions on issues. Later, the ancient Romans modified this concept by forming a *republic*. Unlike a direct democracy in which all qualified citizens vote on laws and public policies, in a republic elected representatives, usually from an elite upper class, vote on the people's

Roman Senate

behalf. The Founding Fathers formed a government that ultimately combined elements of both. Although they intended to set up a republic ruled by an "enlightened" elite, it soon became apparent that they had established a **representative democracy** in which white men (and later women and minorities as well) from any class and background could be democratically elected to represent the people in Congress and local assemblies.

The United States Government

PRECOLONIAL INFLUENCES

Signing of Magna Carta

Even before the end of the Middle Ages (period of history dating from the 5th to the 16th centuries AD), England felt the first rumblings of **limited government**. This is government that is limited in how much it can interfere in the private lives of citizens and must, itself, obey a set of laws. These laws are usually in the form of a written document. In 1215, a group of English nobles forced King John I to sign such a document. Known as the **Magna Carta** or "Great Charter," it granted nobles (upper class Englishmen) various legal rights and prevented the King from imposing taxes without the consent of a council. This idea of a council eventually gave birth to the British *Parliament*. Originally formed in the 13th century, Parliament came to be comprised of two houses. The upper house, known as the House of Lords, consisted of appointed noblemen. The lower house, known as the House of Commons, was made up of elected officials and provided English citizens a voice in their national government. Parliament established an example of representative democracy that greatly influenced the models of government that arose in the British colonies.

In 1689, Parliament gained additional power as a result of the **English Bill of Rights**. Under the English Bill of Rights, the monarch could not interfere with Parliamentary elections, nor could he/she impose taxes without Parliament's consent. It also granted citizens the right to a speedy trial, forbade cruel and unusual punishment and granted citizens the right to petition the government. The US Constitution eventually guaranteed such rights as well.

English government was also limited by **common law**. First established during the Middle Ages, common law is law based on tradition or past court decisions, rather than on a written statute. Today, the idea of relying on past legal decisions where no formal statute (written law) exists is an important aspect of the US legal system.

Iroquois Indians

Europeans were not the only ones to influence later ideas about colonial and US government. In the late 1500s, the Iroquois tribes of what is today the northeast United States agreed to stop fighting amongst themselves and banded together to form the **Iroquois League**. This union served to greatly strengthen the Iroquois and made them the dominant tribe among eastern Native American peoples.

COLONIAL INFLUENCES

Established in 1619, Virginia's **House of Burgesses** was the first body of elected officials in the English colonies. Although only white males who owned property were permitted to vote, it demonstrated a belief among colonists that citizens should have a voice and established representative government in the colonies.

Benjamin Franklin

In New England, the first efforts at self-government were defined in the **Mayflower Compact**. The Puritan settlers at Plymouth drafted this document while still on board the *Mayflower* (the ship that brought them to Massachusetts). It established an elected legislature and asserted that the government derived its power from the people of the colony. It also recognized the colonists' desire to be ruled by a local government, rather than England. More than a hundred years later, in 1754, a group of colonial representatives met in Albany, New York at the outset of the French and Indian War (war fought between Great Britain and France for control of North America) to discuss how the British colonies might be better unified for waging war against France and its Native American allies. It was there that one of the delegates, Benjamin Franklin, proposed the **Albany Plan of Union**. Franklin's plan called for a permanent union of the colonies under one representative government and was modeled, in part, after the Iroquois League. Although the colonies rejected the plan, Franklin's proposal provided a model of unity that later influenced the framers of the Constitution.

THE DECLARATION OF INDEPENDENCE

In May 1775, the Second Continental Congress assembled to discuss how to deal with the outbreak of fighting between the colonies and Great Britain. The following year, in June 1776, delegates to the assembly declared independence from England and appointed a committee to prepare a statement outlining the reasons for this separation. One of the committee's members, a young delegate named Thomas Jefferson, drafted the statement. Jefferson was a man greatly influenced by the *Enlightenment* and the ideas of John Locke. The Enlightenment was a time that featured revolutionary ideas in philosophy and political thought. Locke was one of the most noted political philosophers to arise out of this period. His thoughts on government challenged the old view that monarchs possess a

Thomas Jefferson

God-given right to rule with citizens obligated to obey. Locke believed that people were born with certain **"natural rights"** that no government could morally take away. These rights include life, liberty and property. He also advocated what is often referred to as *social contract theory*. According to this philosophy, there is an implied contract between government and citizens. Citizens are born with freedom and rights. However, for the good of society, people agree to give up certain freedoms and empower governments to maintain order. Locke believed that the right to govern came from the people and if a government failed to fulfill its proper role, then that government should be replaced. Many colonial leaders used his views to justify the American Revolution.

The United States Government

In CONGRESS, July 4, 1776.

The unanimous Declaration of the thirteen united States of America,

On July 4, 1776, the delegates to the Second Continental Congress formally adopted the **Declaration of Independence**. The document echoed many of the principles put forth by Locke and others. Appealing to the belief that governments get their power from the people, the Declaration of Independence proclaimed that the United States of America was forevermore a free nation. It also asserted the principle of **egalitarianism** (the idea that all men are created equal) and proclaimed that men are born with certain **"unalienable rights"** (natural rights that government cannot take away. Often, they are also referred to as *inalienable rights*). Among these rights are "life, liberty and the pursuit of happiness." Claiming that Great Britain had failed to fulfill its duty to respect and uphold these rights, the Declaration of Independence concludes with a list of complaints against the king and asserts the colonies' right to declare independence.

Sadly, it was not until many years later that minorities and women began to enjoy the same rights as white men.

THE ARTICLES OF CONFEDERATION

Once the colonies declared independence, they became individual states. As such, they quickly drew up their own state constitutions (documents that lay out the laws and principles of a government). However, they also needed a national body of laws. Cautious about giving too much power to a central government, Congress drafted the **Articles of Confederation**. Finally ratified in 1781, this document did not give enough power to the federal (national) government for it to lead effectively. In order for any law passed by Congress to be final, at least nine of the 13 states had to agree. Since the states often had different interests, such agreement was rare. Also, the Articles did not grant Congress the power to impose taxes. The federal government had to *ask* the states for money. As you might imagine, this was not very effective and made it practically impossible to administer the government or provide for a national defense. Due to an economic crisis that engulfed the new nation after the Revolutionary War and a series of other challenges, it became evident that a stronger central government was needed. In 1787, leaders called a convention to revise the Articles of Confederation. Soon after gathering, however, the representatives from almost every state (only Rhode Island did not send delegates) decided to do away with the Articles and draft a new document altogether.

Practice 1.1 Historical Influences on US Government

1. A form of government in which citizens democratically elect officials to make decisions on their behalf is known as what?

    A. direct democracy

    B. limited government

    C. representative democracy

    D. common law

2. What document established the principle of *limited government* during the middle ages?

   A. the United States Constitution

   B. the Magna Carta

   C. the Declaration of Independence

   D. the Iroquois League

3. List and define some of the principles on which the Declaration of Independence is based.

1.2 THE UNITED STATES CONSTITUTION

DEBATE AND COMPROMISE

CONSTITUTIONAL CONVENTION

All the delegates in attendance at the *Constitutional Convention* agreed that change was necessary. However, how the national government should be reorganized was a matter of much debate. As a result, a number of compromises (decisions reached as a result of disagreeing parties being willing to give up a little of what they want) emerged. Edmund Randolph and James Madison of Virginia introduced the *Virginia Plan*. They proposed a federal government made up of three branches: a legislative branch to make the laws, an executive branch to enforce the laws, and a judicial branch to make sure that the laws were administered fairly. For the legislative branch, the Virginia Plan called for two houses with representatives from each state. In each house, the number of representatives per state would be determined by population. The greater a state's population, the more representatives it would have. Larger states loved the idea, but smaller states hated it because they would be left with less representation. As a result, one of New Jersey's delegates proposed the *New Jersey Plan*. Like the Virginia Plan, it also called for three branches of government, but it wanted the legislative branch to consist of only one house with each state getting a single vote. In the end, the delegates decided on a compromise. It became known as the **Great Compromise** or the *Connecticut Plan*, because it was proposed by Roger Sherman of Connecticut. It established a legislative branch with two houses. One house, called the *House of Representatives*, would be elected directly by the people and each state granted a certain number of seats based on population. The other house, called the *Senate*, would be elected by state legislatures with each state having two senators, regardless of population. Together, the two houses would comprise Congress.

Slavery also proved to be a point of contention. Northern states had fewer slaves and argued that, since slaves were not voting citizens, they should not be counted as part of the population. Southern states, however, had far more slaves and wanted to count them. The answer to this question was important because it affected how many representatives each state would have in Congress. Again, a compromise was reached. It was known as the **Three-fifths Compromise** because it stated that each slave would count as "three-fifths of a person." In other words, for every five slaves, a state would be credited for having three people. Meanwhile,

The United States Government

Northerners who opposed the slave trade agreed to allow it to continue for twenty years, after which time Congress could impose regulations. This was important to Southerners who insisted that their economy could not survive without the slave trade.

Although the new document was an amazing improvement from the Articles of Confederation, it was not without controversy. A number of states refused to ratify it, claiming it did not do enough to guarantee the rights of citizens. Finally, in late 1788, the last of the nine states needed approved the Constitution once Congress agreed to consider a number of amendments protecting civil liberties (Maryland was the seventh state to ratify the Constitution). Only North Carolina and Rhode Island held off until after these amendments had actually been submitted to Congress. When Congress met in 1789, one of its first orders of business was to pass the **Bill of Rights**. It consists of the first ten amendments (additions) to the Constitution and stems from many of the principles expressed in the Declaration of Independence.

FEDERALISTS VS. ANTI-FEDERALISTS

The controversy surrounding the new Constitution concerned what role and powers the national government should have. Many favored the Constitution because they believed that the United States needed a strong federal government with a powerful president at its head. Others opposed the Constitution because they feared that a powerful federal government would trample on their rights. Because of the debate, political leaders split into opposing factions. A faction is a group of people who are bound by a common belief or in a common cause,

Alexander Hamilton   Thomas Jefferson

usually against another group bound by an opposing belief/cause. The faction that favored a strong central government and supported the Constitution was called the *Federalists*. Among their leaders were Alexander Hamilton, James Madison and John Jay (first chief justice of the Supreme Court). The faction that opposed them and wanted to see stronger state governments was called the *Anti-federalists* (author of the Declaration of Independence, Thomas Jefferson, was an Anti-federalist). Federalists had a **loose interpretation** of the Constitution. They believed that the *elastic clause* (also known as the *"necessary and proper"* clause) of the Constitution allowed the federal government to take certain actions not specifically stated so long as such actions were deemed necessary for carrying out the government's constitutional responsibilities. By contrast, Anti-federalists held to a **strict interpretation**. They believed the federal government could only do what the Constitution specifically said. The Anti-federalists feared that the central government would become too powerful and infringe on the rights of citizens. Eventually, with the support of men like George Washington, Alexander Hamilton and John Adams, the Federalist view won. Anti-federalists did succeed, however, in securing the Bill of Rights.

> The *elastic clause* of the US Constitution states that Congress shall have the power:
>
> *"To make all laws which shall be necessary and proper for carrying into execution the foregoing powers, and all other powers vested by this Constitution in the government of the United States, or in any department of officer thereof."*
>
> **In other words, Congress can pass the laws it needs to in order to carry out its constitutional responsibilities.**

22

PRINCIPLES OF THE CONSTITUTION

US Capitol

The Founding Fathers drafted the Constitution based on certain key principles:

Consent of the governed: The Constitution opens with the Preamble (sentence stating the intent of the document) that begins, "*We the people...*" Like the Declaration of Independence, the Constitution makes it clear that the right of the government to rule and the powers the government possesses comes from the free consent of the people it governs. Thus, the people have the right to elect and/or replace their leaders.

Majority rule: Although the Founding Fathers had reservations about unlimited democracy and preferred that the nation's leaders come from the more educated classes, they still believed that these leaders should be elected, either directly or indirectly, according to the will of the majority. As a result, they established a government based on **popular sovereignty**, in which the people would choose their representatives, at least in the House of Representatives, by democratic elections.

Limited government: One of the most important principles of the Constitution is the idea of limited government. As stated earlier this is the idea that government is restrained by laws and is restricted in how much it may interfere in the private affairs of citizens. So important was this principle to people in the US after the revolution, that many refused to support the Constitution until a bill of rights was added placing restrictions on the government and guaranteeing the rights of citizens.

Separation of powers: In order to prevent any one leader or branch from becoming too powerful, the framers divided powers among three branches of government (legislative, executive, and judicial). To make sure that no one branch tried to use its authority to overpower the others the Constitution also included a system of **checks and balances**. In other words, although one branch might enjoy a certain power, another branch can still "check" or "balance" its power if need be. For example: Congress has the power to propose and pass bills that become laws. The president, however, has the authority to "check" this power by vetoing (rejecting) the bill Congress passes, thereby preventing it from becoming a law. In turn, if Congress has enough votes, it can override the veto (voting to ignore the president's rejection) in which case, the bill becomes law anyway. This is just one example of how checks and balances work.

23

The United States Government

Federalism: Federalism is when two levels of government share power. In the United States, the national and state governments each have authority, with the national government's being supreme. Certain powers belong to the federal government (negotiating treaties, declaring war, establishing foreign trade, etc.) and some are given to the states (regulating public schools and local governments, deciding how elections will be run, etc.). A few are shared by both (i.e., the authority to build roads or impose taxes). Powers directly given to the national government by the Constitution are called *delegated powers.* Powers "not restricted by the Constitution, nor delegated to the US government" are called *reserved powers* because they are "reserved" for the states. Finally, powers that are shared by both the states and the national government are called *concurrent powers.* Both federal (national) and state governments must adhere to the **rule of law**. That is, they must operate within the guidelines of the US Constitution and, in the case of state governments, the state constitution as well.

Supreme Court in Session

Flexibility: The representatives to the Constitutional Convention wanted to ensure that the Constitution would last a long time and remain relevant to changing circumstances. Therefore, they provided a process by which it could be *amended.* An **amendment** is simply a change to the Constitution that is added later. There are two ways that amendments may be added to the Constitution. First, if two-thirds of both houses of Congress vote in favor of a change it is then presented to the states. If three-fourths of the states approve the proposed amendment then it is added to the Constitution. The second way that an amendment can be added is when two-thirds of the states call for a *constitutional convention.* Any amendments adopted by the convention must then be ratified by three-fourths of the states in order to become part of the Constitution. Amazingly, in its over 200 year history, the Constitution has only been amended 27 times. Due to the fact that it tends to emphasize principles and leaves room for interpretation and debate, the document has proved to be flexible and able to adjust to changing times. For this reason, it has often been referred to as a **"living document."**

PROS AND CONS OF US GOVERNMENT

Separation of powers, checks and balances and *limited government* are all principles that help to ensure that the liberty of all US citizens remains secure. As a result, our government is able to function with stability, unconcerned with any serious threat of armed rebellion or civil war. At the same time, the peaceful way in which power is transferred from outgoing leaders to incoming ones is all but unheard of in many nations around the world. However, these same principles sometimes hinder our government as well. While separation of powers might help prevent tyrannical leadership, it also means that the government sometimes performs inefficiently. Important laws are often bogged down in debate or disputes between branches of government. Federalism sometimes means that states and the federal government are unable to work together on certain issues. The fact that officials are elected means that they sometimes act to secure votes rather than do what is truly in the best interest of the people. As you can see, the principles on which the US Constitution is founded both serve to assist and impede effective government.

24

Chapter 1

Practice 1.2   The United States Constitution

1. The fact that even Congress, the president and the courts are bound by the Constitution and public officials are limited in how much they may interfere in the lives of citizens is evidence of which of the following principles?

   A.   popular sovereignty
   B.   limited government
   C.   federalism
   D.   democracy

2. The president appoints a promising young judge to the United States Supreme Court. However, to ensure that the appointee is qualified, the US Senate must first confirm (approve) the nomination. This is an example of what?

   A.   checks and balances
   B.   judicial review
   C.   legislative process
   D.   impeachment

3. The fact that the Constitution delegates some powers to the federal government while reserving other powers for the states is evidence that the US government is based on:

   A.   republicanism
   B.   democracy
   C.   separation of powers
   D.   federalism

1.3 THE GOVERNMENT ESTABLISHED BY THE CONSTITUTION

THE PREAMBLE AND ARTICLE I (THE LEGISLATIVE BRANCH)

The first sentence of the US Constitution is known as the *Preamble*. It serves to explain the purpose and intent of the document. It reads as follows:

> *"We the people of the United States, in order to form a more perfect union, establish justice, insure domestic tranquillity, provide for the common defense, promote the general welfare, and secure the blessings of liberty to ourselves and our posterity, do ordain and establish this Constitution for the United States of America."*

Congressional Debate

The Preamble is followed by three articles that establish the three branches of US government. *Article I* establishes the **legislative branch**, known as Congress. It is the role of the legislative branch to make the laws. Congress consists of two houses. Population determines how many representatives each state has in the **House of Representatives**. The greater a state's population, the more representatives that state has. Voters elect representatives to the House every two years. Once in office, these representatives then elect a **speaker of the House** (usually from the majority party) to preside over the House of Representatives.

The United States Government

Speaker of the House
Rep. Nancy Pelosi

Sen. Robert Byrd
President Pro Tempore
of the Senate

The second house is the **Senate**, which is comprised of two senators from each state. Originally, state legislatures rather than the people elected senators. However, in 1913, the Seventeenth Amendment changed this. Now, citizens directly elect US senators who serve six year terms. Under Article I / Section 3, one-third of the sitting senators are elected every two years. States usually stagger senatorial elections (make sure that their two senators are elected in different election years) so as to always have at least one experienced senator in Congress at all times. The senator who has represented a particular state in Congress the longest is referred to as that state's "senior senator," while the senator who has served less time is referred to as the "junior senator." The Senate is presided over by the vice president, however, there is also a **president pro tempore** (also known as the president of the Senate). This person is usually the most senior member of the majority party and is the highest ranking member of the Senate. He/she presides over the Senate in the vice president's absence.

POWERS AND LIMITATIONS OF CONGRESS

The Constitution grants each house of Congress certain powers and responsibilities. Some powers are shared by both houses. Others belong to one house, but not the other. For instance, both houses must approve a bill (a proposed law) before it can become a law (a rule which society is legally bound to uphold and abide by). On the other hand, only the House of Representatives may introduce tax bills or impeach public officials, while only the Senate has the power to block or confirm presidential appointments (people the president nominates to fill cabinet positions, seats on the federal courts, or other public offices) and ratify treaties. Below are some of the powers given to one or both houses of Congress and limitations specifically stated in the Constitution.

President George W. Bush

POWERS:

1. Power to *impeach* (charge with wrongdoing while in office) public officials.

2. Power to try impeachment cases and decide the guilt or innocence of impeached public officials.

3. Confirm (accept) or reject presidential appointments.

4. Ratify or reject treaties with foreign nations.

5. Power to propose taxes and means of raising revenue.

6. Introduce bills and pass new laws and/or resolutions.

7. Power to raise revenue in the form of taxes etc. for the purpose of maintaining a national defense and the general welfare of the US.

8. May borrow money and regulate foreign and interstate trade.

9. Authority to coin money, establish rules by which foreign immigrants become citizens, establish bankruptcy laws, post offices, and provide copyrights and patents protecting artists and inventors.

10. May declare war and maintain a national military force.

26

LIMITATIONS:

1. Congress cannot suspend *Writ of Habeas Corpus*. This is the right of an arrested person to go before a judge within a reasonable amount of time to determine if their incarceration is justified. Congress may not suspend this right except in cases of rebellion, invasion, or to ensure public safety.

2. Congress may not pass "bills of attainder" which are legislative acts convicting people of a crime without a trial.

Vice President Cheney

3. Congress may not establish *ex post facto* laws (laws that make some past activity illegal, even though it was not illegal at the time) For instance, if the government established a law making profanity on television illegal, it could not prosecute people for using profanity on TV prior to the law being passed.

4. Congress may not grant "titles of nobility." Sorry, but no matter what you do, Congress cannot name you the *Duke* or *Duchess of Maryland*.

5. Congress is limited in what kinds of taxes and duties it may establish and how it may govern trade.

ARTICLE II (THE EXECUTIVE BRANCH)

Article II establishes the **executive branch** of government to enforce the laws. The **president of the United States** serves as the chief executive of this branch and the nation's head of state (leader). Under Article II / Section 2, the president is elected to office by the **Electoral College**. This is a body of delegates that meets every four years solely to elect the president and the **vice president**. Originally, the vice president was simply whoever had the second highest number of votes in the Electoral College. However, in 1804, the Twelfth Amendment changed this by stating that the delegates to the Electoral College are to cast separate votes for the two offices. Each state's delegation in the Electoral College equals its number of representatives and senators in Congress. Today, this body serves as more of a formality since delegates' votes are predetermined

Al Gore

in a general election. Whichever presidential candidate wins the most votes in a particular state is awarded *all* of that state's votes in the Electoral College (called *electoral votes*). For example, based on the 2000 US Census (official US population count that is conducted every ten years) the state of Maryland has 10 electoral votes. Let's say Randolph and Helen are facing one another in a presidential election. After months of heavy campaigning in Maryland, Randolph barely wins with 51% of the state's vote over Helen's 49%. As a result, Randolph gets all 10 of Maryland's electoral votes even though almost half the state voted for Helen. Under the Constitution, it is the presidential candidate who wins the majority of electoral votes, rather than individual votes (called the *popular vote*) who is elected president. If, however, no candidate wins a majority of electoral votes, then the election is decided by the House of Representatives. This has happened twice: 1800 and 1824,. Usually, the winner in the Electoral College is also the winner of the popular vote. However, a few times in history this has not been the case. Most recently, this occurred in 2000 when Democrat Al Gore actually won the popular vote, but Republican George W. Bush won the electoral vote. Under the Constitution, it was Bush, not Gore, who was elected.

The United States Government

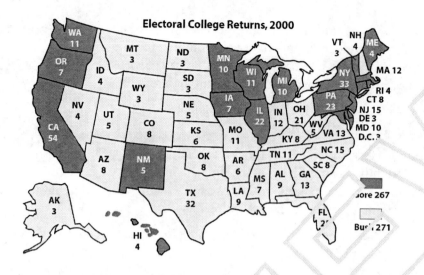

Electoral College Returns, 2000

ELECTORAL COLLEGE MAP

WA 11, OR 7, CA 54, NV 4, ID 4, MT 3, WY 3, UT 5, AZ 8, CO 8, NM 5, ND 3, SD 3, NE 5, KS 6, OK 8, TX 32, MN 10, IA 7, MO 11, AR 6, LA 9, WI 11, IL 22, MS 7, AL 9, TN 11, KY 8, IN 12, MI 10, OH 21, WV 5, GA 13, SC 8, NC 15, VA 13, PA 23, NY 33, VT 3, NH 4, ME 4, MA 12, RI 4, CT 8, NJ 15, DE 3, MD 10, D.C. 3, FL 25, AK 3, HI 4

Gore 267

Bush 271

Once elected, the president and vice president are then inaugurated (swear an oath to uphold the duties of their respective office and the Constitution) and serve four year terms. Although the Constitution did not originally place limits on how many terms a president may serve, none served more than two terms until 1940. That year, Franklin Delano Roosevelt broke tradition and became the only president in history elected to a third term (he was elected four times). Later, in 1951, the *Twenty-second Amendment* limited presidents to no more than two terms.

Franklin D. Roosevelt

RESPONSIBILITIES OF THE PRESIDENT AND VICE PRESIDENT

The Constitution lists the qualifications for president in Article II / Section 5 and defines his/her powers and responsibilities in Article II / Sections 3 – 4.

POWERS OF THE PRESIDENT:

1. The president is to serve as "commander in chief" of the nation's military. In other words, he/she is the top military commander.

2. The president is responsible for negotiating treaties with other nations (treaties must be ratified by the Senate before they are official).

3. He/She appoints public officials (i.e., heads of federal departments and federal judges) which must be approved by the Senate.

4. The president is the head of the executive branch and is ultimately responsible for enforcing federal laws.

As in the case of Congress, the Constitution also takes steps to make sure that the president is bound by the rule of law. Article II / Section 4 states that the president may be **impeached** (charged with criminal behavior) by the House of Representatives if he/she is suspected of treason, bribery, or "other high crimes and misdemeanors." If this occurs, the president then stands trial in the Senate. If two-thirds of the Senate finds him/her guilty, then he/she is removed from office.

The vice president is also part of the executive branch and he/she presides over the Senate. He/she has no vote, however, unless there is a tie; in which case the vice president casts the tie-breaking vote. Article II / Section 1 says that if the president cannot fulfill his/her term in office, then the vice president shall assume the duties of the presidency. This wording was originally confusing, however, because it was not clear whether or not this meant that the vice president became president, or if it merely meant that he/she remained vice president but assumed the responsibilities of the president. In 1967, the *Twenty-fifth Amendment* settled this issue by plainly stating that, if the president could not fulfill his/her term, then the vice president would become the president.

**Secretary of State
Condoleeza Rice**

THE PRESIDENT'S CABINET

One part of the executive branch that has evolved into an important part of US government but is not officially established by the Constitution is the **president's cabinet**. The cabinet evolved over time and consists of the heads of various federal departments. It serves as the president's official panel of advisors and representatives regarding certain issues. For instance, the secretary of state advises the president on foreign affairs and often acts as the president's representative in dealing with leaders of foreign governments. The secretary of defense presides over the defense department and, as a civilian, has authority over the nation's military commanders and helps form and implement policies regarding the armed forces. The attorney general is the nation's top law

**Attorney General
Alberto Gonzalez**

enforcement official and, as head of the justice department, presides over agencies like the FBI. These are just a few examples of officials who serve on the president's cabinet. They are appointed by the president and must be approved by the Senate before they can take office. Usually, they serve until the president who appointed them leaves office; although it is not uncommon for some to resign sooner.

ARTICLE III (THE JUDICIAL BRANCH)

Article III creates the **judicial branch**. This branch consists of the federal court system with the Supreme Court acting as the highest court in the land. The role of the judicial branch is to make sure that laws are applied appropriately. Since Article III is somewhat vague about how this branch should be organized and what powers the Supreme Court shall hold, Congress passed the Judiciary Act of 1789 to establish both the federal court system and the authority of the Supreme Court.

Supreme Court Building

The United States Government

One of the most important powers of the judicial branch is not specifically granted by the Constitution, but rather was established by precedence in 1803. **Precedence** means a court uses past legal decisions to make rulings because the law is open to interpretation or there is no written statute. In 1801, Thomas Jefferson (an Anti-federalist) became president. However, just before leaving office, his predecessor, John Adams (a Federalist), appointed a number of federal judges. Although the Senate had confirmed these judges and Adams had signed their appointments, the documents making their appointments official had not yet been delivered when Jefferson took office. Fearing that Federalist judges might interfere with his plans, Jefferson refused to deliver the documents (commissions), preventing some of the judges from ever taking office. When several of the appointees challenged this move, the Supreme Court intervened to hear the case. In *Marbury v. Madison (1803)*, Chief Justice John Marshall stated

John Marshall

that the appointees were entitled to their commissions *but that the US Supreme Court did not have authority under the Constitution to force the president to issue them. In so doing, Marshall led the court in striking down part of the Judiciary Act of 1789 which gave such authority to the Court, thereby establishing the Court's authority of **judicial review**. Judicial review is the Courts' power to declare acts of Congress and/or state legislatures "unconstitutional." This means that even if Congress passes a law and the president signs it, the federal courts can still nullify the law by ruling that it violates the Constitution.

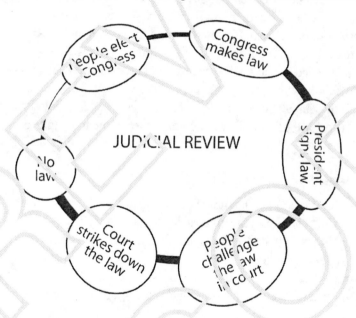

Unlike the president, vice president and members of the legislative branch, judges who serve in the judicial branch are not elected. Rather, they are **appointed** (given their position) by the president for life. The reason they are appointed rather than elected is so that they will be free to make their decisions based strictly on the law without having to worry about popular opinion or political pressures. The Supreme Court consists of nine judges, called *justices*. One justice serves as the *chief justice* (lead justice) while the other eight serve as *associate justices*. These justices serve as the highest court in the land and have appellate jurisdiction (the authority to review the decisions of lower courts) over all federal and state court cases. Under Article III / Section 2, the Supreme Court also has original jurisdiction (authority to hear a case first) over, "cases affecting ambassadors, other public ministers and consuls and those in which a state shall be a party."

Chapter 1

Underneath the Supreme Court are the US Court of Appeals, US District Courts and US Special Courts. In each case, judges who preside on these courts must be appointed by the president and **confirmed** (approved) by the US Senate before they take the bench.

Supreme Court Justices

U.S. Court System

UNITED STATES SUPREME COURT

Highest court in the nation which has appellate jurisdiction over all lower courts and original jurisdiction over cases affecting ambassadors, other public ministers and consuls, and those in which a state shall be a party. It may also hear cases appealed from state supreme courts.

UNITED STATES COURT OF APPEALS

Federal mid-level appellate court. Appellate jurisdiction over decisions rendered by the US District Courts and US Special Courts,.

US DISTRICT COURTS

Act as the federal court system's trial courts for both criminal and civil cases that involve the federal government or alleged violations of federal laws.

US SPECIAL COURTS

Have original jurisdiction over special kinds of cases (i.e., international trade).

Some cases are heard ONLY by federal courts rather than state courts. They include:

- cases over which the Supreme Court has original jurisdiction.
- cases that involve violations of a federal rather than a state law.
- cases concerning bankruptcies, patents and/or copyrights.
- civil suits brought against the US government.

The United States Government

Practice 1.3   The Government Established by the Constitution

1. Congress passes a new federal law making it illegal to call public officials "boneheads." The president gladly signs it. However, the Supreme Court nullifies the law by ruling that it violates citizens' First Amendment right to free speech. What power has the Court exercised?

   A.   the power to impeach
   B.   judicial appointment

   C.   judicial review
   D.   constitutional amendment

2. Which of the following BEST describes how the president of the United States is elected?

   A.   Whichever candidate wins the most individual votes becomes president.

   B.   Whichever candidate is elected by both houses of Congress becomes president.

   C.   Whichever candidate wins the most states becomes president.

   D.   Whichever candidate wins the majority of electoral votes becomes president.

3. What are some of the differences between the House of Representatives and the US Senate?

1.4 THE FEDERAL LEGISLATIVE PROCESS

CONGRESSIONAL COMMITTEES AND VOTING ON BILLS

HOW BILLS BECOME LAWS

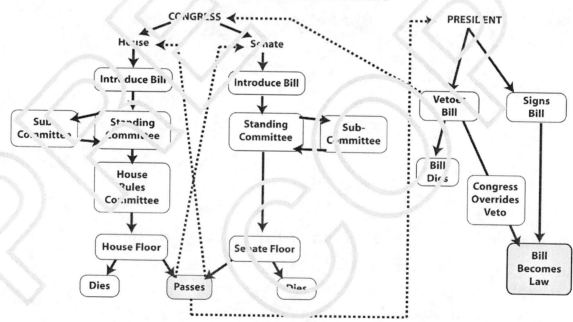

In order for a proposal (idea for a new law) to become a national law, it must first be introduced as a **bill** in either the House of Representatives or the US Senate. The president of the United States may submit bills to Congress for consideration, but they must be formally introduced by members of either the House or

Senate who support the president's proposal. In addition to the guidelines of the Constitution, a legislative process has evolved over time by which bills become laws. A key element in this process is the role of **committees**. These are panels within each house of Congress that are responsible for studying proposed bills and recommending to their respective house whether or not the bill should pass.

Once a bill makes it out of committee, it goes before the entire house for debate and a vote. The House of Representatives generally puts limits on how much time can be spent debating a bill. In the Senate, however, no such limits exist. Therefore, senators will sometimes attempt to stop a vote on bills they oppose by means of a **filibuster**. This is a strategy in which a senator will continue to talk until either the bill is withdrawn, or other senators can convince colleagues to vote "no." If, however, three-fifths of the senators present vote in favor of closing the debate, then the filibuster is ended and a vote can occur. This process is called **cloture.** If the majority in one house of Congress votes in favor of the bill, then it goes on to the other house. If the majority in that house also votes for the bill, then the bill is said to have "passed" both houses of Congress. If either house of Congress fails to pass a bill, then that bill will either have to be reintroduced (usually with changes) or "dies" without ever becoming a law. Bills that do pass both houses are sent to the president for his/her signature. If the president signs it, the bill becomes a law.

PRESIDENTIAL VETOS

Often, the president may *veto* a bill. A **veto** is when both houses of Congress pass a bill, but the president refuses to sign it. If this happens, the bill does not become law unless two-thirds of both the Senate and the House vote to override the president's veto. Occasionally, the president may exercise a *pocket veto.* Under the Constitution, the president has ten days (not counting Sundays) to either sign or veto legislation. If he/she does nothing, then the bill becomes law. The one exception is if Congress adjourns (ends its session) prior to the ten days expiring. If this happens and the president takes no action, then the legislation effectively dies. A **pocket veto** is when the president intentionally takes no action on a bill because he/she knows Congress is not in session, and the bill will die. He/she is said to "put the bill in his/her pocket."

Practice 1 : The Federal Legislative Process

1. A proposal that has been introduced by a member of Congress to be considered as a potential law is called what?

   A. a resolution

   B. an act of Congress

   C. a bill

   D. a veto

2. Of the following, which one is NOT a power enjoyed by the president during the legislative process?

   A. veto

   B. overriding judicial reviews

   C. pocket veto

   D. signing bills into law

3. What point do you believe the above political cartoon is trying to make?

1.5 THE BILL OF RIGHTS

The **Bill of Rights** was not originally part of the Constitution. It was added in 1790 for the purpose of protecting individual rights and providing **equal protection** under the law. "Equal protection" simply means that the document is intended to guarantee the rights of *all citizens*, not simply a privileged few.

The **First Amendment** guarantees citizens *freedom of speech, freedom of the press, freedom to petition the government, and freedom to assemble.* It also protects *freedom of religion* and establishes the principle of separation of church and state through the *free exercise clause,* which forbids Congress from making any law prohibiting the free exercise of one's religious beliefs; and the *establishment clause,* which forbids Congress from establishing a religion.

Bill of Rights

Chapter 1

Right to Protest

The **Second Amendment** guarantees the *right to bear arms*. Although there is much debate today about the extent to which firearms should be available to private citizens, in the early days of the nation this right was considered crucial for maintaining local militias. In fact, the first shots of the revolution were fired because the British attempted to take arms stored by private citizens at Concord, Massachusetts.

The **Third Amendment** restricts *quartering* (housing) of federal troops in the homes of US citizens. Prior to the revolution, the British angered colonists by forcing them to house British soldiers.

The **Fourth Amendment** protects citizens against *unreasonable searches and seizures*. Supporters of the Bill of Rights insisted on this amendment because Great Britain had used search warrants known as *writs of assistance* to board and search American ships prior to the colonies declaring independence.

The **Fifth Amendment** clearly defines criminal proceedings by which a person may be arrested and charged with a crime. It ensures that no person shall be imprisoned or deprived of his or her property without *due process*. In other words, the government must obey the laws governing criminal and civil proceedings before it can put someone in jail or strip him or her of his or her property. Due process prevents government abuse and ensures that citizens who are charged with a crime are not denied their rights during judicial proceedings. In addition, this amendment also protects citizens from *double jeopardy* (being charged with the same crime again after being found "not guilty"), *self-incrimination* (having to testify against oneself in court or being forced to confess to a crime) and places limits on **eminent domain**. Eminent domain is the government's power to take private property for public use. Under the Constitution, the government cannot take a citizen's property without paying "just compensation" (i.e., if the government takes someone's house, then they must pay that person what the house is worth).

The **Sixth Amendment** protects the rights of the accused. This includes the right to a *public and speedy trial by jury*. A trial by jury simply means that a group of an accused person's peers decides his or her guilt or innocence, rather than a single government official. This amendment also guarantees a defendant's right to be informed of the nature of the charges against him/her, the right to call and confront witnesses and the right to be represented by *legal counsel* (a lawyer). The **Seventh Amendment** extends the right to a trial by jury to civil cases (i.e., when one person sues another for money).

The **Eighth Amendment** protects those arrested or found guilty of a crime. It prohibits the government from imposing *"excessive bail/fines."* Bail is money an arrested person must pay to get out of jail until the date of his/her trial, while fines are amounts of money imposed as punishment for a crime one has been found guilty of. The Eighth Amendment also forbids *"cruel and unusual punishment"* of those convicted of a crime. Of course, what constitutes "cruel and unusual" punishment is often an issue of debate.

The United States Government

The **Ninth Amendment** simply says that the rights specifically mentioned in the Bill of Rights are not necessarily the only ones enjoyed by the people. Meanwhile, the **Tenth Amendment** says that those powers not restricted by the Constitution, nor delegated to the US government, are *"reserved for the states."* In other words, the Constitution grants the states the authority to decide certain matters of law.

Practice 1.5   The Bill of Rights

1. The Second Amendment is designed to protect which of the following rights?

   A.   the right to free speech

   B.   the right to peaceful assembly

   C.   the right to religious freedom

   D.   the right to bear arms

2. Which of the following statements is **false** regarding the Bill of Rights?

   A.   The rights listed in the first ten amendments are the only ones the government is obligated to recognize.

   B.   It is comprised of the first ten amendments to the US Constitution.

   C.   It was not originally part of the Constitution, but rather was added later.

   D.   It proclaims that certain powers are reserved for the states.

3. What is the purpose of the Bill of Rights?

CHAPTER 1 REVIEW

Key Terms and Concepts

democracy

representative democracy

limited government

Magna Carta

English Bill of Rights

common law

Iroquois League

House of Burgesses

Mayflower Compact

Albany Plan of Union

natural rights

Declaration of Independence

egalitarianism

unalienable/inalienable rights

Articles of Confederation

Great Compromise

Three-fifths Compromise

Bill of Rights

loose interpretation of the Constitution

strict interpretation of the Constitution

consent of the governed

majority rule

popular sovereignty

separation of powers

checks and balances

federalism

rule of law

amendment

living document

legislative branch

House of Representatives

Speaker of the House

Senate

president pro tempore

executive branch

president of the United States

vice president

Electoral College

US Census

president's cabinet

judicial branch

precedence

Marbury v. Madison

judicial review

appointed

confirmed

bill

congressional committees

filibuster

cloture

veto

pocket veto

equal protection

First Amendment

Second Amendment

Third Amendment

Fourth Amendment

Fifth Amendment

due process

eminent domain

Sixth Amendment

Seventh Amendment

Eighth Amendment

Ninth Amendment

Tenth Amendment

The United States Government

Multiple Choice and Short Answer

1. The idea that government officials cannot do whatever they want but rather must obey a set of laws that restricts how much government may interfere in private citizens' affairs is called what?

   A. popular sovereignty

   B. representative democracy

   C. limited government

   D. checks and balances

2. The idea of courts using *precedence* to decide cases where the written law is not clear or specific is closely related to which of the following?

   A. the Magna Carta

   B. natural rights

   C. social contract theory

   D. common law

3. Which of the following is **not** a principle on which the US Constitution is based?

   A. federalism

   B. limited government

   C. state religion

   D. representative democracy

4. Which of the following statements is **true**?

   A. The House of Burgesses met on board a ship to draft the first document establishing government in New England.

   B. Both the Declaration of Independence and the US Constitution proclaim that government is empowered by the people.

   C. The Magna Carta established three branches of government in the colonies

   D. The only known influences on colonial ideas about government came from England.

5. The US Constitution was ratified in 1788 after Congress agreed to do what?

   A. grant the states their independence

   B. ratify the Declaration of Independence

   C. make the president the commander in chief

   D. consider amendments protecting civil liberties

38

6. Congress is composed of two houses known as what?

   A. House of Representatives and the Senate

   B. Parliament and the Legislature

   C. House of Lords and the House of Commons

   D. Senate and the House of Delegates

7. What dispute was the "Great Compromise" meant to settle and how did it do so?

   A. It settled the manner in which states would be represented in the judicial branch and did so by allowing each house to send delegates based on its population.

   B. It settled the issue of slavery by allowing states to count slaves as 3/5 of a person in their populations.

   C. It settled the issue of representation in the legislative branch by establishing two houses, one based on population and the other on equal representation for each state.

   D. It settled the issue of civil liberties by adding ten amendments to the Constitution

8. Which of the following **most** accurately depicts the process by which a law is created?

   A. A bill is first signed by the president who then presents it to Congress. Congress then sends it to a committee in each house. If the committee approves the bill, it is presented to both houses of Congress for a vote. If both houses vote in favor of the bill, it becomes law

   B. If one house of Congress votes in favor of a bill, it then goes to a committee within that same house. If the committee recommends the bill, it then goes to the other house of Congress for a vote. If that house also votes in favor of the bill, it then presents the bill to one of its own committees. If that committee recommends the bill, then it becomes law.

   C. Once a bill is introduced by either a senator or a representative, it then goes to a committee. Once a committee is done debating a bill and decides to send it to the house of Congress of which the committee is a part, the bill is then debated and voted on. If it passes by a majority vote, it then goes to the other house. Once a bill passes both houses, it goes to the president who will either sign or veto it.

   D. Bills must originate in the House of Representatives. Once this occurs, they go to a committee. Once the committee recommends the bill, it then goes to the whole House for a vote. Once the House passes it, it then goes to the president, who will either veto or sign it.

The United States Government

9. Which of the following bodies of government was **not** officially established by the Constitution?

   A. the office of vice president

   B. the president's cabinet

   C. the Supreme Court

   D. the US Senate

10. Why did the framers of the Constitution establish a government based on *separation of powers* and *checks and balances*? How can such principles both assist and hinder effective government?

11. What is the difference between *popular vote* and *electoral vote* in a presidential election, and what role does each play in determining who is elected president?

GOVERNMENT

HSA

Chapter 2
Maryland State and Local Governments

This chapter addresses the following expectation(s) from **Core Learning Goal 1 Political Systems**

Expectation 1.1	The student will demonstrate understanding of the structure and functions of government and politics in the United States *Indicator 1.1.2*

2.1 STATE GOVERNMENT

THE MARYLAND CONSTITUTION

The state of Maryland has had four state constitutions. The first was adopted in 1776 just a few months after the Declaration of Independence was signed. The fourth and most current was ratified in 1867 and has been amended (revised or changed) numerous times. The **Maryland Constitution** serves as the highest authority of law in the state. It begins with a **Declaration of Rights** which is similar to the US Constitution's Bill of Rights. This declaration begins with a preamble and consists of numerous articles defining the rights of Maryland's citizens.

Maryland Flag

Longer than most state constitutions, the Maryland Constitution is based on many of the same principles as the US Constitution. Its guidelines ensure a *limited government* based on *popular sovereignty* and *representative democracy*. Like the national government, the Maryland Constitution establishes a government based on *separation of powers* and *checks and balances*. In fact, while the US Constitution merely implies the principle of separation of powers, the Maryland state Constitution expressly states that, "The legislative, executive and judicial powers of government ought to be forever separated and distinct from each other..."

As mentioned earlier, the Maryland Constitution can also be amended. However, while the federal document always attaches amendments at the end, the state constitution actually inserts amendments into the body of the document itself. The General Assembly proposes amendments by means of a three-fifths vote in both the House of Delegates and the Senate. Once a proposed amendment passes both houses, it then must go to the voters of Maryland in a **referendum**. In other words, the public votes on whether or not to ratify (approve) the amendment. If the majority of state voters favors the amendment, it becomes part of the constitution. One provision in the state constitution mandates that every 20 years the people of Maryland be given the option of calling a constitutional convention to revise the document. Such a convention is held if the majority of voters requests it.

THE EXECUTIVE BRANCH

**Governor
Martin O'Malley**

**Lieutenant Governor
Anthony G. Brown**

Article II of the Maryland Constitution establishes the executive branch of government for the purpose of enforcing the laws of the state. The *governor* is the head of this branch and has several powers and responsibilities. He/she is the commander-in-chief of the state's military forces (i.e. the National Guard). The only exception to this is when the president of the United States nationalizes (calls up for federal duty) these forces. Even then, however, the governor may establish and maintain additional state military forces as need be (i.e., the Maryland Defense Force). The governor also appoints a number of public officials (these officials must be confirmed by the Senate), sits as head of the **Governor's Executive Council**, chairs the Board of Public Works and must annually submit a budget to the General Assembly for its consideration. The governor also has the power to grant pardons (forgive people who have committed crimes so that they are not punished), commute (shorten) sentences, call special sessions of the General Assembly and veto proposed legislation. The governor is elected to a term of four years and is not eligible to serve more than two terms consecutively. Likewise, the **lieutenant governor** is also elected to a four year term. He/she is the second highest ranking executive officer and is responsible for whatever duties the governor delegates to him/her. As part of the Governor's Executive Council, he/she is the first in line to succeed the governor should he/she be unable to fulfill his/her term.

Maryland Governor's Mansion

The Maryland Constitution also establishes the **Board of Public Works** as part of the executive branch. This board consists of the governor, the comptroller of Maryland and the state treasurer. Elected by the people to a term of four years, the *comptroller of Maryland* is responsible for supervising the fiscal affairs (affairs involving state revenue and spending) of the state. In comparison, the General Assembly elects the *state treasurer* who is responsible for the state's treasury and oversees decisions regarding how to invest state funds and pay for the obligations of state government. He/she serves a four year term that coincides with that of the elected governor. The Board of Public Works is responsible for approving certain state expenditures.

Chapter 2

THE GOVERNOR'S EXECUTIVE COUNCIL

As part of the executive branch, the governor also appoints the **Executive Council** known as the **governor's cabinet**. This body consists of twenty-three members. Among them are the *lieutenant governor*, the *secretary of state*, the *secretary of higher education*, the *adjutant general* (head of the state's military department) and the heads of the nineteen principal executive departments. While the lieutenant governor is elected, the other members are appointed by the governor and must be approved by the state Senate.

Maryland's 19 Principal Executive Department Heads	
Secretary of Aging	*Secretary of Human Resources*
Secretary of Agriculture	*Secretary of Juvenile Services*
Secretary of Budget & Management	*Secretary of Labor, Licensing and Regulation*
Secretary of Business & Economic Development	*Secretary of Natural Resources*
Secretary of Disabilities	*Secretary of Planning*
State Superintendent of Schools (Education)	*Secretary of Public Safety & Correctional Services*
Secretary of the Environment	*Secretary of State Police*
Secretary of General Services	*Secretary of Transportation*
Secretary of Health and Mental Hygiene	*Secretary of Veterans Affairs*
Secretary of Housing and Community Development	

THE LEGISLATIVE BRANCH

The Maryland **General Assembly** comprises the legislative branch of state government. It is a bicameral (two house) body, consisting of the state **Senate** and the **House of Delegates**. The General Assembly currently has 188 members (47 senators and 141 delegates). There are 47 legislative election districts within Maryland and each one is represented in the General Assembly by one senator and three delegates. Members of both houses are elected to four year terms, with districts being redrawn every ten years after the US Census to ensure that each citizen is adequately represented.

Maryland Statehouse

Just as Congress makes federal laws, the General Assembly's role is to make the laws that govern Maryland. State legislators introduce bills (proposed laws) for consideration that must then be voted on. Once the bill passes both houses, it then must go to the governor. If the governor signs it, the bill becomes a law. If, however, the governor vetoes the bill, then the bill dies *unless* three-fifths of the total number of both houses vote to override the governor's veto. If this happens, then the bill becomes a law anyway.

Maryland State and Local Governments

In addition to passing legislation, the General Assembly also has other powers. It may establish executive departments, levy taxes, create special taxing districts and propose state constitutional amendments which must then be ratified by the voters of Maryland. Although only the governor may call a special session of the Assembly, members of the legislative branch can *force* the governor to do so on petition of a majority of each house. Only the House of Delegates has the power to impeach public officials, while the Senate tries such cases and determines if an impeached official is to be removed from office. Before an impeached official may be found guilty, two-thirds of the senators must agree with the decision. The Senate must also approve those whom the governor appoints to public offices. The General Assembly also elects the state treasurer, and, if the election for governor ends in a tie or the elected individual is unable to fulfill the office, the governor as well. If the office of lieutenant governor becomes vacant, then the General Assembly must approve whomever the governor nominates to fill the office.

LEGISLATIVE LEADERSHIP

Thomas V. "Mike" Miller
President of Senate

Each house of the General Assembly has leadership which it elects from among its members. The Senate is led by the **Senate president**, while the House of Delegates is led by the **speaker of the House**. Each presides over the daily affairs of his/her respective house and almost always is elected from the majority party (Democrat or Republican). If both the governor and the lieutenant governor are unable to serve, then the Senate president also acts as governor until the General Assembly can meet and elect a replacement. Like the United States Congress, the Maryland General Assembly also has **committees** within each house for the purpose of examining proposed bills and making recommendations regarding whether or not the bill should be approved.

THE JUDICIAL BRANCH

The judicial branch of state government is comprised of the courts of Maryland. The Maryland court system consists of four levels. The lowest level is the **District Court of Maryland**. The district courts have *original jurisdiction* (authority to hear cases first) in matters involving minor criminal and civil offenses and in most cases involving motor vehicle laws. Judges on the district court are appointed by the governor and, provided their nomination is confirmed by the Senate, serve ten year terms. The chief judge of the District Court of Maryland is appointed by the chief judge of the court of appeals.

The next level is the **circuit courts**. These courts are the trial courts of general jurisdiction within the state of Maryland. Their original jurisdiction includes more serious criminal and civil cases. They also have *appellate jurisdiction* (authority to rule on the decisions of lower courts) over cases heard in district courts and decisions made by certain administrative agencies. There are eight *judicial circuits* within the state of Maryland. Circuit court judges are appointed by the governor but then must run for the office in an election in which he/she may be opposed by qualified candidates. Once elected, these judges serve a term of 15 years.

Historic 1799 Courthouse

Chapter 2

Chief Judge, Court of Appeals
Robert M. Bell

The second highest court in Maryland is the **Court of Special Appeals**. It consists of 13 judges, only three of which usually hear a given case. The Court of Special Appeals has appellate jurisdiction over lower court decisions, except those of criminal cases involving the death penalty. Judges who sit on this court are appointed by the governor, approved by the Senate and serve ten year terms.

Finally, there is the Maryland **Court of Appeals**. This is the highest court in Maryland and has appellate jurisdiction over cases heard in lower Maryland courts. Often, decisions are based on whether or not lower court procedures properly upheld the constitutional rights of defendants. The court of appeals also often rules on whether or not laws passed by the state legislature are constitutional. In this way, it exercises judicial review much like the US Supreme Court. The Court of Appeals consists of seven judges, each appointed by the governor and representing a different judicial circuit. Once appointed, these judges must be approved by the Senate and then run for election unopposed to be either accepted or rejected by the people. If rejected, the office remains vacant and a new appointment must be made. If accepted, the judge then serves a ten year term. The Court of Appeals is headed by a chief judge appointed by the governor. This judge serves as the administrative head of Maryland's judicial system. Although the highest court in the state, it is important to remember that even the decisions of the Court of Appeals can be appealed to the US Supreme Court for review.

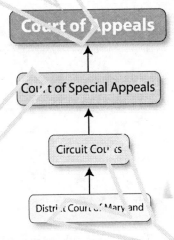

Maryland State and Local Governments

Structure of Maryland's Government

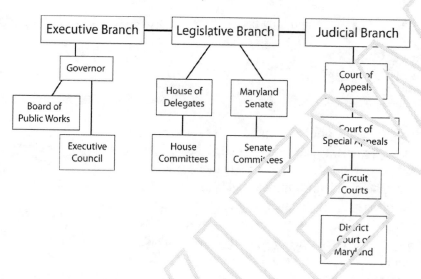

Practice 2.1 State Government

1. Which of the following statements is **false** regarding Maryland's state government?

   A. It depends on a bicameral legislature to carry out the duties of the legislative branch.

   B. The governor is elected directly by the people, unless the election is a tie.

   C. Once appointed by the governor and approved by the Senate, most state judges serve for life without ever having to be elected.

   D. The governor of Maryland can veto any bill that passes the Senate and House of Delegates, but the General Assembly can override the veto if it has enough votes.

2. Which of the following is an example of how separation of powers is established by Maryland's state constitution?

   A. Members of both the Senate and the House of Delegates are elected to four year terms.

   B. The executive branch is responsible for enforcing the laws of the state, but the legislative branch must first pass the laws.

   C. The General Assembly is a bicameral legislature.

   D. Leaders of state government are bound to obey the guidelines of the Maryland Constitution.

3. What are the four levels of Maryland's judicial branch of government and what role does each play?

2.2 MARYLAND'S LOCAL GOVERNMENTS

COUNTY GOVERNMENTS

Counties of Maryland

With only 23 counties, Maryland ranks among those states with the fewest number of local governments. There are three different types of county government in Maryland. **Commissioner counties** are counties that are legislated directly by the General Assembly. While these counties have a board of commissioners that performs both executive and legislative duties, its powers are limited to what is authorized or allowed by the state legislature. Eight counties operate using this form of government.

Ratified in 1966, Article XI-F of the state constitution allows for another form of county government known as **code home rule**. A county may adopt code home rule if two-thirds of the county commissioners vote in favor of the resolution and it is approved by the voters of the county at the next general election. Commissioners in code home rule counties have broader legislative powers than those in commissioner counties, although only the General Assembly may enact laws dealing with taxes or fees. Six Maryland counties currently operate under this model of government.

Finally, there is the **charter** government, which separates the executive and legislative branches of county government. To become a charter county, a charter board must draft a charter that outlines the structure of the proposed government, then have it approved by the county's voters. Charter counties have authority over almost all local matters except the power to regulate elections and to regulate or license the sale of alcoholic beverages. Currently, nine counties use this form of government. In most charter counties, powers are divided between an elected executive and an elected legislative body. In a few, however, the executive is actually appointed by an elected council.

MUNICIPAL GOVERNMENTS

Municipal governments are city or town governments that operate independently of the county (although they may depend on the county for certain services, i.e. law enforcement). There are roughly 157 town and city governments operating within Maryland. They are usually incorporated by the General Assembly, although some have been established by referendums as well.

Among Maryland's municipal governments, **Baltimore** is unique. As the largest city in Maryland, Baltimore is generally considered to be the same as county level governments because of its size and population. The city is also unique because it is not part of any county in the state. Since Baltimore County is actually a separate entity, Baltimore is often referred to as "Baltimore City" to distinguish it as independent. Baltimore is governed by an elected mayor and city council.

Maryland State and Local Governments

Practice 2.2 Maryland's Local Governments

1. Which of the following are most directly legislated by the General Assembly?

   A. commissioner county governments

   B. charter county governments

   C. code home rule governments

   D. municipal governments

2. Which of the following models of county government is specifically designed to separate the executive and legislative branches of government?

   A. commissioner government

   B. code home rule government

   C. bicameral government

   D. charter government

3. In what ways is Baltimore unique among Maryland's municipal governments?

Chapter 2

CHAPTER TWO REVIEW

Key Terms and Concepts

Maryland Constitution
Declaration of Rights
referendum
governor
Executive Council/Governor's Cabinet
lieutenant governor
Board of Public Works
General Assembly
Senate
House of Delegates
Senate president

speaker of the House
legislative committees
District Court of Maryland
circuit courts
Court of Special Appeals
Court of Appeals
commissioner counties
code home rule counties
charter counties
municipal governments
Baltimore

Multiple Choice and Short Answer

1. Which part of the Maryland Constitution is the following phrase **most likely** found in?

    "...all government of right originates from the People, is founded in compact only, and instituted solely for the good of the whole; and they have, at all times, the inalienable right to alter, reform, or abolish their Form of Government in such a manner as they may deem expedient

    A. the Declaration of Rights

    B. the Bill of Rights

    C. Article II – the powers of the executive branch

    D. Article III – the powers of the legislative branch

2. Of the following, which one is **not** a role fulfilled by the governor of Maryland?

    A. He/she submits a proposed budget to the General Assembly.

    B. He/she appoints judges, many of whom must then stand on their own for election.

    C. He/she chairs the Board of Public Works.

    D. He/she officially introduces all bills considered by the General Assembly.

3. Which of the following is a principle on which the Maryland Constitution is based?

    A. unlimited government

    B. limited monarchy

    C. popular sovereignty

    D. suppression of rights

4. The General Assembly comprises which branch of state government?

    A. municipal   B. county   C. legislative   D. judicial

5. Which of the following **best** describes the role of legislative committees in the General Assembly?

    A. They consider bills and make recommendations to their respective houses.

    B. They elect the state treasurer every four years.

    C. They try impeached public officials.

    D. They are responsible for approving nominations to the Executive Council.

6. Brandon is arrested and charged with a string of armed robberies in which several people were seriously wounded, and one was even killed. Brandon's case will likely be tried first at which level of the Maryland court system?

    A. district court

    B. circuit court

    C. court of special appeals

    D. court of appeals

7. Betty is convicted of a state crime in Maryland and sentenced to 40 years in prison. She appeals the conviction because she feels that her rights were violated at her trial. Her case goes before a panel of three judges who rule that her rights were not violated and uphold her conviction. Betty now appeals to the highest court in the state. Betty's first appeal was most likely heard in which court?

    A. district court

    B. circuit court

    C. court of special appeals

    D. court of appeals

50

Senate Says "No" to
Governor's Budget Despite
House Support

8. The above headline illustrates what principle of Maryland's government?

9. Describe the difference between commissioner counties, charter counties and code home rule counties in terms of how they carry out government. How does a county establish either a charter or code home rule model of government?

Chapter 3
The Government and Public Issues

This chapter addresses the following expectation(s) from **Core Learning Goal 1 Political Systems**

Expectation 1.1	The student will demonstrate understanding of the structure and functions of government and politics in the United States *Indicator 1.1.3*
Expectation 1.2	The student will evaluate how the United States government has maintained a balance between protecting rights and maintaining order. *Indicator 1.2.2*

3.1 HEALTH, ENVIRONMENT AND ENTITLEMENTS

PUBLIC HEALTH AND HEALTH CARE

Of all the modern issues that face the United States, perhaps none is as important as **public health** and **health care**. Public health refers to the status of the public's health overall, while health care refers to the system of prevention, treatment and management of illnesses (both physical and/or mental) provided by the nation's health professionals. While people in the US arguably have the best health care in the world, there are challenges. *Obesity* (being overweight) is becoming more and more of a problem for US citizens and at an earlier age. Obesity often leads to other health problems that affect quality and length of life. *Diseases* like cancer, AIDS, heart disease, etc., continue to afflict and take the lives of millions of people. More and more citizens report taking prescription medications for depression, anxiety, the inability to maintain a long-term attention span and numerous other mental and physical disorders. Meanwhile, *substance abuse* puts added pressure on the US healthcare system as resources are needed to help those who are battling addictions to alcohol, illegal drugs, prescription pain killers, etc. Longer average lifespans also pose a problem. Although advances in medical technology greatly improve countless lives and allow most citizens to live longer, increased lifespans mean added strains on the US healthcare system as individuals grow older and their medical needs increase. At the same time, *medical costs* continue to skyrocket, leaving many citizens with limited or no health insurance unable to pay their bills or afford needed procedures and/or medicines.

Over the years, the government has attempted to address the healthcare problem with programs and legislation. In 1965, as part of President Lyndon B. Johnson's "Great Society" domestic programs, Congress established Medicare and Medicaid. **Medicare** is an insurance program administered by the US government. It is designed to cover citizens over the age of 65 or who meet certain other requirements. **Medicaid** is a US health insurance program for low income individuals and families. Unlike Medicare, it is administered and partially funded by the states. Almost 30 years later, President Bill Clinton proposed *healthcare reform* (changes that would improve the US healthcare system). Early in his first term, Clinton introduced legislation to Congress designed to guarantee affordable, government sponsored health coverage to every US citizen. However, Congress rejected the plan after roughly a year of debate. Many insurance and business interests opposed the plan and did an effective job of lobbying and building political support against it. In addition, many conservatives felt that it was too expensive. Critics also argued that government control would ultimately hurt the quality of health care in the US and pointed to examples in other countries to support their claim. A decade later, in 2003, President George W. Bush signed the *Medicare Prescription Drug, Improvement and Modernization Act*. The act represented the largest overhaul in Medicare history and was intended to make it easier for senior citizens to afford needed prescription drugs. While some view the plan as a positive step, others criticize it as being too confusing and failing to adequately improve prescription benefits.

President Lyndon B. Johnson

Health care for Senior Citizens

ADVANTAGES AND DISADVANTAGES OF GOVERNMENT HEALTH CARE

Today, the issue of US health care continues to inspire much debate and be of great concern. While most agree that the cost of medical care is ballooning out of control and must be made more affordable, political leaders often differ greatly regarding how to accomplish this. Some advocate more government restrictions and regulation. They point out that government run health care would provide health care for every citizen at affordable costs. Opponents, however, quickly respond that by regulating health care, the government runs the risk of greatly diminishing the quality of healthcare services provided. They also point out that such services would have to be paid for with higher taxes. These same critics often argue that the best approach is to lessen government restrictions and make it more difficult for healthcare professionals to be sued. By doing so, they claim, healthcare professionals and institutions will not have to pay as much for insurance and can pass the savings on to consumers. Look for the issue of health care to be a key topic in both state and federal elections in the years to come.

THE ENVIRONMENT

Environmental issues also require government attention. Political leaders have acted in the last few decades to place more government regulations on corporations to ensure the environment is protected. Laws like the **Clean Air Act of 1970** and **Clean Water Act of 1972** regulate how much pollution companies can legally release into the environment and how they dispose of things like radioactive waste. In addition, the government has declared certain areas as public lands that are "off limits" to development. While environmentalists applaud the government for restricting industrial development, others complain that such measures produce shortages and economic hardship.

Clean Air Act 1970	Clean Water Act 1972
Congress passed this act in 1970 in order to ensure cleaner air by restricting the amount of pollutants that can be emitted by industries, automobiles and so on.	Congress passed this act in 1972 in order to lower water pollution by restricting the amount of toxic wastes that may be dumped into rivers, streams and other bodies of water.

DEBATE ON GLOBAL WARMING

Today there is a growing call from environmentalists for the government to pursue alternative sources of fuel. Many environmentalists point to the rising global temperatures in recent years as evidence that the burning of *fossil fuels* (i.e., exhaust from automobiles) produces gases that destroy the earth's ozone (protective barrier that prevents harmful rays from the sun from hitting the earth) and contribute to creating a layer of gases that holds in heat from the sun rather than letting it escape into space. They believe that this **"greenhouse effect"** is contributing to **global warming** (process of the earth's average temperature increasing over time). People who hold this view believe that discovering alternative sources of energy is ultimately a matter of survival as well as a matter of independence from foreign oil suppliers. While many scientists advocate this theory, debate still rages because there are also respected scientists who question whether any such "greenhouse effect" actually exists and, if it does, how much damage it causes.

Environmental issues can sometimes be tricky for government leaders because environmental concerns often conflict with other government priorities. For instance, the need to escape dependence on Middle Eastern oil and be more independent requires exploring other energy sources and/or drilling for oil within US territories. Environmentalists, however, have grave concerns about the effects of off-shore oil drilling on marine life. Areas of Alaska are known to be very rich in oil reserves, yet environmentalists oppose drilling in many of these areas because of the damage it could do to portions of the Alaskan wilderness. Environmentalists often express concerns when it comes to coal mining and nuclear energy as well. Although a number of scholars and scientists dispute some of these environmentalist claims, most government energy policies are now careful to take into account possible effects on the environment.

Oil Pipeline

Actions Taken to Protect the Environment

- Automobile manufacturers now strive to produce cars that emit less pollutants and develop automobiles that burn alternative fuels.

- Industries adhere to stricter guidelines to make sure that production does not damage or pollute the environment.

- Federal and state governments provide funding to help protect and conserve natural resources.

- Individual citizens buy products that are biodegradeable and recycle such things as plastic, aluminum and paper.

- The government often places regulations on businesses and corporations designed to protect the environment.

ENTITLEMENTS AND SOCIAL SECURITY

Another issue of intense debate is *entitlements* **Entitlements** are guarantees of benefits. For instance. millions of US citizens receive **welfare**. In the United States, welfare is the distribution of money to impoverished citizens (and in some cases, entities) without the expectation of those citizens producing anything in return. For example, under certain circumstances, low income families and/or single parents may receive benefits from the government. These benefits might come in the form of money or **food stamps** (vouchers that can be exchanged for food). A number of welfare programs began as part of President Franklin Roosevelt's "New Deal" during the Great Depression of the 1930s as a means for helping citizens make it through the economic crisis Today, much debate rages concerning welfare and the extent to which it should be offered. Many see welfare programs as being

too expensive and criticize them as encouraging laziness and irresponsible living rather than helping people to better their lives. Proponents of welfare claim that certain programs are essential for helping those who would otherwise suffer due to a lack of education, poor health or an inability to help themselves. In 1996, President Clinton won re-election to the White House largely because he was willing to sign national *welfare reform*. The plan eliminated federal guarantees of cash assistance in favor of block grants (money the federal government gives state or local governments, that allowed states to run their own welfare programs. The reforms also placed lifetime limits on the amount of aid families could receive, required most adults to find work within two years of applying for aid and placed more conditions on qualifying for food stamps.

The Government and Public Issues

One of the nation's best known federal programs is **Social Security**. First established in 1935, Social Security provides retirement income for all US workers once they reach the official age of retirement. Originally, this age was 65. Now, however, one's official age of retirement depends on the year he/she was born. For those born before 1938, it is still 65. For those born after, it is 66 or 67. In some cases, Social Security benefits can also be received at an earlier age and/or for reasons other than retirement (i.e., becoming disabled). Employed citizens pay for Social Security by means of payroll taxes. Every time you get paid at work, a certain amount of money is taken out of your paycheck to pay for Social Security. While people often like the idea of receiving money from the government after they retire, many are concerned about Social Security and feel that the system is in desperate need of change. A number of leaders have expressed the view that there may not be adequate money to finance Social Security in coming decades. Many US citizens think that when they pay Social Security taxes, the money goes into their own account until they need it for retirement. In reality, however, that is not how Social Security works. Take your teacher, for example. The money taken out of his/her check for Social Security is actually used to pay benefits to someone who is already retired. The belief is that when your teacher reaches retirement, someone else will be working and can pay his/her benefits. However, since people now live longer and the cost of living is constantly increasing, it takes more people working to pay for one person's benefits than it used to. The fear is that by the time future generations retire, there just won't be enough people working to provide benefits unless something is done. So why doesn't the government just change it? For one, there is much debate about what approach is best. Some politicians want to raise taxes to set aside more benefits. Some want to lessen benefits and encourage younger citizens to save more money privately. Still others are afraid to change things much at all because they fear the political consequences if they are perceived by voters as tampering with Social Security benefits. A few even question if there is anything to fear at all. For these reasons and others, Social Security is a hot topic at election time.

Practice 3.1: Health, Environment and Entitlements

1. Which of the following results from longer average US lifespans?

    A. concerns about fossil fuels

    B. more strain on the US healthcare system

    C. increased obesity among teens

    D. fewer tax dollars required to pay government retirement benefits

2. Over which of the following would state governments have the MOST control?

    A. Social Security

    B. Medicare

    C. Medicaid

    D. the EPA

3. What are *entitlements* and what are some of the arguments for and against them?

4. What is MOST LIKELY the intended message of the above cartoon?

    A. Citizens can feel secure about the future of retirement benefits.

    B. The government should stop granting entitlements.

    C. Healthcare costs are too high.

    D. Social security may not be around in the future.

3.2 SOCIAL AND ECONOMIC EQUALITY

Equality refers to the degree to which people in the United States are treated fairly and receive equal opportunities and consideration. Throughout US history, various factors have traditionally affected how people are treated in society. Race, gender, religion, age, socioeconomic status (what level of society one comes from based on income level, cultural/social background, etc.) and nationality are just a few of the characteristics which sometimes determine how people are perceived and/or treated. As a result, debate has often raged concerning to what degree the government should act to promote equality in society. While nearly everyone believes that all citizens should have equal opportunities for success and should be treated fairly under the law, opinions differ over how much the government should try to regulate equality. Should the government force private businesses to adhere to policies designed to promote equality? When should the federal government act and when should issues of equality be left to the states and local governments? What is *equality*? Because of different experiences and perspectives, people from different racial, religious, cultural and/or socioeconomic backgrounds often differ in how they define the concept.

AFRICAN-AMERICANS AND AFFIRMATIVE ACTION

For decades, *racial segregation* (the separation of people based on race) was practiced in the United States and even upheld by the US Supreme Court. Whites and African-Americans were often required to use separate public facilities, attend separate schools, use different waiting rooms and restrooms, sit in different sections on public transportation and so on. Since whites were the ones in positions of power, white facilities were usually far superior and policies usually favored whites. Then, beginning in the 1950s, the *civil rights movement* began to change things. It was a movement that unified African-Americans in an effort to end racial segregation and achieve equal treatment. It led to a number of court cases that helped strike down segregation (a few of these cases will be discussed in chapter 5) and inspired important civil rights legislation. Shortly after President Lyndon Johnson became president, Congress passed the **Civil Rights Act of 1964**. The act prohibited segregation in public accommodations (hotels, restaurants, theaters that served an interstate clientele, etc.) and discrimination in education and employment. Although originally designed to protect the rights of African-Americans, it was ultimately amended to protect the rights of women and other minorities as well. That same year, the states ratified the **Twenty-fourth Amendment** to the Constitution. This amendment served to protect minority voting rights by making the poll tax illegal. The poll tax was a tax put in place in a number of southern states to prevent African-Americans from voting. Since most African-Americans were poor and unable to pay, the "tax" kept many blacks from exercising their right to vote.

Martin Luther King, Jr.

Congress passed another key piece of legislation in 1965. That year, civil rights protesters in Selma, Alabama decided to bring national attention to their cause by marching 50 miles to the state's capital in Montgomery. When the 500 marchers reached Selma's city limits, 200 state troopers and sheriff's deputies beat them with clubs and whips, released dogs on them, and showered them with tear gas. People across the US were shocked by televised scenes of the violence. The event became known as "Bloody Sunday" and was called an "American tragedy" by President Johnson. Thousands of whites and blacks descended on Selma to continue the march. Two weeks after "Bloody Sunday," Martin Luther King, Jr. led more than 3,000 marchers out of Selma, including a core of 300 people who walked the entire journey. Four days later, they arrived in Montgomery. Soon after, on August 6, 1965, President Johnson signed the **Voting Rights Act of 1965**. It authorized the president to suspend literacy tests (another method used to prevent blacks — many of which were poorly educated at the time — from voting) and to send federal officials to register voters in the event that county officials failed to do so. This new law led to a huge increase in African-American voter registration as well as an increase in the number of African-American candidates elected to public office.

Related to the issue of racial equality is the concept of **affirmative action**. Often referred to as *"positive discrimination,"* affirmative action is a policy by which minorities are given preferential consideration or are actively recruited for jobs, admittance to universities and/or other positions as a means of helping them "catch up" to whites who have enjoyed years of advantage. Many civil rights activists justify affirmative action policies as necessary to correct past injustices and discrimination. In 1965, President Johnson publicly advocated affirmative action during a speech at Howard University (a predominantly African-American institution). In his support for the policy, Johnson used the analogy of a race. He said that you cannot take someone who's been shackled for years, liberate him, put him on the starting line with people who've been free to train and then claim that the race is now fair. In the same way, Johnson argued it is not enough to simply remove discrimination; minorities need the help of policies that will enable them to make up lost ground.

Affirmative action remains an issue of political controversy. Critics feel that such policies are unfair, claiming that they deny opportunities to qualified whites in favor of less qualified minority candidates. For this reason, they often label affirmative action *"reverse discrimination."* Meanwhile, many proponents feel it is a necessary step to achieving true equality for all. Still others believe that it fails to achieve the goals for which it was implemented and even hurts minorities in the long run.

WOMEN, SENIOR CITIZENS AND OTHER ETHNIC MINORITIES

The US government has also dealt with issues of equality regarding women, senior citizens and other minorities. Under the **Equal Pay Act of 1963**, Congress made it illegal for employers to pay female employees less money than male employees who do "equal work" requiring "equal skill" and that are performed under similar circumstances. Almost a decade later, in 1972, Congress passed the **Higher Education Act** which included **Title IX**. This legislation guaranteed equality between men and women in federally funded schools. It prohibits sexual discrimination and focuses on access and admission to federally funded institutions, equal educational opportunities and equal opportunities for men and women when it comes to athletic programs. Increased enforcement of Title IX in recent years has created controversy. While many point out that the law is simply meant to provide equal opportunities for women, critics claim that the law has hurt, and even ended, some male sports programs because of the additional money and scholarships that must now go to women's athletics.

Ageism is discrimination against individuals because of their age. Although people of any age can be unfairly discriminated against, ageism is most often associated with discrimination against *senior citizens* (older citizens in society). In particular, seniors are often discriminated against when it comes to employment. The federal **Age Discrimination in Employment Act (ADEA)** prohibits such discrimination. Meanwhile, the **Maryland Antidiscrimination Act** prevents businesses within the state from practicing age discrimination when it comes to hiring and firing employees.

NATIVE AMERICANS

In addition to blacks, Native Americans have also suffered from discrimination and prejudice. To help address issues dealing with Native Americans, the US government established the *Bureau of Indian Affairs (BIA)*. This agency is part of the Department of the Interior and is responsible for both Native American lands and educational services within the United States. In addition, Congress has passed several key pieces of legislation in an attempt to address important issues and correct past injustices against Native Americans.

The Government and Public Issues

In 1924, Congress passed the **Snyder Act**, which granted full citizenship and the right to vote to Native Americans. Half a century later, Congress passed the **Indian Education Act of 1972** which addresses the educational needs of Native American students in the United States. This act was reactivated in 2001 as part of the No Child Left Behind Act signed by President George W. Bush. The 1990 **Native American Graves Protection and Repatriation Act (NAGPRA)** requires that "cultural items," such as artifacts, human remains and other revered objects be returned to Native American peoples/tribes. Although the act was criticized by some for interfering with archaeological research, many agreed that it was necessary to help make up for past wrongs against Native American peoples. The law gives Native Americans control over artifacts and archaeological discoveries related to their own heritage. Finally, in 1996, Congress passed the **Native American Housing and Self-determination Act (NAHASDA)** aimed at improving housing conditions for poorer Native Americans.

Officially recognized Native American tribes also enjoy special privileges in terms of *sovereignty* (the ability to govern themselves and make their own decisions). The federal government currently recognizes over 500 Native American tribes in the US. These tribes are basically granted the same rights as states when it comes to self-government. In 1968, the US Congress passed the **Indian Civil Rights Act** for the purpose of making sure that the rights of US citizens protected by the Bill of Rights are extended to those living under tribal governments as well. Some tribes have been granted recognition within certain states but not by the federal government. Others, such as the Piscataway tribe of Maryland, have been denied official recognition altogether. In order to receive recognition, a tribe must be able to prove its continuous existence since 1900. This is sometimes tricky because, in the past, many Native Americans were inclined to deny their Native American heritage in order to escape prejudice and discrimination.

LATINOS

Although the plight of African-Americans in the South is often identified with the struggle for civil rights, many people fail to realize that Latinos (those of Hispanic descent) historically faced similar struggles in the southwest United States. In places like Texas and California Latinos (in particular Mexican-Americans) often faced the same kind of discrimination and suffered from laws to keep them disenfranchised (unable to vote) just like blacks. For this reason, the same legislation that helped empower African-Americans in the South often meant more equality for Latinos as well.

In recent decades, the US Latino population has grown tremendously. One of the greatest reasons for this is *immigration* from Latin American countries (i.e, Mexico and Central America). One of the effects of this increase in population has been a controversial acceptance of *bilingualism* (accommodating for the use of more than one language). As the number of people in the US who speak Spanish as a first language grows, more and more states and government institutions are

60

beginning to use Spanish as well as English. In public schools, there is some emphasis on *bilingual education*. First mandated by Congress in 1968, this is the practice of providing students with access to public education taught in their own language. Some have argued that such practices are destructive because they hinder newcomers to the United States from learning English and serve to divide rather than unite people in the US. Proponents point out that it enables immigrants to learn more easily and maintain their cultural identity. They also argue that, because the United States has no official language, there is no reason why education and public information should not be offered in other languages as well as English. Recently, in the midst of ongoing debates about immigration policies, a number of states have introduced bills establishing English as the official language and/or no longer mandating bilingual education. Such actions have only served to inspire more debate and remind citizens of how controversial such issues can be.

While there are many people who immigrate to the US legally each year, a growing number tend to be **illegal immigrants** who enter the United States unlawfully across its southern border. Because of this, many citizens want existing immigration laws strictly enforced and illegal immigration halted. Advocates of such positions point out that the millions of illegal immigrants who live in the US cause a drain on the nation's healthcare system and public services without contributing enough taxes to cover the costs. Critics of this position, however, point out that the vast majority of illegal immigrants are decent, hard working people who just want a better way of life. They also claim that many of these immigrants are necessary to sustain the nation's economy because they do many of the menial tasks and manual labor jobs that most US citizens will not. In 2006, the debate surrounding illegal immigration led to many in the US Latino community uniting as a political force to oppose policies that might make it harder for Latinos to enter the US. Proponents of stricter enforcement of US immigration laws, however, usually insist that their views have little to do with race or ethnic background and more to do with necessity and national security.

RECENT IMMIGRATION LEGISLATION

In 1986, Congress passed the **Immigration Reform and Control Act**. Criticized by some for granting amnesty (forgiveness for committing a crime) to illegal immigrants already working in the US, the act was intended to halt the flow of illegal immigrants into the country. Twenty years later, the number of illegal immigrants has only increased and many point to the Immigration Reform and Control Act as proof that offering amnesty is a poor way of dealing with the illegal immigration problem. In 1996, Congress passed the **Illegal Immigration Reform and Immigrant Responsibility Act**. This act authorized the hiring of at least 1,000 new border patrol agents, mandatory detention of immigrants convicted of certain crimes, gave the government greater authority to detain aliens and made it easier to deport illegal immigrants back to their nation of origin.

The events of 9/11 have also contributed to a call by many for the US to deal with illegal immigration by controlling its borders. Many opinion surveys show that most citizens believe that, until the US adequately secures its borders, it is easy for foreign terrorists to enter the United States. The **Real ID Act** of 2005 seeks to deter terrorism by setting national standards for photo IDs and allowing for the construction of barriers along the US border. Meanwhile, recent bills were introduced in both the Senate and the House of Representatives for the purpose of dealing with illegal immigration and securing the nation's borders against the threat of terrorism. Both bills sparked intense debate and public outcry, revealing the huge divisions that exist in the United States over the immigration issue. In 2006, the president authorized the use of National

Guardsmen to help secure the borders and signed measures approving the construction of a fence along a large portion of the US-Mexico border. People on both sides of the immigration issue now anxiously await to see how much of the fence actually gets built and what effect it will have on illegal immigration.

DISABILITIES AND SEXUAL ORIENTATION

Gender, ethnicity (a person's race and/or ethnic background) and nationality (what country a person is from) are not the only areas that inspire debates over equality. In 1990, Congress passed the **Americans With Disabilities Act** This law guarantees equal opportunity for people with disabilities in public accommodations, employment, transportation, government services and telecommunications. It also protects the rights of those who are not disabled themselves, but are responsible for caring for a disabled person. This act makes it illegal to refuse to hire someone for a job they are qualified for simply because they are disabled. It also requires government buildings and many public facilities to be accessible to disabled persons (i.e., be equipped with wheelchair ramps, etc.). Other key pieces of legislation have been the **Rehabilitation Act of 1975** and the **Individuals with Disabilities Education Act (IDEA)** Congress passed both of these laws to ensure that children with disabilities have access to public education.

Of all the groups demanding equal treatment, perhaps none inspires such heated debate as the *homosexual* community (those who are sexually attracted to members of their own gender). Homosexuals claim that they should be afforded all the same rights as *heterosexuals* (those who are sexually attracted to members of the opposite gender). While many citizens agree that a person's **sexual orientation** (whether or not they are homosexual or heterosexual) should not interfere with civil rights, there is often much debate about what is a "right." For instance, many homosexuals claim that they have a "right" to be married to members of the same gender. Opponents often claim, however, that *marriage*, by its very nature and definition, is a union between a man and a woman. Some of these opponents say that homosexuals should have the same legal rights as married couples under what is often referred to as "civil unions," but not be recognized as "married." Others oppose legal recognition of any kind of union for homosexual couples. As a result, civil unions, homosexual "marriage" and even the idea of a constitutional amendment specifically defining marriage as a union between a man and a woman have all become hot political topics in recent years.

To add to the controversy, there is often not agreement as to *why* certain individuals are homosexuals and others are not. Many homosexuals claim that they were "born this way" and that their sexual orientation is determined genetically. For this reason, they claim they should be viewed as any other minority group and have their civil rights protected in the same manner. Others point out that there is no definitive scientific evidence to prove this and, therefore, view homosexuality as a behavior and lifestyle choice. Because they hold this view, such individuals usually refuse to put homosexuals in the same category as ethnic minorities.

How has the government addressed the issue of sexual orientation? In 2003, the US Supreme Court struck down laws prohibiting consensual homosexual acts as unconstitutional in *Lawrence v. Texas*. Before that, in *Rimer v. Evans (1996)*, the Court also ruled that state and local governments cannot pass laws prohibiting legislative action designed to protect homosexuals from discrimination based on their sexual orientation. Meanwhile, Maryland's legislature also passed the **Maryland Antidiscrimination Act** (discussed earlier in regards to ageism) which bans discrimination based on sexual orientation in employment, housing and/or public accommodations.

Chapter 3

SOCIOECONOMIC EQUITY

Socioeconomic status refers to an individual's social and/or financial standing in society. Next to the rest of the world, most US citizen compare favorably on a socioeconomic basis. However, within the United States, there is a great deal of disparity. The bulk of the nation's wealth is (and historically has been) in the hands of a relatively small percentage of US citizens. Meanwhile, on average, white US citizens tend to do better economically than minority citizens. Due to *urban flight* (trend in which middle class citizens leave the cities to live in the suburbs) inner cities tend to be economically worse off than the suburbs. In addition, poorer communities generally tend to lag behind in education and earning potential (how much money individuals can expect to earn in their lifetime). How to deal with the reality of economic disparity and to what degree the government should implement policies designed to encourage *socioeconomic equity* are often issues of debate. *Conservative* politicians tend to advocate less government control. They believe that the government should simply provide equal opportunity for all citizens to pursue success without hindering the process with high taxes or excessive regulation. By contrast, more *liberal* politicians believe that it is up to the government to get involved. They tend to favor higher taxes for raising revenue that can then be pumped into government programs designed to help those who are economically disadvantaged.

CRIME AND CENSORSHIP

Many critics of the criminal justice system say that **crime** and how it is punished is also a symptom of inequality. They point to the fact that, statistically, the ratio of minorities in prison to whites in prison tends to be much higher than the ratio of minorities to whites in the general population. This fact, they often claim, is evidence of racial prejudice in how laws are applied and/or the fact that minorities tend to be more disadvantaged socioeconomically. Such critics often point to *capital punishment* (the death penalty) as the most drastic example of inequality in the criminal justice system. Capital punishment is when an individual is sentenced to die for his/her crimes. The death penalty is not used in every state. It is, however, used in Maryland where first degree murder is the only offense punishable by death. Lethal injection (a process by which poisonous chemicals are injected into a condemned person's veins) is generally used as the state's method of execution, although Maryland does have the option of the gas chamber for prisoners sentenced before March 25, 1994. In addition to claiming the death penalty violates Eighth Amendment restrictions against "cruel and unusual punishment," many highlight statistics suggesting that capital punishment is not fairly applied because men and minorities are more likely to be sentenced to death than women and whites. Proponents of the death penalty argue that the solution is to execute more whites and females who are convicted of heinous crimes rather than abolishing capital punishment. In 1972, the Supreme Court struck down the death penalty as a method of punishment. It ruled in *Furman v. Georgia (1972)* that the death penalty was not constitutional in the way that it was applied because, in some cases, those committing serious crimes (murder, rape, etc.) were sentenced to death, while in other similar cases, convicted persons received life in prison. Four years later in *Gregg v. Georgia (1976)*, the Court upheld the death penalty so long as proper and consistent guidelines are provided to juries in deciding whether or not to sentence someone to die. Together, the two cases established that the death penalty does not constitute cruel and unusual punishment, so long as it is applied in a fair and consistent manner.

Gas Chamber

Censorship is when the government limits certain information from being dispersed to the public. In the United States, most information can be spread freely thanks to the **First Amendment** (see chapter 1, section 1.3). However, there are times when the government finds it necessary, and the courts have upheld censorship of certain types of information. For instance, the First Amendment does not protect speech or printed material that could cause injury, threaten national security or damage a person or entity's reputation through *slander* (verbally spreading false information) or *libel* (printing false information). In addition, there is certain information which may be censored because it is of a private nature. Such information includes medical records, information exchanged between lawyers and clients and juvenile records. The **Family Educational Rights and Privacy Act of 1974** both entitles parents to have access to all school records regarding their child, while simultaneously ensuring that such records remain confidential between the school and the parents/student. We will discuss a number of important Supreme Court cases involving the First Amendment in chapter 5.

Forms of Speech Which May be Censored by the Government
• Speech that is considered "indecent" may not be broadcast over public airwaves (radio/television). What constitutes "indecent" is sometimes an issue of controversy. • Speech or printed matter that would threaten national security (i.e. revealing classified information). • Speech or printed material that threatens public safety, such as yelling "fire" in a crowded theater or distributing information on how to kill someone. • libel and slander • documents officially sealed by a court of law

Practice 3.2 Social and Economic Equity

1. What does the term *equality* refer to?

2. Which of the following is the BEST example of an affirmative action policy?

   A. A school principal decides to hire the same number of math teachers as she does English teachers.

   B. A corporation decides to award a promotion to an African-American who is more qualified than any other candidate.

   C. A business decides to give special consideration to African-American job applicants because it wants its workforce to reflect more cultural diversity.

   D. A less qualified white applicant is turned away by a university in favor of a more qualified black applicant.

3. Who would benefit MOST from Title IX?

   A. a woman in a wheelchair who wants to work

   B. a young man hoping to get a football scholarship

   C. a homosexual demanding that his civil rights be protected

   D. a young woman wanting a chance to play intercollegiate sports

4. Why do many US citizens want laws against illegal immigration more strictly enforced, and what are some of the arguments against such enforcement?

5. Which of the following is an acceptable form of censorship?

   A. state officials making it illegal to pray in public

   B. newspapers being fined for criticizing the president

   C. government worker arrested for attempting to reveal military secrets to the press

   D. Latino citizen arrested for criticizing immigration policy

3.3 GOVERNMENTAL DEPARTMENTS AND AGENCIES

In order to address the kinds of issues discussed in this chapter, both the federal and state governments have established a number of departments and regulatory agencies. The following are a few examples.

FEDERAL DEPARTMENTS AND AGENCIES

Department of Health and Human Services	This department is responsible for protecting the health of US citizens and for providing essential human services.
Center for Diseases Control	The **CDC** is within the above department and located in Atlanta, Georgia. It conducts research and responds to the threat of potential outbreaks of serious diseases.
US Department of Agriculture	The **USDA** seeks to assure the safety of agricultural products. It also seeks to promote agricultural trade in order to help alleviate world hunger as it attempts to meet the economic needs of US farmers.
Environmental Protection Agency	President Richard Nixon established the **EPA** in 1970. Its goal is to protect the environment while making sure that laws regulating pollution, the use of certain chemicals and pesticides and waste disposal are properly adhered to.
Department of Housing and Urban Development	Congress passed legislation that established **HUD** in 1965. It addresses housing needs and community development for low-income families/communities. It also provides rent assistance to low income citizens.
US Department of Energy	Established in the late '70s by President Carter, the purpose of this department is to coordinate federal programs designed to find alternative sources of energy and promote conservation.
Nuclear Regulatory Commission	Created in 1975, this department has the responsibility of overseeing the operation and construction of nuclear reactors, ensuring the transportation and proper disposal of nuclear waste and making sure that nuclear materials are handled and used according to government guidelines. President Jimmy Carter called for a massive reorganization of the commission after a nuclear power plant accident at Three Mile Island near Harrisburg, Pennsylvania in March 1979. A partial meltdown at the nuclear power plant released radiation into the environment and led to a mass evacuation of those living in the surrounding area. It also hindered future efforts to resort to nuclear power as an alternative source of energy.

Three Mile Island

MARYLAND AND PUBLIC ISSUES

The executive branch of Maryland's state government consists of several departments established to address issues of public concern.

Department of Aging	This department is concerned with ensuring the rights and well-being of Maryland's senior citizens.
Department of Disabilities	This department looks after the needs of state citizens with disabilities and makes sure that they are not being discriminated against and that their rights are being protected.
Department of Health and Mental Hygiene	This department seeks to promote, protect and improve the mental and physical health of Maryland's citizens.
Department of the Environment	This department seeks to protect and conserve Maryland's air, land and water resources in a way that is compatible with the state's economic growth and development.
Department of Natural Resources	Also concerned with environmental issues, this department preserves, protects, enhances and restores Maryland's natural resources and manages the state's public lands. The department is also responsible for protecting any *endangered species* (forms of wildlife in danger of becoming extinct) within Maryland or along its coast.
Maryland Energy Administration	Seeks to develop cleaner energy alternatives, in particular by promoting the development and use of automobiles that use alternative fuels. This administration also works in conjunction with the US Department of Energy to administer such programs as the **Maryland Clean Cities Coalition**. This program is designed to encourage voluntary efforts from local communities to develop alternative sources of fuel, accelerate the sale of hybrid automobiles (automobiles that run on energy sources other than traditional gasoline alone) and inform consumers about the choice they can make to help conserve energy and maintain a cleaner environment.

Meanwhile, local governments often deal with public issues through local laws such as **zoning ordinances**. These ordinances are laws regulating where certain types of structures may be built, where businesses may be located within a community and for what purposes land may be used. For instance, certain areas may be designated for residential neighborhoods while others are for businesses and commercial use. Still others might be areas restricted for environmental reasons. Counties or municipalities often have **zoning boards** that make these kinds of decisions.

The Government and Public Issues

MARYLAND'S EFFORTS AT CONSERVATION

Because of its rich natural resources, Maryland has taken a number of steps to conserve and restore its environment. Since the state relies heavily on the Chesapeake Bay, restoring the state's **wetlands** (state's watershed) is vitally important. Entering 2007, the General Assembly is considering legislation aimed at reducing **stormwater runoff** (pollutants caused by increased development and population that contaminate bodies of water). Current legislation under consideration would require developers to have a comprehensive plan for dealing with and limiting the effects of such pollution.

In 2006, the Maryland General Assembly passed the **Maryland Healthy Air Act**. This law is arguably the strictest power plant emission law on the East Coast. It requires significant reductions in power plant emissions and requires Maryland to become involved in the *Regional Greenhouse Gas Initiative* which is aimed at reducing greenhouse gases. Maryland's Department of the Environment is responsible for enforcing the regulations set forth in this act.

Downtown Baltimore

Practice 3.3 Governmental Departments and Agencies

1. Which agency or department of the US government would be MOST concerned with a corporation that is accused of dumping toxic waste into a nearby river?

    A. HUD

    B. Department of the Environment

    C. Department of Energy

    D. Environmental Protection Agency

2. Which of the following statements is TRUE regarding Maryland's approach to dealing with public issues?

    A. Maryland's government does not address such issues because they are handled by the federal government.

    B. Public issues are only addressed by the executive departments of Maryland's government with the General Assembly having no role.

    C. The General Assembly has the power to pass legislation addressing public issues, while the executive branch consists of several departments to oversee areas of public concern.

    D. In 2006, Maryland replaced the Department of the Environment with the Department of Natural Resources to more effectively address environmental concerns.

CHAPTER 3 REVIEW

Key Terms and Concepts

public health

health care

Medicare

Medicaid

Clean Air Act '70 and Clean Water Act '72

greenhouse effect

global warming

entitlements

welfare

food stamps

Social Security

equality

Civil Rights Act of 1964

Twenty-fourth Amendment

Voting Rights Act of 1965

affirmative action

Equal Pay Act '63

Higher Education Act/Title IX

Age Discrimination in Employment Act

ageism

Maryland Antidiscrimination Act

Snyder Act

Indian Education Act of 1972

NAGPRA '90

Native American Housing and Self-determination Act

Indian Civil Rights Act

illegal immigrants

Immigration Reform and Control Act

Illegal Immigration Reform and Immigrant Responsibility Act

Real ID Act

Americans with Disabilities Act

Rehabilitation and Individuals with Disabilities Education Acts

sexual orientation

socioeconomic status

crime

censorship

First Amendment

Family Educational Rights and Privacy Act

Department of Health and Human Services

CDC

USDA

EPA

HUD

Department of Energy

Nuclear Regulatory Commission

Department of Aging

Department of Disabilities

Department of Health and Mental Hygiene

Department of the Environment

Department of Natural Resources

Maryland Energy Administration

Maryland Clean Cities Coalition

zoning ordinances

zoning boards

stormwater runoff

Maryland Health Air Act

The Government and Public Issues

Multiple Choice and Short Answer

1. The status of the public's health overall is referred to as what?
   - A. public health
   - B. public status
   - C. US health care
   - D. healthcare reform

2. A working, low-income, single mom who is dealing with a chronic illness would **most likely** benefit from which of the following?
   - A. Medicare
   - B. Medicaid
   - C. services of the EPA
   - D. affirmative action

3. Which of the following laws would the EPA **most likely** appeal to as justification for its actions?
   - A. The Clean Air Act
   - B. The Americans with Disabilities Act
   - C. The Snyder Act
   - D. The Voting Rights Act

4. The CDC would be **least** concerned with which one of the following?
   - A. an outbreak of a mysterious flu in New England
   - B. the discovery that rats in New York City are infected with a deadly virus
   - C. the fact that welfare benefits for low-income families have been cut
   - D. policies implemented by the Department of Health and Human Services

5. Which of the following is the **best** example of an entitlement?
   - A. an insurance company paying for the medical care of one of its policy holders
   - B. an out of work father receiving government unemployment benefits until he can find another job
   - C. a government agency making sure that its facilities are accessible to disabled persons
   - D. a US citizen receiving a tax refund.

6. A building inspector visits the construction site of a new post office. While there, she informs the workers that they will have to remember to include a wheelchair ramp in their building plans. This inspector is making sure that the builders comply with what law?
   - A. Native American Housing and Self-determination Act
   - B. Americans with Disabilities Act
   - C. Individuals with Disabilities Education Act
   - D. Rehabilitation Act

70

7. Which of the following statements is **true** regarding the ratio of minorities to whites in US society?

    A. The ratio of minorities to whites is higher in prison than in the general population.

    B. The ratio of minorities to whites is lower in prison than in the general population.

    C. On average, whites are more likely to be sentenced to capital punishment than minorities.

    D. There have historically always been more blacks in prison than whites.

8. The above cartoon is making what point?

    A. Minorities have fewer rights.

    B. People with disabilities deserve more access to public education.

    C. People with disabilities need equal opportunities for job advancement.

    D. The government should enforce fewer regulations on corporations.

9. What are *zoning boards* and what kinds of decisions are they responsible for?

10. What is *socioeconomic status* and how do conservative and liberal politicians propose dealing with the issue of socioeconomic equity differently?

11. In terms of sovereignty, what privileges are enjoyed by officially recognized Native American tribes and what is the purpose of the Indian Civil Rights Act?

GOVERNMENT

Chapter 4
The Citizen's Role in Government

This chapter addresses the following expectation(s) from **Core Learning Goal 1 Political Systems**

Expectation 1.1	The student will demonstrate understanding of the structure and functions of government and politics in the United States *Indicator 1.1.4*

4.1 POLITICAL PARTIES

Citizen involvement is a key part of the US political system. One of the ways citizens play a role in their nation's politics is by joining and actively supporting **political parties**. Political parties are organizations that promote political beliefs and sponsor **candidates** (people running for political office) under the organization's name. Many of the world's democracies operate on what is called a *multi-party system*. In such a system, there are numerous political parties that hold government seats. The Netherlands, Israel and Denmark are just a few examples of countries operating on this kind of system. In a multi-party system, parties are usually given representation in government proportional to the number of votes they receive in an election. For example, say that there are 10 seats available in Parliament. Party A receives 40% of the vote, party B receives 30%, and parties C, D and E each receive 10%. Proportional representation means that party A gets 4 seats, party B 3 seats and parties C D and E each get 1 seat. All five parties will be represented in Parliament, with party A having most of the influence.

Party Symbols:
Elephant (Republican) and Donkey (Democrat)

Ross Perot

Bill Clinton

George H. W. Bush

By contrast, the United States operates on a *two-party system.* This is a system in which only two primary parties dominate a nation's politics. In the United States, these two parties are the **Democrats** and **Republicans**, and both operate at the federal, state and local levels of government. Why does the US feature a two-party system while many other nations have multi-party systems? The answer is largely due to the way the US conducts elections. Take, for example, congressional elections. In a multi-party system based on proportional representation, each party receives a number of seats based on the number of votes it gets. But in the United States, things are done differently. If a state is entitled to 15 representatives, then that state is divided into 15 individual voting districts. Each district then elects one winner to represent them. This means that if the Democratic candidate wins 51% of the vote, the Republican 42%, the Libertarian 6%, and the Reform Party 1%, then there is still just one winner — the Democrat. Only the Democratic candidate will go to Congress; the other three are flat out of luck. As a result, it is more beneficial in the United States to align oneself with one of the two major parties that actually have a chance of winning. Sometimes, however, **third parties** (parties other than the Republicans and Democrats) and **independents** (those not affiliated with a party) do play an important role in US politics. Third parties usually arise and gain momentum when citizens don't feel that either of the two major parties adequately represents their views. In the late 1800s, the Peoples Party (also known as the Populists) initiated a number of key reforms. In 1912, Theodore Roosevelt actually won more votes for president as the Progressive Party candidate than did the incumbent Republican. In 1992, Bill Clinton (a Democrat) won the election with only 43% of the popular vote, in large part due to Ross Perot's independent campaign that pulled support away from President George HW Bush. Historically, however, while third party candidates and independents have won some government offices and, at times, influenced policies, they generally do not win the White House or a large number of seats in Congress. This is largely because they face challenges that the major parties do not. They are neither as well funded nor have anywhere near the number of members as the Republican and Democratic parties. Also, many citizens are traditionally tied to one of the major parties and are unwilling to vote for third party candidates they doubt can win. Because third parties usually rally around a single issue or regional concern, they often have trouble appealing to a widespread audience as well.

National Convention

Some countries use a *one party system* in which only one party is allowed to operate. As a result, citizens' ability to have a say in their government is greatly limited under such a system. China's Communist Party is an example of a one-party system.

US PARTY STRUCTURE AND FUNCTION

Political parties serve several functions. They nominate candidates for office, structure the voting choice (limit the list of candidates to those who have a real chance of winning — usually the Republican and Democratic candidates), coordinate the actions of government officials (i.e., facilitate the different branches of government working together) and establish party *platforms.* The *platform* is the party's statement of programs and policies it will pursue once its candidates are in office. It is made up of several *planks*. The term "plank" refers to an individual policy within the platform. For example, if the Republican platform states that the party opposes abortion, favors increased military spending and supports a constitutional amendment against flag burning, then each one of these issues represents one plank of the platform. Parties normally adopt their platform every four years at their national convention. The **national convention** consists of delegates (representatives) from each state and US territory that meet to nominate (choose) candidates for president and vice president in the upcoming general election.

Practice 4.1 Political Parties

1. Party leaders gather at the national convention to nominate their candidates for president and vice president. While there, they draft a list of policies and programs the party will support. What is this list of policies and programs called?

   A. the party plank
   B. the party platform
   C. the party machine
   D. the party system

2. In the United States, only the Republican and Democratic parties truly dominate the political scene. This demonstrates that the US operates on which kind of political system?
   A. multi-party
   B. a republic
   C. two-party
   D. coalition

3. How does the manner in which the United States conducts elections contribute to its two-party system?

4.2 POLITICAL CAMPAIGNS AND ELECTIONS

CAMPAIGNS

Citizens also impact politics by participating in **political campaigns** (strategy for winning / process of candidates running for public office). Effective campaigns are essential in order for candidates to win an election. If the candidate is his/her party's nominee, then he/she can count on the support of the party. In addition, campaigns are often supported by **political action committees (PACS)**. These are groups organized to ensure that the candidates who will back issues most important to the PAC get elected and remain in office. PACs primarily contribute money to the campaigns of candidates they support. Most funding for campaigns comes from private resources, such as PACs or private donors. However, since 1976, presidential candidates also have access to *public funding*. Candidates must first demonstrate that they have broad support and be able to raise a certain amount of money privately. Once they have, candidates may accept public funds; but to do so, they must agree to limit their campaign spending.

Money is just one aspect of successful campaigns. They also require wise strategy and lots of hard work. To get their supporters to the polls (place where people vote on election day), candidates and parties often rely on *"grassroots efforts."* Like the roots that lie unseen below the surface — yet are necessary for grass to grow — grassroots campaign efforts are those efforts made by volunteers and local party members who actively educate, campaign and encourage citizens to get out and vote for the party's candidates. Although their labor is "unseen" by many, it is crucial for effective campaigns.

Volunteer Campaigning Door-to-Door

Propaganda

To win votes, campaigns also produce a great deal of campaign propaganda. **Propaganda** is information meant to influence voters to support a specific candidate over another. The information may or may not be true; but it is always biased (meant to favor one candidate). Propaganda can take the form of television, radio or printed ads and can be geared towards either molding a positive public image of the candidate it supports (called **positive campaigning**) or a negative public image of the candidate it is aimed at defeating (called **negative campaigning**). In order to avoid alienating voters, candidates often speak in *"glittering generalities"* during election campaigns. In other words, they say things that appeal to emotions or are consistent with popularly held values without getting so specific as to offend voters. For example, a candidate may say something like, "We must protect Social Security at all costs," but he/she will not say that they intend to raise taxes to do so. This is because they realize that most citizens support Social Security but hate paying taxes.

ELECTIONS

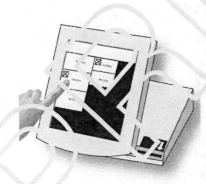

Local, state and federal officials are voted into office by means of a **general election**. General elections are held in November of an election year (usually even numbered). This is the time in which voters choose between the Republican, Democratic and any third party/independent candidates for public office. However, before the general election is held, each party must first decide which candidate will be its representative. After all, there may be ten Democrats who want to be the party's nominee for president, or six Republicans who want to run for governor. To decide on a single nominee, each major party holds primary elections a few months prior to the general election. In **primary elections** voters choose between candidates within the same party. The candidate who wins the majority of votes receives the party's nomination. Sometimes, in both general and primary elections, the candidate who receives the most votes fails to win the majority of votes (more than half). This is usually because more than two candidates were on the ballot. When this happens, the top vote winners (usually the top two) will meet again in a **run-off election**, with the top vote getter in the run-off election winning. It is important to note, however, that run-off elections do not occur in presidential elections because they involve the Electoral College. If a presidential candidate fails to win a majority of electoral votes, then the winner is decided by the House of

Representatives. Some states (i.e., Iowa) choose their party's nominee for president by means of a **caucus** rather than a primary. In the caucus system, party members hold local meetings to choose delegates who vote in favor of nominating a certain candidate at the national convention.

Practice 4.2   Political Campaigns and Elections

1. The Democratic and Republican candidates for lieutenant governor have just squared off in a tough election. After all the votes were counted, the Democratic candidate pulled out a narrow victory. He will be the state's next lieutenant governor. This describes what?

    A.   the results of a general election
    B.   the results of a primary election

    C.   the results of the state caucus
    D.   the results of the Electoral College

2. Miriam's congressional campaign has just launched a series of ads. Half of the ads feature her past accomplishments and talk about her patriotism. The other half criticize her opponent and point out that he was investigated by the IRS. ALL of Miriam's ads are examples of what?

    A.   negative campaigning
    B.   positive campaigning

    C.   canvassing
    D.   propaganda

3. What is a run-off election and why would one be held? How is the president of the United States elected if no candidate wins a majority of electoral votes?

4. What point is the above cartoon trying to make about political campaigns? Give reasons for your answer.

4.3 MEDIA AND POLITICAL ACTIVISM

INFLUENCE OF THE MASS MEDIA

US culture is greatly influenced by its mass media. Nowhere is this more evident than in politics and public opinion. The term **"mass media"** refers to the journalists, celebrity personalities, writers, etc. who have an impact on society via television, radio and printed materials. Through news reports, opinion polls and other forms of communication, the mass media plays a major role in forging the nation's *public agenda* (what issues are most important to US citizens). Because the public tends to focus its attention on whatever issues the media chooses to highlight, the mass media ultimately has great impact on US politics. As a result, some have even nicknamed the media the **"fourth branch of the government."** Issues like US military actions, concerns about the environment, unemployment, health care and minority rights are all examples of issues that have impacted politics and influenced the decisions of elected officials, in part due to their coverage in the media. Since elected officials know they must appeal to voters in order to remain in office, they often feel they must mold their policies to address issues about which the media has helped to arouse public concern.

While most agree that the mass media helps define the important issues of the day, citizens are often divided on whether or not they believe the mass media is guilty of *bias* (favoring one stance or political position over another). Since journalists are expected to accurately report facts rather than support political agendas, any news agency or publication thought guilty of bias tends to lose credibility. News agencies and networks accused of bias claim that they simply report the facts they uncover. Critics say that reporters often go in search of what they *want* to find, rather than objectively reporting all sides of a story.

CITIZEN ACTION

Political activism refers to the act of being politically involved. It is the means by which private citizens can make their opinions known and their voices heard. Voting is one way people are politically active. Another way citizens exercise influence is through **referendums**. A referendum is a direct vote by the people on a policy or law. Often, referendums are used to vote on whether or not to overturn or accept a proposed piece of legislation. For instance, before changes can be made to Maryland's constitution, they must first be approved by the state's voters by means of a referendum. Citizens can also *force* a vote on a particular issue that might otherwise go unaddressed or not be given the level of priority the public demands by getting enough citizens to sign a **petition** (a document/form signed by citizens in support of a certain change or government action). Such a process is called an **initiative**. If citizens are extremely displeased with a public official they can ask for a **recall election**. Recall elections are special votes called to determine if voters want to remove a sitting official from office before his/her elected term is up because of questionable behavior or failing leadership. This occurred in California in 2003 when Governor Gray Davis was recalled and defeated by Arnold Schwarzenegger. More radical activists (those who engage in political activism) might take part in political **protests**. Marches, sit-ins, hunger strikes, etc., in the name of a certain cause are all forms of political protest. Such protests are usually carried out in opposition to a government policy.

INTEREST GROUPS AND LOBBYISTS

Interest groups are different from political parties because, unlike parties that sponsor candidates and support a number of issues, interest groups tend to focus on a single issue and seek to use the political process (supporting candidates, campaigning for their position, lobbying politicians, etc.) to either encourage or prevent change to existing policies. In most important debates, there are interest groups fighting for both sides. Since third parties rarely win elections in the US, most interest groups choose to align themselves with one of the two major parties, rather than branching out on their own. This leads to interesting coalitions. *Coalitions* are the banding

**Civil Rights Marchers
(Library of Congress)**

together of different groups for the purpose of achieving political success. For instance, auto workers in Michigan and civil rights activists in the South may, on the surface, not seem to have much in common. However, they may band together for the purpose of supporting candidates that will back both their interests. Some groups within a party might be seen as *radical* because they hold extreme opinions. For instance, those advocating massive government reforms and/or government control over certain institutions are often tagged as "radicals" (i.e., those favoring government control of businesses or health care). Other groups are seen as *reactionary* because they "react" to what they view as radical changes or movements. Reactionary groups tend to value the status quo or want to see a return to more traditional ways. Since both groups tend to be seen as "too extreme" by many citizens, they find it advantageous to be part of a larger coalition within one of the major parties.

Lobbying

To help get laws passed that are favorable to their cause, many interest groups hire **lobbyists** who work to influence legislation in Congress and/or state legislatures. Many believe that the name goes all the way back to the administration of Ulysses S. Grant. Grant may have been the Union general who was able to defeat the Confederate army and end the Civil War, but he couldn't convince his wife to let him smoke cigars in the White House. One of the places he *could* smoke was in the lobby of one of the local hotels. While Grant sat in the lobby puffing away, those wanting to make requests, seek his backing or ask political favors would line up to meet with him. Hence the term, *"lobbyist."* Today, many corporations and special interest groups pay big money to lobbyists who can influence Congress and state legislatures. Beginning in the 1980s, there has been increased concern about former elected officials turned lobbyists using their connections in Congress to win special consideration. In 2006, scandals surrounding lobbying practices on Capitol Hill led to the introduction of new legislation aimed at preventing corrupt deals between lobbyists and lawmakers.

CAMPAIGN FINANCE REFORM

Because of the large amounts of money funneled to candidates through PACs and used by lobbyists to cater to legislators, many have called for more regulation of these practices. One key figure in the battle for **campaign finance reform** has been Senator John McCain of Arizona. In 2000, McCain ran for the Republican nomination for president but lost to eventual President, George W. Bush. Since 1992, McCain has called for legislation to regulate campaign financing. In 2002, Congress passed the McCain-Feingold bill, which places limits on financial contributions to political candidates. Although it was challenged on the grounds that it violated free speech, the law was narrowly upheld by the Supreme Court.

Sen. John McCain

LEGISLATIVE HEARINGS

Finally, citizens can make their voices directly heard at **legislative hearings**. Such hearings can be as local as a town meeting at a school or community center, or as formal as testifying before members of the General Assembly or Congress. Public hearings allow citizens to attend government meetings and, in many cases, voice their opinions. Meanwhile, public *forums* are special meetings called to specifically give citizens a chance to express their feelings about an issue prior to any final government decisions.

Practice 4.3 Media and Political Activism

1. Which one of the following would NOT be considered part of the mass media?

    A.   NBC's nightly news broadcast

    B.   *The New York Times* newspaper

    C.   the president's State of the Union Address

    D.   *Newsweek* magazine

2. Why would political bias be a negative thing for journalists?

3. What are *interest groups,* who are *lobbyists* and how are they connected?

CHAPTER 4 REVIEW

Key Terms and Concepts

political parties	positive campaigning	referendum
candidates	negative campaigning	petition
Republicans and Democrats	general election	initiative
third parties	primary election	recall election
independents	run-off election	protests
national convention	caucus	interest groups
political campaigns	mass media	lobbyists
PACs	"fourth branch of government"	campaign finance reform
propaganda	political activism	legislative hearings

Multiple Choice and Short Answer

1. A *political party* is **best** defined by which of the following?

    A. a system based on proportional representation

    B. an organization that promotes political beliefs and sponsors political candidates for office

    C. a group with political interests that often hires lobbyists to influence legislation

    D. a national convention held to nominate political candidates

2. The results of an election are very close. Candidate A wins 49% of the vote, candidate B wins 48% of the vote and candidate C wins the remaining 3% of the vote. There is a good chance that candidates A and B will have to meet again in what kind of election?

    A. a primary election

    B. a recall election

    C. a general election

    D. a run-off election

3. The Democrats meet for their national convention and decide to support a woman's right to abortion on demand, oppose a constitutional amendment against flag burning and support certain civil rights legislation. This list of policies and programs which the party supports is known as what?

    A. the party platform

    B. the party plank

    C. the party agenda

    D. the party delegate

4. Abigail is passionate about seeing her candidate win the upcoming primary election. She volunteers her time and energy to pass out flyers, put up campaign signs and make phone calls. Abigail is part of what?

    A. a television campaign

    B. a political protest

    C. a PAC

    D. a grassroots campaign effort

5. Before Joe can be his party's candidate for president, he must first defeat other members of the party who want to be the party's nominee in a series of what?

   A. general elections

   B. national caucuses

   C. primaries and caucuses

   D. run-off elections

6. The fact that US and Maryland state politics is dominated by only the Republican and Democratic parties is evidence that the US operates on what kind of political system?

   A. direct democracy

   B. representative democracy

   C. primary election

   D. two-party

7. Phil and Linda founded an organization called *Equality First* which is dedicated to fighting for the rights of low-income families. Over the past three years, they have amassed a large number of members and succeeded in influencing some state and local legislation. To increase their influence, their organization hires Olivia to convince congressmen and state legislators to support laws that *Equality First* supports. Which of the following statements is **most** accurate?

   A. Phil and Linda are founders of a political party.

   B. *Equality First* is a PAC and Olivia is the candidate it supports for office.

   C. *Equality First* is an interest group and Olivia is a lobbyist.

   D. *Equality First* is a political party and Olivia has been hired to represent the party platform.

8. The Maryland General Assembly has just passed a resolution to amend the state constitution. Before such an amendment can be added, however, the state's voters must first approve it. The vote in which Maryland voters decide in favor of or against the proposed amendment is called what?

   A. referendum   B. recall vote   C. initiative   D. primary

9. Walter is outraged that the local government is allocating thousands of dollars to renovate City Hall but hasn't done anything to improve the local park and library. He decided to launch a drive to force a city-wide vote on how the money should be spent. Which option is best for Walter?

   A. introduce a referendum

   B. run for Congress in his district

   C. insist on a mayoral recall vote

   D. get enough citizens to sign a petition to force an initiative

10. Define what is meant by *mass media* and describe several ways it influences politics and elections.

Chapter 5
Government Action and Civil Rights

This chapter addresses the following expectation(s) from **Core Learning Goal 1 Political Systems**

Expectation 1.2	The student will evaluate how the United States government has maintained a balance between protecting rights and maintaining order. *Indicators 1.2.1 and 1.2.3*

5.1 LANDMARK SUPREME COURT CASES

In chapter 3, we discussed some of the legislation and issues that face our nation regarding civil rights. In particular, we examined attitudes and laws regarding affirmative action, socioeconomic equity, the rights of women, immigration, etc. Now, we will examine additional actions by the government and important rulings by the US Supreme Court which have affected civil rights as well.

POWERS AND AUTHORITY OF THE FEDERAL GOVERNMENT

One of the most important powers the judicial branch has is the power of *judicial review*. As mentioned earlier, this is the authority to declare certain laws passed by Congress, or even state legislatures, unconstitutional (in violation of the Constitution). This power is not specifically delegated to the courts by the Constitution. Rather, it was established in a landmark court case known as ***Marbury v. Madison (1803)***. We discussed this case in chapter 1, however, due its significance, it is worth reviewing again. Just before leaving office, President Adams appointed a number of Federalist judges whom his successor, President Jefferson, did not want on the bench. For this reason, Jefferson refused to deliver the commissions appointing these judges. Marbury (one of the appointed judges) and several others sued, taking the case to the Supreme Court. The justices agreed that the judges were entitled to their commissions but ruled that the Supreme Court did not have authority to force the president to deliver them under the Constitution. In so doing, the Supreme Court declared part of the Judiciary Act unconstitutional and established the Court's power of *judicial review.*

John Marshall
Chief Justice
Marbury v. Madison
McCullough v. Maryland

Another important case was *McCullough v. Maryland (1819)*. In this case, the court dealt with the question of whether or not Congress had the right to establish a national bank; and, if it did, could the state of Maryland impose state taxes? The Court ruled that the *elastic clause* allowed Congress to establish a national bank because it was an action "necessary and proper" for carrying out its constitutional duties. It also ruled that Maryland did not have the authority to impose taxes on a federal institution. The case both reinforced the principle of "implied powers" (the idea that Congress has powers other than those specifically mentioned in the Constitution) and the *supremacy clause* which states that federal powers exceed those of the states.

Both *Marbury v. Madison* and *McCullough v. Maryland* would eventually become key precedence for cases involving civil rights. *Marbury* eventually allowed the court to use judicial review to strike down laws it deems to be violations of the Bill of Rights. Meanwhile, *McCullough* reinforced the federal government's authority over states and allowed Congress to take any action it felt necessary to fulfill its responsibilities. Both principles would be very important later when the Court addressed state laws limiting the civil rights of citizens.

RACIAL SEGREGATION

Segregation is a term that refers to the separation of groups (i.e., blacks and whites). There are two types of segregation. *De jure segregation* is segregation sanctioned by law. For instance, when buses in the South used to require blacks to sit separately from whites, this was de jure segregation. *De facto segregation* is segregation that is brought about by social or economic circumstances rather than written law. When blacks and whites tend to live in separate neighborhoods because, on average, one community is financially better off than the other, this is an example of de facto segregation. The Supreme Court has made landmark decisions affecting both.

Thurgood Marshall
Chief Justice
Brown v. BOE Topeka

The Court originally sanctioned de jure segregation in *Plessy v. Ferguson (1896)*. Homer Plessy, a man who was one-eighth black, was arrested for riding in a "whites only" railway car in Louisiana. With only one justice dissenting (disagreeing with the final decision of the Court) the Supreme Court ruled that segregation is lawful so long as the facilities provided for both races are equal. This came to be known as the **"separate but equal"** doctrine. In 1954, the NAACP (National Association for the Advancement of Colored People) argued a case before the Supreme Court that challenged the *Plessy* decision. The case revolved around a young, African-American girl named Linda Brown. Brown had been denied enrollment at a school close to her home because it was all white. In *Brown v. Board of Education of Topeka (1954)*, the Supreme Court overruled the *Plessy* decision by striking down segregation in public schools on the grounds that separate facilities are inherently "unequal" because they do not present minority students with the same opportunities that are offered in white schools.

Fifteen years later, in 1969, the Supreme Court made another key decision regarding school desegregation in Mississippi. When the state dragged its feet integrating its schools, the US Supreme Court stepped in and ruled in ***Alexander v. Holmes County Board of Education*** that the state's school districts must immediately operate as integrated school systems and that no student could be excluded from any school because of race or color.

Closely related to the issue of desegregation (also called *integration*) is the topic of *busing*. First implemented in the early 70s, busing is a method of integration in which students are required to attend schools outside the boundaries of what would normally be their school district. It is meant to deal with the de facto segregation that occurs in education because blacks and whites often live in different districts. The practice was challenged in the courts and reached the Supreme Court on appeal. In ***Swann v. Charlotte-Mecklenburg Board of Education (1971)***, the Court agreed with a lower court decision allowing busing as a means for integrating public schools.

DUE PROCESS

As noted in chapter 1, ***due process*** refers to the principle that a citizen who is accused of a crime is entitled to certain rights and that the government must obey certain laws when carrying out its investigation, prosecution and/or sentencing of a defendant. From 1961 to 1966, the Supreme Court ruled on landmark criminal cases involving the Fourth, Fifth and Sixth Amendments. In 1914, the courts established the ***exclusionary rule***, which holds that evidence gathered in a manner that violates the Constitution is inadmissible (cannot be used against a defendant at trial). However, at the time, it only applied to federal cases. Then, in 1961, the Supreme Court ruled in ***Mapp v. Ohio*** that the exclusionary rule applies at the state level as well. Mapp involved a case in which law enforcement had seized evidence without a proper warrant. The court ruled that this constituted an illegal search and therefore the evidence could not be used at trial.

Two years later, the Court ruled in ***Gideon v. Wainwright (1963)*** that states are required under the Sixth and Fourteenth Amendments to provide attorneys for criminal defendants who cannot afford them. The case involved a man named Clarence Gideon who was convicted of burglary. Because he was not able to afford to hire an attorney, Gideon was forced to defend himself and was ultimately found guilty. He appealed to the Supreme Court, which ruled that Gideon's Sixth and Fourteenth Amendment rights to legal counsel had been violated. The conviction was overturned.

That same year, a Mexican immigrant named Ernesto Miranda was arrested and interrogated by police without the presence of a lawyer. During the interrogation, he confessed to the crimes of kidnapping and rape. After his conviction, the case was appealed all the way to the Supreme Court. In ***Miranda v. Arizona (1966)***, the Court ruled that both Miranda's Fifth Amendment protection against "self-incrimination" and his Sixth Amendment right to counsel had been violated. The case established the *Miranda Rule*, which states that law enforcement agencies must inform anyone they arrest that they have these rights. Often called "Miranda Rights," you hear them recited whenever you watch your favorite cop show on TV and hear the words, "You have the right to remain silent… you have the right to an attorney…"

THE BILL OF RIGHTS AND PUBLIC EDUCATION

Few settings have provided as many notable court cases as US public schools (i.e., *Brown v. Board of Education* and *Swann v. Charlotte-Mecklenburg Board of Education*). Again and again, the courts have been asked to rule on the extent to which the Bill of Rights applies in an educational setting. In *New Jersey v. TLO (1985)*, the Court ruled that Fourth Amendment rights do apply to students, but are more limited than in other public environments. The case involved the searching of a student's purse at a New Jersey high school. The search revealed that the student both used and sold marijuana. The Court ruled that, in order for school officials to conduct such a search, they must first have "reasonable suspicion" that a student is guilty of wrongdoing. In this case, the Court upheld the search because the student had been caught smoking.

A number of cases involving schools have centered on the First Amendment. One of the most notable was *Tinker v. Des Moines (1969)*. The case involved students who wore black armbands in protest of the Vietnam War. In response, the school suspended the students. The case went to the Supreme Court which ruled that the student's First Amendment rights had been violated because their actions were an expression of free speech that did not disrupt the educational mission of the school.

THE FOURTEENTH AMENDMENT

Ratified in 1868, the **Fourteenth Amendment** is special because it defines US citizenship to include all races and proclaims that any citizen of the US is automatically a citizen of the state in which he/she resides as well. The amendment also makes it illegal for any state government to pass laws denying liberties guaranteed under the Bill of Rights. For example, since the Fifth Amendment guarantees due process, no state may do anything to deny due process in a state case. In short, the Fourteenth Amendment guarantees the same rights under state governments that are guaranteed under the national government.

Practice 5.1 Landmark Supreme Court Cases

1. Congress passes a law making it illegal to burn a US flag. The president signs it. The Supreme Court, however, strikes down the law, ruling that it violates the First Amendment. What court case provides the Supreme Court with the authority it needs to make such a ruling?

   A. *Brown v. Board of Education of Topeka*

   B. *McCullough v. Maryland*

   C. *Marbury v. Madison*

   D. *Tinker v. Des Moines*

2. The police go to Amy Smith's apartment and, without warning, break the door down. Once inside, they discover a bloody knife in the bathroom. Later, the knife is used as evidence to convict Amy of murder. Amy appeals the decision because the police had no search warrant when they entered her residence. What court case will the courts most likely look to for precedence in this case?

   A.   *Gideon v. Wainwright*
   B.   *Miranda v. Arizona*
   C.   *New Jersey v. TLO*
   D.   *Mapp v. Ohio*

3. What do the cases of *Tinker v. Des Moines* and *New Jersey v. TLO* have in common?
   A.   They both involved the Fourth Amendment.
   B.   They both involved the First Amendment.
   C.   They both addressed the issue of how the Bill of Rights should be applied to public school settings.
   D.   They both involved freedom of speech in the public schools.

4. What is *due process* and how does the Supreme Court's ruling in *Miranda v. Arizona* seek to protect it?

5.2 EXECUTIVE ACTIONS

EXECUTIVE ORDERS AND THE PATRIOT ACT

In addition to the legislative and judicial branches of government, the executive branch also plays a role in the protection and/or suppression of civil liberties. Often, such action comes in the form of **executive orders**. Executive orders are issued by the president and carry the weight of law. The president assumes the power to issue such orders under Sections 1 and 3 of Article II of the Constitution, which grant the president "executive power" and state that he/she is to "take care that the laws (of the country) be faithfully executed...." Below is a list of some of the executive orders that have impacted civil rights.

1. The *Emancipation Proclamation (1863):* This order, handed down by President Lincoln, declared African-American slaves in those states in rebellion against the Union (Confederate states) to be free. It is important to note that the order did not free slaves in states loyal to the Union nor give them the rights of citizens. Such actions came later because, at the time, Lincoln could not afford to risk alienating those loyal to the Union who owned slaves or who opposed citizenship for African-Americans.

2. *Executive Order 8802 (1941):* Signed by President Franklin D. Roosevelt, this order prohibited discrimination in the defense industry which was growing rapidly and in need of labor during World War II.

3. ***Executive Order 9066 (1942):*** Also issued by Roosevelt, this order became one of the most notorious in US history. Because the Japanese attack on Pearl Harbor fueled suspicion of Japanese people in the United States, fear grew that Japanese Americans living on the West Coast might assist Japan through sabotage (engaging in activity to undermine the US government/military) and espionage (spying) in its war against the US. As a result, on February 19, 1942, President Roosevelt signed Executive Order 9066, ordering all Japanese Americans away from military facilities

Japanese Internment Camp

The US military then forced more than 100,000 Japanese Americans from their homes and businesses during the war and placed them in internment camps. These camps tended to be located in remote areas owned by the federal government. Many of these Japanese American citizens lost everything as a result. In 1944, a Japanese American named Fred Korematsu challenged the executive order on the grounds that it violated his civil rights. In *Korematsu v. United States,* the Supreme Court ruled that the government internment of Japanese Americans was not unlawful because "the military urgency of the situation..." justified it. Eventually, in 1983, the United States government formally recognized its injustice and authorized payments of $20,000 each to all living Japanese Americans who suffered under this policy.

4. ***Executive Order 9835 (1947):*** Following WWII, President Harry Truman and much of the US public were concerned about the threat of communism spreading to the United States. In 1947, Truman signed an executive order that came to be called the "Loyalty Order." This order empowered officials to investigate government employees and determine which ones were a security risk because of their political beliefs.

Harry S. Truman

5. ***Executive Order 9981 (1948):*** While Truman's "Loyalty Order" served to limit the rights of those with different political views, the order he signed in 1948 actually promoted civil rights by prohibiting discrimination in the armed forces.

6. ***Executive Order 11246 (1965):*** Signed by President Lyndon Johnson, it prohibited employment discrimination on the basis of race, religion, gender or nationality.

7. ***Executive Order 11478 (1969):*** President Nixon signed this order to prevent discrimination in the competitive service of the federal civilian workforce.

8. ***Executive Order 13087 (1998):*** Issued by President Bill Clinton, Order 13087 expanded Executive Order 11478 to prohibit discrimination based on sexual orientation.

Richard M. Nixon

9. ***Executive Order 13166 (2000):*** President Clinton signed this order during his final months in office. It required federal agencies to make sure that those with a limited understanding of English could still have access to government services.

10. *Executive Order 13224 (2001):* Since September 11, 2001, much of the executive branch's attention has been focused on combatting terrorism. Less than two weeks after the attacks, President George W. Bush signed Executive Order 13224 disrupting the financial activities of those believed to be associated with terrorist organizations.

In addition to executive orders, presidents also support the actions of Congress and the courts. Following Supreme Court rulings requiring the desegregation of public schools in the 1950s and 1960s, both President Eisenhower and President Kennedy authorized federal troops and/or law enforcement to make sure that the policies were properly enforced. More recently, President George W. Bush passionately fought for and continues to defend the **PATRIOT Act**. Congress passed this act at the president's urging in response to the 9/11 terrorist attacks. Its purpose is to battle terrorism by loosening restrictions on law enforcement when it comes to conducting investigations and gathering evidence. Supporters of the law say that it is crucial to the United States' ability to detect terrorist threats before future attacks occur. They claim that the law has saved, and will continue to save, the lives of US citizens. Critics of the law say that it goes too far and violates citizens' civil liberties. Despite opposition, Congress renewed the PATRIOT Act in March 2006.

EXECUTIVE AGENCIES AND THEIR IMPACT ON RIGHTS, ORDER AND PUBLIC SAFETY

The executive branch of the federal government is responsible for enforcing the laws Congress passes. In order to fulfill its role, a number of agencies and departments have been established. These agencies attempt to protect and ensure public welfare. Inevitably, however, their actions sometimes cause controversy regarding government authority and civil rights. For instance, the **Federal Bureau of Investigation (FBI)** is part of the **US Justice Department** (executive department responsible for most federal law enforcement) and is the federal government's top law enforcement agency. Its primary role is to investigate violations of federal crimes and crimes that cross state lines. One of its main objectives since 2001 has been to battle terrorism. Under the PATRIOT Act, the FBI has enjoyed more flexibility in how it is able to legally conduct searches and gather information. However, as mentioned earlier, this law relaxes some of the Constitutional restrictions placed on law enforcement to allow them to secure evidence more easily. As a result, debate rages as some claim the law is an important part of the war on terror, while others condemn it as a violation of civil liberties.

Also involved in the battle against terrorism is the **Department of Homeland Security**. Created after the 9/11 attacks, this department is responsible for preventing future terrorist attacks in the US, reducing the threat of such attacks, and minimizing the effects of such an attack should one occur. This department is also responsible for dealing with the effects of natural disasters such as earthquakes and hurricanes. The agency within the department that is responsible for planning for and responding to such disasters is the **Federal Emergency Management Administration (FEMA)**. This organization came under intense criticism in 2005 for its failure to adequately plan and provide relief for victims of Hurricane Katrina after it struck the Gulf Coast.

The **Central Intelligence Agency (CIA)** was created after World War II and is the federal agency charged with conducting espionage. It is up to the CIA to spy and gather intelligence on the activities of foreign countries. Since 9/11, many of its operations have been geared towards locating terrorists and uncovering terrorist plots. While many, including the president, insist that it is essential for the CIA to be able to carry out the bulk of its operations in secret, others claim that the agency must be more accountable. They claim that, without more congressional oversight, the CIA is prone to violate the civil rights of those both inside and outside the US. Opponents of this view respond that the agency operates within the limits of the law and that those who are not US citizens are not guaranteed the same rights under the Constitution as those who are.

Other law enforcement agencies that sometimes find themselves caught between protecting national security and safeguarding civil rights include the *Bureau of Alcohol, Tobacco, and Firearms (ATF)* which enforces federal laws regarding firearms and explosives as well as laws dealing with the manufacture, transportation, and distribution of alcohol and tobacco; the *Drug Enforcement Agency/Administration (DEA)* which enforces laws against drug trafficking and, unlike the FBI has the authority to pursue US drug investigations outside the United States; and the *United States Citizenship and Immigration Services (CIS)* which is part of the Department of Homeland Security and enforces laws and administers procedures for dealing with immigration and foreign visitors to the United States.

There are a number of other agencies concerned with public safety and which to some degree limit civil liberties as well. The **FDA (Food and Drug Administration)** upholds government guidelines to ensure that only the safest foods and medicines reach consumers. While the regulations it enforces help protect public health, its actions often mean that citizens are not free to buy the medicines and/or foods that they want and would willingly pay for. As a result, many citizens have started importing prescription drugs not yet approved in the United States. Similarly, the **US Department of Agriculture (USDA)** also seeks to ensure public safety by enforcing government regulations on agriculture. As with the FDA, however, this can mean limiting consumers' rights to purchase certain products and/or farmers' freedoms to engage in the most profitable means of production. As mentioned in chapter 3, the **EPA (Environmental Protection Agency)** makes sure that government environmental guidelines are adhered to. Again, while most applaud the government for protecting the environment, such regulations sometimes mean that businesses are not free to produce goods in the most efficient way or that people are not permitted to behave as they would like. The **FTC (Federal Trade Commission)** ensures consumer protection by making sure companies do not engage in false advertising and that they disclose crucial information (i.e., health concerns or issues regarding safety). The FTC also makes sure that businesses do not violate antitrust laws, thereby placing restrictions on how private businesses and business owners conduct themselves. The **FCC (Federal Communications Commission)** enforces federal regulations regarding modes of communication, such as television and radio broadcasts. It also regulates all interstate and international (provided at least one of the communicating parties is in the US) telecommunications. To a degree, the regulations enforced by the FCC limit free speech.

Practice 5.2 Executive Orders

1. Federal executive orders are issued by which of the following?

   A. Congress
   B. the president
   C. the governor
   D. the Supreme Court

2. Which of the following is the best description of executive orders issued by President Harry S. Truman?

   A. They were paranoid and served to maintain the status quo.
   B. They were discriminatory in nature.
   C. Some limited civil liberties while others promoted civil rights
   D. They were offensive to Democrats because they tended to favor communism.

3. What is the PATRIOT Act and what are some of the arguments in favor of and against it?

4. In what ways do the FDA, EPA and FCC limit civil liberties?

5.3 STATE ACTIONS AND CIVIL LIBERTIES

LEGISLATION

States must also deal with the conflicts that sometimes exist between public welfare and personal freedoms. One area of public concern is *highway safety*. Like all states, Maryland has state laws limiting how citizens may operate motor vehicles. In 1997, Maryland's **Primary Seat Belt Law** gave Maryland law enforcement officers the authority to ticket drivers and passengers who fail to use their seat belts. In 2005, Maryland also enacted stricter guidelines for **drivers under the age of 18**. Under the new law, new drivers must have a valid *learner's permit* for at least six

months and complete 60 hours of driving practice before obtaining a license. In addition, drivers under 18 are restricted from using cell phones while behind the wheel and cannot have another adolescent in the car with them for the first five months unless it is a direct family member or they are accompanied by an adult. While traffic laws help to decrease accidents and improve highway safety, they also interfere with citizens' freedom to decide for themselves whether or not to wear seat belts and/or under what conditions they will drive within the state of Maryland.

State laws also affect other areas as well, such as discrimination, due process and the environment (i.e. the Maryland Healthy Air Act mentioned in chapter 3). In many states, both state and local governments have passed **smoking legislation** which limits where and when tobacco users may "light up." For instance, in Maryland, smoking is prohibited in enclosed workplaces (except for designated areas), on public transportation and in schools. In addition, any smoking that occurs in restaurants or bars must be confined to specific areas that do not exceed 40% of the establishment. Maryland also places certain restrictions on those who own or want to purchase **firearms**. The state requires a seven day waiting period before buying a handgun and limits purchases of such firearms to one per month. The minimum age for purchasing a handgun is 21 and the state police maintain records of all such transactions. Recently, the General Assembly also passed legislation that will require guns sold in Maryland to be equipped with built-in child safety locks and will mandate safety training for gun purchasers. While such restrictions are applauded by many, others protest such laws as violations of citizens' rights.

A particularly emotional area that often involves conflict between individual rights and public concern is the issue of convicted **child predators** (adults who have been convicted of sexually molesting children). Most states, including Maryland, require that those convicted of sexual offenses against children register where they are living with local law enforcement officials. Many local communities also restrict where such offenders may live. A number of child advocates (people who fight for the protection and rights of children) argue that laws often do not go far enough. They believe that the government should alert private citizens when convicted sexual offenders move into their communities so that parents can better protect their children. Civil rights advocates, however, often respond that such requirements would violate the civil rights of a convicted child molester because he/she has already been punished for his/her crime and is entitled to the same "right to privacy" as any other citizen. They often argue that to take such action would, in effect, subject offenders to "double jeopardy" by punishing them twice for the same crime.

GUBERNATORIAL ACTIONS

Current Governor of Maryland Martin O'Malley

Like the president of the United States, governors can also issue **gubernatorial executive orders**. These are executive orders that are issued from the state's top executive officer. For example, in 2003, following the terrorist strikes of September 11, Maryland Governor Robert Ehrlich issued an executive order establishing the **Governor's Office of Homeland Security** for directing and coordinating efforts to protect the state against terrorist strikes. From time to time, governors will also declare a **state of emergency** throughout or in certain parts of the state following some catastrophic event or natural disaster. Such action could include deploying the national guard to maintain order, prevent looting (stealing) and/or enforce curfews (set times at which the public is to be off the streets).

State actions are intended to protect society and provide for the public welfare, but they also restrict civil liberties. Drivers are not free to decide for themselves whether or not they want to wear a seat belt. Teenagers are not free to drive cars with the same freedoms as adults. Business owners are not allowed to operate their businesses any way they see fit. Consumers have to accept limitations on their "right to bear arms" and purchase certain products. Executive orders sometimes interfere with citizens' personal freedoms. Finding the balance between public welfare and individual civil liberties has historically been, and will continue to be, a topic of intense debate both in Maryland and throughout the US.

Practice 5.3 State Actions and Civil Liberties

1. Which of the following is true regarding state actions designed to protect the public?

    A. They are always initiated by the legislative branch of government.
    B. They tend to take longer to implement because chief executives at the state level cannot issue executive orders.
    C. They rarely promote public safety without limiting personal rights.
    D. The Governor's Department of Homeland Security is officially responsible for implementing all such actions.

2. David owns a restaurant in College Park. Because he serves a largely college crowd that will frequent his establishment late at night, he wants to allow smoking. Which of the following guidelines must David adhere to?

    A. He cannot allow smoking.
    B. Because it is his place he can have whatever guidelines about smoking he wants.
    C. He must allow at least 40% of the establishment to be reserved for smoking customers.
    D. He cannot allow smoking in more than 40% of the establishment.

3. Why do some civil libertarians oppose making citizens aware that a convicted child molester has moved into their neighborhood?

CHAPTER 5 REVIEW

Key Terms and Concepts.

Marbury v. Madison	US Justice Department
McCullough v. Maryland	Department of Homeland Security
Plessy v. Ferguson	FEMA
Brown v. Board of Education Topeka	CIA
Alexander v. Holmes County Board of Education	FDA
Swann v. Charlotte-Mechklenburg Bd. of Education	USDA
due process	EPA
exclusionary rule	FTC
Mapp v. Ohio	FCC
Gideon v. Wainwrifht	Primary Seat Belt Law
Miranda v. Arizona	restrictions on drivers under 18
New Jersey v. TLO	smoking legislation
Tinker v. Des Moines	firearms
Fourteenth Amendment	child predators
executive orders	gubernatorial executive orders
PATRIOT Act	Governor's Office of Homeland Security
FBI	state of emergency

Multiple Choice and Short Answers

1. A television broadcast violates federal standards by using a word that is not allowed on network TV. As a result, the station that aired the broadcast is ordered to pay a hefty fine and is warned that future violations could result in the loss of its license. The agency that issued this fine and warning is **most likely** which of the following?

   A. FCC B. FTC C. EPA D. FBI

2. Today, it is widely accepted that Congress has powers broader than just those specifically mentioned in the Constitution. The courts have held that Congress may appeal to "implied powers" to justify taking actions that are "necessary and proper" for carrying out its constitutional duties. Which court case helped establish this precedence?

   A. *Marbury v. Madison*

   B. *McCullough v. Maryland*

   C. *Plessy v. Ferguson*

   D. *Miranda v. Arizona*

3. Doug is arrested and charged with the crime of arson. Without being aware that he is entitled to a lawyer and that he does not have to incriminate himself, Doug confesses to the crime. Eventually, the court assigns him a defense lawyer who argues that the confession cannot be used as evidence

against his client. The lawyer claims that Doug was denied due process by not being made aware that he had the right to legal counsel and the right to remain silent. Which of the following court cases will Doug's attorney **most likely** appeal to in order to support his argument?

A. *Marbury v. Madison*

B. *Mapp v. Ohio*

C. *Gideon v. Wainwright*

D. *Miranda v. Arizona*

4. Which of the following **does not** represent a means by which an executive branch of government attempts to deal with issues regarding public welfare?

A. EPA

B. executive orders

C. Maryland's Primary Seat Belt Law

D. state of emergency declared by Maryland's governor

5. A series of devastating storms hits several midwestern states, leaving thousands of US citizens homeless and in need of federal assistance. Which of the following agencies will be responsible for dealing with this situation?

A. EPA
B. FDA
C. FEMA
D. FCC

6. FBI agents raid an apartment in Baltimore and arrest several people suspected of plotting a terrorist attack against the city. They search the premises and uncover photos and blueprints of government buildings, as well as materials for making explosives. Attorneys for the arrested suspects argue that the arrests are unlawful and that the seized evidence cannot be used at trial because the FBI violated their clients' civil liberties. The government argues, however, that federal legislation signed after 9/11 and renewed in March 2006 gives law enforcement broader powers to fight terrorism and therefore the arrests are valid. The government is appealing to which of the following to make its case?

A. the PATRIOT Act

B. the Terrorism Act

C. the Department of Homeland Security

D. an executive order by President George W. Bush issued shortly after 9/11

7. In what ways do the Primary Seat Belt Law and restrictions on Maryland drivers under the age of 18 impact civil liberties?

8. A 20-year-old Maryland resident wants to buy a handgun in Annapolis. Why will she not be allowed to do so and what reasons might the government give for limiting her civil liberties?

9. When might a governor declare a state of emergency and how can such a declaration impact people's individual rights?

10. What issue did both *Plessy v. Ferguson* and *Brown v. Board of Education* deal with? State the Court's ruling in each case and describe how its decision in *Brown* impacted its earlier decision in *Plessy*.

Chapter 6
Criminal and Civil Law

This chapter addresses the following expectation(s) from **Core Learning Goal 1 Political Systems**

Expectation 1.2	The student will evaluate how the United States government has maintained a balance between protecting rights and maintaining order. *Indicators 1.2.4 and 1.2.5*

US society is governed by both criminal and civil laws. **Criminal laws** deal with crime and define the punishments for criminal offenses (i.e., theft and murder are criminal offenses). **Civil laws** are those laws that govern relationships between private individuals and/or entities. For example, say a landlord and a tenant are arguing over who is responsible for paying to fix an insect problem. Since no crime has been committed, this kind of case would be settled in civil court.

6.1 CRIMINAL LAW

CONSTITUTIONAL RIGHTS

Under the United States Constitution, those suspected, accused and/or convicted of a crime have certain civil rights which the government must uphold. Under the *Fourth Amendment*, US citizens have a right to be, "...secure in their persons, houses, papers and effects, against unreasonable searches and seizures." The courts have interpreted this to mean that, in most cases, law enforcement must have a search warrant to search a citizen or their property and that no such warrant can be issued without **probable cause**. In other words, law enforcement

officials must have good reason to believe that evidence of a crime exists before they can obtain a warrant. They cannot randomly search whomever they want or for whatever reason.

The *Fifth Amendment* says that no citizen shall have to answer for an "infamous crime" unless they are indicted by a **grand jury**. A grand jury is a group of private citizens that assembles to hear evidence presented by the government to decide if a suspected person

95

should stand trial for a crime. Their proceedings are usually held in secret without the defendant or his/her attorney being present. An **indictment** is the formal charge put forth by a grand jury that there is enough evidence to warrant that a person stand trial. Under the Fifth Amendment, a person cannot be placed in *double jeopardy*. In other words, the same person cannot be charged for the same crime a second time once they have been tried and found "not guilty" in a court of law. Neither can a person be forced to be a witness against him/herself. Although a **criminal defendant** (person charged with committing a crime) may not lie in court, if he/she feels that testifying truthfully would hurt his/her chances of being acquitted (found not guilty), then he/she does not have to testify at his/her own trial. Finally, the **Fifth Amendment due process clause** protects citizens by stating that no citizen may be deprived of "life, liberty or property without due process of law." Due process simply means that the government must abide by the Constitution and not violate the rights guaranteed to citizens as it carries out criminal investigations/proceedings.

Historic Punishment: Stocks

The *Sixth Amendment* guarantees accused persons the right to a "speedy and public trial, by an impartial jury..." and the right to be informed of the charges against them. This is meant to prevent decisions from being made in secret that might violate a person's rights and ensures that decisions about guilt or innocence are made by a group of private citizens rather than by a single judge. In addition, the Sixth Amendment guarantees the right to legal counsel (a lawyer) and to confront and call witnesses at trial. Finally, the *Eighth Amendment* prohibits excessive bail and/or fines and forbids cruel and unusual punishment once a citizen has been convicted of a crime.

THE FOURTEENTH AMENDMENT

Dred Scott

Ironically, the US Supreme Court actually appealed to the Fifth Amendment's guarantee of due process to strengthen the institution of slavery in 1857. In the case of *Dred Scott v. Sanford,* the Court heard a case involving a Missouri slave named Dred Scott. Scott's owner had taken him into free territory where he lived for four years. The owner later returned to Missouri where he died. After his death, Scott sued for his freedom. The Supreme Court ruled that Scott had no right to sue because, as a slave, he was not a citizen. It also declared that a slave owner could not be deprived of his "property" without *due process of law.* Following the Civil War, however, Congress ratified the **Fourteenth Amendment**. It made the recently emancipated slaves citizens of both the United States and the states in which they lived. It also says that no state may deny due process and/or equal protection under the law to any citizen. In effect, the Fourteenth Amendment guarantees due process in state cases as well as in federal criminal proceedings.

THE CRIMINAL JUDICIAL PROCESS

PRIOR TO TRIAL

The criminal judicial process begins with the commission of a crime. **Misdemeanors** are less serious crimes that are usually punishable by a fine, probation or less than a year in jail. **Felonies** are more serious crimes (i.e., murder, rape, drug trafficking, kidnapping, etc.) and are punishable by longer periods of incarceration and/or capital punishment (execution). Following a crime, a certain law enforcement agency will exercise jurisdiction (authority to investigate the case). This could be a local police department, state or county law enforcement agency or a federal agency (i.e., FBI). Once law enforcement feels it has a likely suspect (someone suspected of committing the crime) it will then make an arrest and take the person into custody. In most misdemeanor cases, law enforcement must first obtain a legal document from the court called an *arrest warrant*. In the case of more serious offenses, or if law enforcement witnessed the crime, the government does not usually need a warrant so long as they have probable cause.

As mentioned before, the person charged with a criminal offense is called the *defendant*. Meanwhile, the attorney representing the government's case against the defendant (i.e., district attorney or US attorney) is known as the **prosecutor**. A defendant can be charged with a crime either by means of an *indictment* or a *complaint*. An indictment is a formal charge that someone has committed a felony and is issued by a grand jury. A complaint is when a prosecutor files charges directly with the court rather than seeking an indictment from a grand jury. When a complaint is used to file more serious charges, the court will hold a *preliminary hearing* to determine if there is enough evidence to warrant a trial. While the Constitution requires that grand juries be used in more serious federal cases, many states have ceased to use grand juries in favor of using the complaint/preliminary hearing approach. Both grand juries and preliminary hearing are meant to protect the rights of the accused.

Under the Constitution, citizens who are accused of a crime are guaranteed **writ of habeas corpus** which means that they are entitled to appear before a judge to determine whether or not their arrest and incarceration is justified. Shortly after an individual is arrested for a serious offense, a judge presides over an *arraignment hearing* in which the defendant is officially informed of the charges against him/her. If the judge rules that there is sufficient evidence to justify the arrest/charges, the defendant is then asked to enter a plea of "guilty," "not guilty" or "no contest." If the defendant pleads guilty then the judge will either impose a *sentence* (punishment for a crime) or set a future date for sentencing. If the defendant pleads "not guilty," then the court will schedule a date for either a trial or a preliminary hearing if one has not yet been held. A plea of "no contest" simply means that a defendant is not admitting guilt but neither will he/she attempt to prove his/he innocence. Defendants who use this plea normally are sentenced as if they had entered a plea of guilty, but have the privilege of not having an admission of guilt on their record.

In reality, many cases never go to trial. This is because defendants often plead guilty. They do this as a result of **plea bargaining**. This is a process in which defendants who know they will likely be found guilty at trial agree to plead guilty in exchange for being charged with a less serious offense or a guarantee of less severe punishment. For instance, suppose Susan is at the mall shopping. Suddenly she sees her boyfriend, Gavin, in the parking lot kissing her best friend. In a fit of rage, Susan rips the arm off of a department store mannequin, rushes to the parking lot and begins beating the couple relentlessly, sending them both to the hospital with head injuries. Because there were a number of witnesses to the attack, Susan knows that she will likely be found guilty of "assault with a deadly weapon" if she goes to trial. In exchange for being charged with the less serious crime of "misdemeanor assault," she agrees to plead "guilty" rather than argue her case in court. This saves the government time and money, ensures the defendant a lighter sentence and prevents the judicial system from being overwhelmed with cases waiting to be tried. Due to the large number of criminal cases that come before the US judicial system every year, plea bargaining is essential because it allows cases to be resolved relatively quickly.

Criminal and Civil Law

CRIMINAL TRIALS

Defendant in Court

At criminal trials, prosecutors present the government's case against the accused, defense attorneys represent the defendant, a trial jury (usually consisting of twelve citizens) hears the evidence and decides if the defendant is guilty and a judge presides over the proceedings. Trial juries in both criminal and civil cases are sometimes called ***petit juries*** because they are generally smaller than grand juries that issue indictments. Under the law, all accused persons come to trial under a **presumption of innocence**. In other words, it is not up to the defendant to prove his/her innocence; rather, it is up to the government to prove his/her guilt beyond **"reasonable doubt."** The prosecution does not have to prove that an accused individual committed the crime beyond *all* doubt; it simply must present evidence that removes doubt in the mind of any "reasonable person" that the accused is guilty of the crime. If a defendant wishes, he/she may waive his/her right to a jury and just stand trial before a judge. Also, juries are often not used in less serious cases. Meanwhile, if a defendant cannot afford to hire a defense attorney, the courts have interpreted the Sixth Amendment to mean that the government must appoint one for him/her, except in less serious cases (i.e. misdemeanors that carry little or no jail time).

Witness Gets Sworn In

During a trial, both the prosecutor and defense attorney will make opening arguments to the jury in which it summarizes its case. Each side will call witnesses and will have an opportunity to cross-examine (ask questions of) the other side's witnesses. Witnesses are called to testify by means of a **subpoena**. These are legal documents ordering a particular person to appear in court to testify. If a witness refuses to show up after receiving a subpoena, he/she can be arrested and charged with "contempt of court." Once on the witness stand, witnesses for both sides are sworn to tell the truth. A witness who lies is guilty of *perjury* and can end up in jail. Finally, each side's attorney will present closing arguments in which they attempt to persuade the jury one last time. The jury will then deliberate (meet in closed session) until it is ready to deliver a verdict. If the verdict is "not guilty," then the judicial proceedings are over and the defendant is free to go. If the verdict is "guilty," then the judge will either pronounce sentence or set a future date for sentencing *unless* it is a capital offense (crime for which the defendant can be sentenced to death). If it is a capital case and the defendant is found guilty, then the jury must deliberate again to decide whether or not the convicted person will be executed or sentenced to life in prison. Sometimes the members of a jury cannot agree on the guilt or innocence of a defendant. Such juries are referred to as "hung juries." The result is a **mistrial**. If a mistrial occurs, the prosecutor must either retry the case or drop the charges against the defendant.

Practice 5.1 Criminal and Civil Law

1. US citizens do not have to worry about random searches of their homes by law enforcement thanks to which of the following?

   A. the Fifth Amendment

   B. the Sixth Amendment

   C. protection from double jeopardy

   D. the Fourth Amendment

98

2. The Fourteenth Amendment had which of the following effects?

   A. It ensured that states must respect a citizen's right to due process.

   B. It stated that criminal defendants are entitled to legal counsel.

   C. It upheld the Supreme Court's ruling in the Dred Scott case.

   D. It mandated that criminal defendants could not be indicted by a grand jury.

3. What is *plea bargaining* and why do prosecutors, defendants and the courts support the practice?

6.2 CIVIL LAW

Unlike criminal trials that are initiated by the government, civil trials must be initiated by individuals, organizations or businesses. Civil cases begin when one side brings a **lawsuit** (claim that a person, business, etc. has been wronged) against another side with which they have a dispute. The side that initiates the lawsuit is called the **plaintiff**. The side against whom the lawsuit is filed is called the **civil defendant**. Unlike criminal cases, where the accused can face incarceration or some other form of criminal punishment, defendants who lose civil cases normally have to pay damages (money) to the plaintiff. If defendants *win* a civil case, then they don't have to pay anything other than their attorney's fees. In some cases, the defendant files a *countersuit* against the plaintiff. If this happens and the defendant wins, then the plaintiff is the one who has to pay damages even though he/she was the one who originally filed the lawsuit.

Often, civil lawsuits have to deal with **contracts.** Contracts are legal agreements between individuals and/or businesses in which each side agrees to provide something (i.e., a service or money) in exchange for something in return. If one party feels that the other party has not stuck to the legal conditions of the contract, then they may sue the defendant for **breach of contract** (not abiding by the conditions of the legal contract). Many civil cases involve **torts**. Torts are lawsuits that involve alleged injuries to one's person, reputation, property or business related to violation of some general community standard rather than a specific contract. Torts often involve charges of **negligence**. Negligence is any action, or lack of action, that is deemed to be irresponsible on the part of the offender and results in some form of injury. For example, say you fail to engage the emergency brake on your car. As a result, your car rolls down the hill and crashes through your neighbor's house while she is enjoying a big bowl of popcorn and watching the latest episode of *American Idol*. The bad news for your neighbor (in addition to missing the end of her favorite show) is that the front of her house is demolished and she has suffered a broken arm. The bad news for you (in addition to the damage to your car) is that your neighbor now has grounds to file a tort lawsuit against you. Why? Your failure to engage the emergency brake was *negligent* and led to an injury to someone else's property and person. Torts can involve such things as causing excessive noise or pollution, spreading slander, striking someone, trespassing, causing someone to slip and injure themselves and so on.

CIVIL COURT PROCEEDINGS

Arbitration Before a Neutral Panel

Both civil plaintiffs and defendants are usually represented by attorneys. However, unlike criminal cases, neither party is guaranteed legal counsel under the Constitution; therefore, the court is not obligated to provide a lawyer for either side. Defendants usually become aware that someone has taken civil action against them by means of a legal document called a **summons**. The summons informs them of the civil charges and tells them what day they must appear in court. Once a civil case goes to court, the plaintiff must prove that the defendant is guilty based on the **preponderance of evidence**. In other words, they must present sufficient evidence to show that the defendant is most likely guilty of the claimed offense. Proving that the defendant is *most likely* guilty of a civil offense is not as strict as having to prove guilt beyond reasonable doubt in a criminal case. For example, in 1995, NFL football great OJ Simpson was accused of murdering his ex-wife and a man named Ronald Goldman. Because the jury felt that the prosecution did not prove his guilt beyond reasonable doubt, Simpson was found "not guilty." However, the victims' families later sued Simpson in civil court, claiming that he was liable (responsible) for the deaths. They won, and Simpson was ordered to pay damages. The evidence, which was mostly the same at both trials, was enough to find Simpson liable in civil court, but not enough to convict him of murder in criminal court.

Civil cases involving small amounts of money (i.e., less than a few thousand dollars) often are settled by a single judge or magistrate. However, under the *Seventh Amendment*, defendants in more serious civil cases are entitled to a trial by jury. Many times, civil cases are resolved by **out-of-court settlements** or **arbitration**. *Settlements* are when the plaintiff and defendant meet together along with their attorneys and come to an agreement both sides can live with. Usually, the settlement involves the plaintiff settling for less money in damages than he/she originally wanted and the defendant paying more than he/she was originally willing. Although both sides have to give up some of what they wanted, they agree to settle rather than invest additional time and money in going to court. By comparison, *arbitration* is when a neutral third party mediates the dispute and is granted authority by both sides to render a decision that is legally binding. Parties in a civil dispute will often turn to arbitration if they feel that the legal process could become too long and expensive.

Practice 6.2 Civil Law

1. Melissa is being sued by her former client because the client claims that she did not perform the services she promised when they entered into a business relationship. Which of the following statements is FALSE?

   A. This is a civil rather than a criminal case.

   B. This is a tort case.

   C. Melissa is being sued for breach of contract.

   D. The person suing Melissa is a plaintiff who will likely hire a lawyer to seek damages.

2. Which of the following describes a tort case?

   A. Bob sues Rachel for failing to honor the conditions of her contract.

   B. Brenda sues Eric for divorce because she is tired of him neglecting her and working all the time.

   C. Wilma sues Antonio because her daughter got seriously hurt on his son's trampoline while the two of them jumped on it without adult supervision.

   D. Robomill, Inc. sues Megastorm Industries for failing to live up to the terms of a business agreement.

3. What is the difference between an *out-of-court settlement* and *arbitration*? Why are both sometimes used to settle civil disputes?

6.3 THE APPELLATE PROCESS

Defendants who are found guilty of a crime or who lose civil cases may file an **appeal**. In other words, they may ask a higher court to review, hoping that it will overturn the lower court's decision. Appeals may be based on either an *issue of fact* or an *issue of law*. An issue of fact appeal claims that certain facts about a case were not given proper consideration (i.e., new evidence). An issue of law appeal argues that the decision of the lower court should be overturned because the court did not properly follow trial procedures or the defendant's rights were in some way violated. Appellate courts are different from trial courts because decisions are usually rendered by a panel of judges, rather than a jury. After hearing arguments from both sides, judges on the appellate court will then vote and come to a decision. The *majority opinion* is a written statement that presents the court's decision and why it decided the way it did. Judges who voted differently might write a *dissenting opinion*, in which they give their reasons for coming to a different conclusion. At times, some judges issue a *concurring opinion*. This is an opinion that agrees with the conclusions of the majority opinion, but for different reasons.

The chart on the following page depicts the appellate process in both the federal and Maryland state courts.

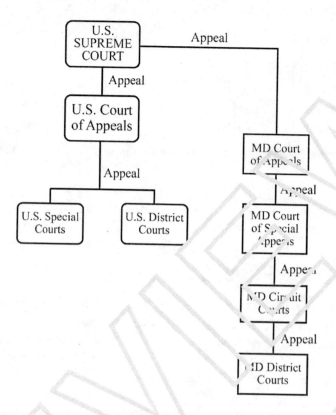

Practice 6.3   The Appellate Process

1. Barbara is convicted of a serious crime. However, because her attorney believes her constitutional rights were violated prior to trial, he and Barbara will ask the Maryland Court of Special Appeals to review the case and overturn the lower court conviction. This process is called what?

   A. a dissenting opinion

   B. an appeal

   C. writ of certiorari

   D. a judicial review

2. Marcus is part of a panel of judges which has just overturned a lower court's decision. However, Marcus disagrees with his colleagues' decision and believes that they should have upheld the decision instead. As a result, he writes his own opinion as to why he disagrees. What is Marcus' opinion called?

   A. majority opinion

   C. concurrent opinion

   b. minority opinion

   D. dissenting opinion

3. What is the difference between an appeal based on an issue of fact and one based on an issue of law?

CHAPTER 6 REVIEW

Key Terms and Concepts

criminal laws
civil laws
probable cause
grand jury
indictment
double jeopardy
criminal defendant
Fifth Amendment due process clause
Fourteenth Amendment
misdemeanors
felonies
prosecutor
writ of habeas corpus
plea bargaining
petit jury
presumption of innocence

reasonable doubt
subpoena
mistrial
lawsuit
plaintiff
civil defendant
damages
contracts
breach of contract
torts
negligence
summons
preponderance of evidence
out-of-court settlements
arbitration
appeal

Multiple Choice and Short Answers

1. Law enforcement officials in Landover want to search the apartment of a young couple that they are positive is selling illegal drugs and firearms out of their home. However, before they can make such a search, which of the following will have to occur?

    A. The police will have to first talk to the couple's attorney so as not to violate any Sixth Amendment rights.

    B. The police will first have to show probable cause as to why they believe the couple is guilty of these charges so they can obtain a search warrant.

    C. The police will have to get a subpoena so that, once the couple is under arrest, they can search the apartment.

    D. The police will first have to convince a grand jury that there is probable cause to issue an indictment against the couple.

2. Bill is a defendant in court. If Bill is found guilty at trial, the maximum he could be sentenced to is 30 years in prison and be ordered to pay a fine of at least $75,000. Bill has been charged with what?

    A. a felony   B. a misdemeanor   C. a civil offense   D. a capital offense

3. Walter's defense attorney informs him that the prosecutor has a video showing Walter holding up the liquor store he is accused of robbing. As a result, Walter's attorney convinces him to plead guilty in exchange for having the prosecutor charge him with a less serious crime. Walter has just accepted what?

    A. a pre-trial settlement

    B. a tort deal

    C. a jury deliberation

    D. a plea bargain

4. Janice has just received a written notice that one of her customers is suing her for failing to honor her contract. The document informing Janice of these charges and letting her know what day to report to court is called what?

    A. a subpoena

    B. a summons

    C. a writ of certiorari

    D. a brief

5. A state senator in Maryland wants to introduce a bill in the General Assembly that would allow the state to imprison a state citizen and/or take his or her property for state use without having to give any justification for its actions. He claims that this law would allow law enforcement to do a more effective job battling drug dealers and terrorists. One of his colleagues, however, points out to him that the state cannot pass such a law. Which of the following is the **best** basis for the colleague's opinion?

    A. Fourth Amendment

    B. Fifth Amendment

    C. Sixth Amendment

    D. Fourteenth Amendment

6. Emily is accused of embezzling thousands of dollars from the company she works for. As a result, she has been indicted and faces more than 20 years in prison if convicted. She hires Sam to defend her in court, while the government has appointed Michelle to argue and present evidence showing that Emily is indeed guilty. Which of the following statements is true?

    A. This is a civil case, Emily is the plaintiff, Sam her defense attorney and Michelle the prosecutor.

    B. This is a criminal case, Emily is charged with a misdemeanor, Sam is the prosecutor and Michelle the complainant.

    C. Emily is charged with a felony, Michelle is the prosecutor and Sam may want to plea bargain to get Emily a sentence that is less than 20 years.

    D. Emily is the defendant in a civil case, Sam is her defense attorney and Michelle represents the plaintiff which, in this case, is the government.

7. After hearing all of the evidence and arguing amongst themselves for three weeks, members of the jury in Pete's armed robbery trial cannot come to a consensus on whether or not he is guilty. Five members think he is guilty, five think he is innocent and two cannot make up their minds. As a result, they finally give up and notify the court that they cannot render a verdict in this case. Which of the following **best** describes this scenario?

   A. This is a petit jury convinced beyond reasonable doubt

   B. This is a hung jury and the judge will declare a mistrial.

   C. The prosecutor will have to drop the charges against the defendant.

   D. This is a preponderance of evidence that will result in a plea of "no contest."

8. Amanda sues Phil because she insists that he failed to perform the services for which he was hired and yet refuses to reimburse her. Phil refuses to reimburse her because he insists he did provide the required services and any problems she is having are due to her own irresponsibility. Without going to court, Amanda and Phil, along with their attorneys, get together to discuss the problem. Between the four of them, they work out a solution that, while not perfect, is acceptable to both sides. Phil will pay Amanda a partial reimbursement in exchange for her dropping the lawsuit. This solution is an example of what?

   A. arbitration

   B. breach of contract

   C. out-of-court settlement

   D. plea bargaining

9. What is the difference between torts and civil cases involving breach of contract? Give an example of each.

10. What is meant by the terms "reasonable doubt" and "preponderance of evidence"?

Chapter 7
The United States and World Affairs

This chapter addresses the following expectation(s) from **Core Learning Goal 2 Peoples of the Nation and the World**

Expectation 2.1	The student will evaluate the interdependent relationship of United States politics and government to world affairs *Indicators 2.1.1 and 2.1.2*
Expectation 2.2	The student will compare and evaluate the effectiveness of the United States system of government and various other political systems. *Indicator 2.2.1*

7.1 THE INTERNATIONAL COMMUNITY

Although most acknowledge that the United States is both economically and militarily the world's most powerful and influential nation, it still exists as part of a much larger **international community**. This community consists of all the nations of the world, many of which have different forms of government, different values and priorities, different historical perspectives and vastly different cultures than the United States. Some of these countries have traditionally been friendly towards the US. Others have been more hostile. Learning to work with and coexist with countries that operate differently and have different interests is important for maintaining global peace and stability.

Map of the World

Chapter 7

POLITICAL DIFFERENCES

DEMOCRACIES

As we learned in chapter 1, the United States is a **representative democracy**, which means it is ruled by the people. (Review chapter 1, section 1.1 concerning the difference between a *direct democracy* and a *representative democracy*.) US citizens elect representatives in free elections who then make government decisions on the citizens' behalf. As a result, the United States views the world through the eyes of a democracy that assumes all human beings are born with "natural rights" and expects the government to respect and uphold these liberties. Many other nations of the world also operate using some form of democratic government. However, even among democracies, there can be great differences in how they conduct their governments. As we discussed in chapter 4, some nations might have a multi-party system, while the US relies on a two-party system.

British Parliament

Another difference is that while the US relies on a **presidential system** of democracy, many of the world's other democracies use a **parliamentary system**. In a *presidential system*, power is divided between an elected legislature and a separately elected president. In a *parliamentary democracy*, however, the nation's chief executive is selected by the legislature (usually referred to as *parliament*) rather than being elected directly by the people. This executive (usually called the *prime minister*) is the head of the party that controls Parliament (see chapter 4, section 4.1), meaning that the voters influence the choice for prime minister *indirectly* when they vote one party or another into power. Whereas the US model of democratic government is based on a separation of powers between the legislative, executive and judicial branches, in a parliamentary government, power usually rests solely in the legislature with the prime minister as its head. Its actions are not subject to checks from a separate executive or judicial branch. Even among the world's numerous parliamentary democracies, there are often differences in how these nations conduct government and implement policies.

AUTHORITARIAN GOVERNMENTS

Adolf Hitler

An **authoritarian government** is one in which the government is controlled by a ruler and/or a ruling party that is not subject to the will of the people. Many times these governments can be **totalitarian**. In a totalitarian state, the nation is far more important than individuals. The government controls nearly every aspect of society and does not permit political opposition (i.e., Nazi Germany under Adolf Hitler). The "natural rights" championed by the United States' Founding Fathers would mean little in a totalitarian form of government.

Authoritarian governments can take several forms. Under an autocracy, power rests in the hands of a single individual, such as an emperor, dictator or king. An **absolute monarchy** is ruled by a king or queen whose power is not limited by any laws or other bodies of government, although they may be limited somewhat by social norms and/or traditions. In a **limited monarchy** (often called a **constitutional monarchy**) the king or queen must behave according to certain laws and usually shares power with other branches of government.

The United States and World Affairs

England at the time of the American Revolution had just such a government, in which the king and Parliament shared power. Obviously, limited monarchies are less authoritative than absolute monarchies. Under a **dictatorship**, a single individual or party leads without being checked by any laws or regulations. The government is unlimited in what it can do. Saddam Hussein's former government in Iraq and North Korea's ruler, Kim Jong-il, are both modern day examples of dictators. A small group of people, usually from among the upper classes (called the *aristocracy*), control the government in an **oligarchy**. Such governments tend to offer little chance for poorer people to break out of poverty and change their social status, because the upper class uses its power to protect the status quo (keep things the way they are).

Some societies base their government on religion. This kind of government is called a **theocracy**. The Taliban government overthrown by US forces in Afghanistan in 2001 was an example of a theocracy, because it was based on an interpretation of Muslim law. Historically, there have been a few radical movements that advocated *anarchy*. Anarchy is the concept of having no government at all. No society, of course, can exist very long in a state of anarchy.

Taliban Forces

Just because two nations share the same model of government doesn't mean that they will always be allies or that their interests are the same. For instance, the United States has at times allied itself with monarchs and dictators in order to further US economic and/or political interests. In 1991, the US (a democracy) and Saudi Arabia (a monarchy) joined forces to repel Iraq's invasion of Kuwait during the Persian Gulf War. During the Cold War, it was not uncommon for the US to support dictators (some of which were corrupt) who helped suppress communist revolutions. By contrast, the US has also experienced conflict with other democracies. For instance, France refused to support the US led coalition that launched a war against Iraq in 2003. As you can see, how governments are structured is not necessarily the determining factor in whether or not they cooperate or enjoy friendly relations with one another.

FEDERATIONS, CONFEDERATIONS AND UNITARIAN MODELS OF GOVERNMENT

In Chapter 1, we examined *federalism*. Federalism is the principle of dividing power between two levels of government. In the United States, power is divided between the national (federal) government and the states. Although the states enjoy a certain amount of autonomy (right to make their own decisions), they are still subordinate to the national government and must operate within the limitations of the US Constitution. Such a model of government is called a *federation*. Although similar in some ways, a federation is different from a *confederation*. Under a confederation, government authority is still divided between national and state governments, however, it is the states that have most of the power. The states loosely agree to cooperate as a national body on certain matters (i.e., national defense) but still remain sovereign. In a confederation, the laws of the state are superior and take precedence over the laws of the national government. Originally, the United States tried to organize its government as a confederation, but the attempt failed because the nation needed a stronger national government. (Review chapter 1 section 1.1 regarding the *Articles of Confederation*.)

Map of Confederate States

In 1860, a number of southern states seceded from the Union because they felt that the federal government was threatening the sovereignty of state governments. They set up their own government and called their new "nation" the *Confederate States of America*. As the name implies, it was intended to be a confederation in which the states could rule themselves while being loosely affiliated with one another. As in the case of the earlier attempt to establish a confederation after the American Revolution, the South's model of government also proved impractical for sustaining any kind of national, united front. The Confederacy collapsed, in part, because of the inability of its states to cooperate effectively with one another.

Finally, there are **unitary governments**. These are governments in which there is no official division of power; all the power rests in the hands of a national, central government. In some unitary states, autonomous territories do develop. However, this generally tends to occur because the national government has granted them some degree of self-rule and the central government usually retains the authority to revoke such independence and subject these areas to central rule again if it sees fit. Great Britain and Japan are both examples of unitary governments.

CULTURAL DIFFERENCES

In addition to political differences nations of the world also have **cultural differences**. People are ethnically diverse, come from different regions of the world, have different historical perspectives, practice different religions and so on. These differences mean that people see the world in different ways. Capitalists in the US might look at socialism (government based on state ownership of property, state run medical care, massive income redistribution and welfare programs, etc.) and see something repressive and to be feared. Meanwhile, peasants in a developing country who suffer in extreme poverty might look at the same model of government and see it as a reform to be embraced. In the United States, religion and government are usually viewed as separate entities that should operate free and independent from each other. In other countries, however, religion is seen as a driving force behind the government and a major consideration behind government policies. People in the United States view the world through the eyes of a nation that has never been invaded, conquered or colonized by a foreign imperial power. By contrast, many other nations know what it is like to watch foreign armies march across their borders or to be oppressed by foreign peoples.

In some societies (i.e. the US) the preservation of human life is usually viewed as the highest priority in its *value system* (principles/qualities a society holds to be important). In others, however (i.e. the Middle East), the most important thing is the preservation of one's personal or national honor. Therefore, a compromise that might end fighting between opposing factions in western nations often fails in other cultures who regard it better to die with honor than to compromise and be shamed. Inevitably, such different experiences and viewpoints affect how different peoples perceive and react to world events.

A Muslim Man

The United States and World Affairs

THE UNITED NATIONS

Following the destruction of two world wars, countries decided there was a
need for an international body to resolve conflicts peacefully. As a result, the
international community founded the **United Nations (UN)** in 1948.
Centered in New York City, the UN is intended to provide a place where
countries can negotiate rather than go to war. It also acts to provide
humanitarian relief to areas of the world that are experiencing economic
woes and/or the distress of natural disasters (ie, famines, the aftermath of a
tsunami or earthquake, etc.) Within the UN, there is a *Security Council* that
consists of representatives from the United States, Russia (originally the
Soviet Union), Great Britain, France and China. In addition to these permanent members, there are also
temporary seats on which other nations serve two year terms. The Security Council has the authority to
investigate disputes and even authorize military action. Such actions, however, require the approval of all
five of its permanent members.

United Nations Building

Practice 7.1   The International Community

1. Which of the following BEST describes the difference between a *presidential* and a *parliamentary* system of democracy?

    A. A parliamentary system is ruled by the legislature, whereas a presidential system usually divides power between the legislature and a separately elected chief executive.

    B. A presidential system has a chief executive, whereas a parliamentary system has no specified leader.

    C. A parliamentary system has only a separation of powers, while a presidential system has both a separation of powers and a system of checks and balances.

    D. In a parliamentary system, the chief executive is directly elected by the people, while in a presidential system, he/she is elected indirectly.

2. A small group of elite businessmen and influential intellectuals run a certain country and make all the governmental decisions without the people having any real say. What form of government is this?

    A. totalitarian

    B. an oligarchy

    C. a theocracy

    D. limited monarchy

3. Describe the basic differences between a *federation*, a *confederation* and a *unitary government*. Under which of these categories would you place the United States and why?

4. What are some of the cultural differences that affect how nations and peoples see the world?

7.2 US FOREIGN POLICY

US foreign policy refers to the United States' policies towards other countries and its approach to dealing with international situations/conflicts. Under the Constitution, it is the role of the executive branch to dictate and carry out the nation's foreign policy. For this reason, US policies tend to change to some degree each time one presidential administration ends and another takes over. Like all powers of the federal government, however, there are checks and balances. Although the president has the authority to set policies and negotiate with foreign nations, the US cannot enter into any formal treaties or appoint foreign ambassadors without the consent of the Senate. In addition, Congress passed the **War Powers Act** of 1973. This law places limits on the president by requiring him/her to notify Congress within 48 hours of deploying military troops. If Congress does not approve the deployment within sixty days, then the troops must be recalled (brought back to the US.

ECONOMICS

The United States has arguably the strongest and most influential economy in the world. Yet, it is by no means independent. The US is affected by how the economies of other countries are doing. For this reason, the US has an interest in other countries' economies remaining healthy and stable. Many times, the same companies that operate in the US also operate and/or own interests in other nations as well. For example, *multinational conglomerates are corporations that own a variety of companies in more than one country.* As a result, they are concerned with how the economies of other nations are doing as well as the economy of the US. Meanwhile, advances in worldwide communications and the capability to travel relatively quickly anywhere in the world, have resulted in the **economic globalization** (worldwide connection and interdependence) of business and national economies. As a result, global economies rely on one another as never before.

INTERNATIONAL TRADE

International trade is the process by which nations exchange goods with one another. *Exports* are goods that a nation sells to other countries. *Imports* are goods that a nation buys from other countries. The process of the United States trading goods with other nations is referred to as **foreign trade**. International trade without restrictions is known as **free trade**. Many times, however, governments will intervene to regulate trade. **Tariffs** are special taxes placed on products imported from another country. Governments sometimes use tariffs to raise the price of foreign goods and make domestic products (products made at home) more competitive in the marketplace. For this reason, US manufacturers and labor unions often support tariffs, because they help US industries and tend to protect jobs. Some US businesses, however, oppose tariffs because other countries tend to respond with tariffs of their own, thereby making it more costly for US producers to sell their own goods abroad. Tariffs also raise prices, thereby making it harder for producers to purchase capital and causing consumers to pay more for products because international competition is limited in the market place. In short, free trade and tariffs each have advantages and disadvantages. Free trade increases competition by allowing more foreign products into the marketplace, thereby lowering prices for consumers. However, because the price of US products drops and/or may not sell as well as foreign products, free trade can also result in less profits for US producers and the loss of US jobs. Conversely, tariffs can tend to make US products more competitive at home and allow producers to charge more and increase their profits. However, they also result in higher prices for consumers and possibly less quality as competition decreases.

A recent example of legislation affecting US trade occurred in 1993 under President Bill Clinton. That year, the United States ratified **NAFTA (North American Free Trade Agreement),** which lowered trade barriers between the US, Canada and Mexico. NAFTA caused concerns among some in the US that it might lead to a loss of US jobs. Proponents, however, argued that it would benefit the US economy by allowing US businesses greater access to foreign markets.

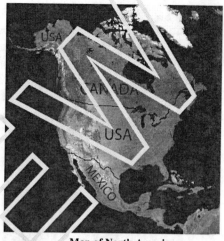
Map of North America

DEVELOPING COUNTRIES AND ECONOMIC STABILITY

The US is one of many nations that are considered to be "**developed countries.**" These are countries which have greater material wealth and whose citizens experience a higher standard of living. They tend to have more stable governments, greater economic opportunities, increased production and access to the latest technological advances. By contrast, many other nations are considered "**developing countries.**" They are poorer and often depend on **foreign aid** from other countries in the form of money, food, technology, capital, etc. for survival. One organization that is geared towards helping developing nations is the **World Bank**. It provides finance and counsel to poorer countries attempting to improve their economic condition. By safeguarding foreign investments, the World Bank helps provide greater incentive for businesses to invest in developing nations. The World Bank works to help countries develop better educational and healthcare systems, improved agricultural methods, needed infrastructure and more stable and honest governments through loans and special grants.

Another key organization is the **International Monetary Fund.** The IMF oversees the international financial system by monitoring exchange rates (how much a certain amount of currency in one country is worth in another country). It also tracks balances on payments between lender and debtor nations and offers financial and technical assistance to different nations worldwide.

Historically, the US has benefitted from helping developing nations and promoting international economic stability. For one, the more advanced the economies of these nations become, the more markets they ultimately create for US businesses. Secondly, the less developed a nation's economy, the poorer its population tends to be. This often gives rise to discontent that can lead to political instability. In the past, such instability made underdeveloped nations susceptible to communism. For this reason, the US has often attempted to bolster the economies of developing nations in the hopes of building alliances and preventing the spread of governments unfriendly to the US. There are also moral reasons. Many in the US believe that it is the nation's responsibility as the most abundant country on earth to help poorer countries succeed as well. Finally, as mentioned earlier, the US is part of a globalized economy. What happens in other countries inevitably impacts the United States. Therefore, by helping to promote economic stability globally, the US helps to promote its own stability as well.

NATIONAL SECURITY

Because international conflicts do arise, the US has to work to maintain its **national security**. In other words, the United States government must implement policies that will protect US citizens and vital US interests against foreign threats. The government uses several methods to accomplish this.

DIPLOMACY

Reagan and Gorbechev

Usually, the first step is **diplomacy**. Diplomacy is a process in which nations meet to talk and negotiate peaceful solutions to their differences. For the United States, this process might be carried out directly by the president or by his/her appointed representative (i.e., the secretary of state, one of the nation's ambassadors or some other official empowered to speak for the US government). Due to the existence of nuclear weapons, many diplomatic talks have often centered around **arms control** (placing limits on the number of weapons nations produce and deploy). During the Cold War, US presidents and Soviet leaders negotiated a number of agreements designed to limit the production of nuclear weapons. Proponents of arms control argue that failure to establish such agreements breeds mistrust between nations and encourages them to produce more powerful weapons in ever increasing numbers to protect their own national security. When nations rush to produce more weapons and build up their militaries rather than agreeing to limit arms production, it is called an *arms race*. While most agree that arms control is a good idea, some point out that it is sometimes difficult to confirm that nations are actually following such agreements. Ironically, many argue that President Ronald Reagan actually helped bring an end to the Cold War and hasten the collapse of Soviet communism by escalating military spending rather than initially advocating arms control. This policy, some argue, made the Soviets realize that their economy could not fund an arms race any longer and forced reforms that ultimately led to the end of the USSR. Only later in his presidency did Reagan sign the INF Treaty with Soviet leader Mikhail Gorbechev which reduced the number of US and Soviet nuclear missiles in Europe.

ECONOMIC SANCTIONS

When diplomacy fails, or if the US for some reason bypasses diplomacy, the nation often invokes more drastic measures for addressing international conflicts. Why does diplomacy sometimes fail? Sometimes nations simply cannot come to an agreement acceptable to both sides. Their interests are clearly too different. Why might the US bypass diplomacy altogether? Sometimes the US does not see the value in diplomacy because it has been aggressively attacked or feels threatened. For example, in 2001, President George W. Bush was not interested in diplomatic talks with the Taliban government which offered safe-haven to Osama bin Laden, the mastermind behind the 9/11 attacks. When the Taliban refused to hand bin Laden over, Bush launched a military

Castro

attack that toppled the government and which was designed to bring bin Laden to justice. In other instances, the US might not engage in diplomacy because it refuses to recognize or deal with a certain government. Until the early 1970s, the US would not enter into diplomatic talks with China because it refused to acknowledge its communist regime as the legitimate government of the Chinese people. By the same token, President George W. Bush has advocated not talking to nations that support terrorism or pursue the development of nuclear weapons. Some support these views, believing that it makes a strong statement about what the US will and will not tolerate. Others criticize such stances, claiming that problems cannot be fixed and animosities overcome until the US and nations hostile to its interests sit down and attempt to come up with peaceful solutions.

Sometimes the US will use **economic sanctions** to deal with nations whose positions and/or actions are considered unacceptable or dangerous. Countries use such sanctions to negatively affect another nation's economy in hopes of making it change its position or give in to certain demands. Perhaps the most drastic example of economic sanctions is an **embargo**. When a nation imposes an embargo, it refuses to engage in trade with a certain country. Embargoes have had notable impact throughout history. In the late 1930s, the United States instituted an embargo against Japan in protest of that nation's military expansion.

Gas Lines in the 1970s

As a result, the Japanese became more aggressive and eventually attacked Pearl Harbor. More than 30 years later, a number of Arab nations all but paralyzed motorists in the United States by imposing an oil embargo that left US citizens sitting in car lines for hours waiting to pay high prices for gas. Fortunately, the embargo did not lead to armed conflict and ended after a few months. In 1979, the US placed an embargo on grain shipped to the Soviet Union in protest of the USSR's invasion of Afghanistan. Finally, for over forty years, the US has kept an embargo in place against Cuba in opposition to the communist government of Fidel Castro. Embargoes are most effective when several nations engage in them against a single country, thereby making it harder for that country to find alternative trading partners. However, to some extent, embargoes also hurt the nations imposing them. After all, no Cuban products means that the cigar shop owner down the street can't sell those world-famous Cuban cigars; US grain farmers in the late 70s lost one of their most lucrative markets when they could no longer sell grain to the USSR; and Arab nations that imposed the oil embargo lost out on millions of dollars they would have normally received from sales to the United States.

MILITARY ACTION

The most drastic method for dealing with international conflict is **military action**. Such action involves the president of the United States ordering US armed forces into combat or into some form of hostile environment in the interest of national security. It is generally reserved as a last resort after diplomacy and economic sanctions have failed. What constitutes "failure" of diplomacy/economic sanctions, however, often turns out to be an issue of political debate. In order to remain prepared for military action, the US has worked hard since WWII to maintain a strong national defense. In other words, the US has devoted lots of money and attention to building and maintaining the world's strongest and most advanced military force.

Some Ways in Which Military Action can be Evoked

- a *declaration of war* in which Congress votes to officially declare war against another nation

- as a congressional resolution in which Congress authorizes the president to use military force as he/she sees fit without a formal declaration of war

- as an executive decision in which the president orders the armed forces to take military action

- as part of a UN coalition of nations, such as during the Korean and Persian Gulf wars

---

NATO Member Nations

6. Iceland
7. Norway
8. Denmark
9. Germany
10. Belgium
1. United Kingdom   11. Netherlands
2. France   12. Hungary
3. Spain   13. Poland
4. Portugal   14. Czech Republic
5. Italy   15. Slovak Republic
16. Greece

17. Estonia
18. Latvia
19. Lithuania
20. Romania
21. Bulgaria
22. Turkey

Since the dawn of the Cold War (political conflict between the US and the former USSR) military alliances have proved important for maintaining national security. These alliances are agreements between the US and other countries to defend one another, at least to some extent, in the event one of the allied nations is attacked. Such an approach is called *collective security* and is designed to maintain the national security of the United States and its allies. **NATO (North Atlantic Treaty Organization)** was one of the first major US alliances. Primarily designed to defend western Europe against Soviet expansion, NATO was an agreement between the US and several western European nations to protect one another. According to this treaty, an attack against one nation would be viewed as an attack against all NATO members.

In an effort to prevent the spread of communism, the United States formed other alliances as well. In Southeast Asia, the US formed the *Southeast Asia Treaty Organization (SEATO)* with Australia, New Zealand, the Philippines, Thailand, Pakistan, France and Great Britain. Unlike NATO, SEATO did not require members to assist one another against military aggression. The United States also led the way in forming the *Organization of American States (OAS)* in 1948. The Cold War meant that the US had strong concerns about the spread of communism in the Western Hemisphere. The OAS was meant to create cooperation and prevent Latin American nations from becoming communist. Later, in 1961, President John F. Kennedy initiated the formation of the *Alliance for Progress*. The Alliance's purpose was to establish economic cooperation between the US and Latin American countries. Kennedy hoped that US economic aid would help deter the spread of communism in the Americas.

In the absence of official treaties, the US will often attempt to build **coalitions** (partnerships with other countries) before launching military action. Often, such cooperation takes the form of actions sanctioned by the UN, such as in the case of the Persian Gulf War. At other times, however, such coalitions might be formed without UN support, such as when the US led an international coalition invading Iraq in 2003. At times, these actions lead to other nations viewing the US as liberators and a positive leader in the international community (such was the case with the Persian Gulf War). At other times, they have produced international resentment and protest (i.e., the War in Iraq).

HUMANITARIAN CONCERNS

Human Rights Protest, Tiananman Square, China

US foreign policy is also shaped by *humanitarian concerns*. How the United States views and chooses to interact with foreign governments often depends on how those governments treat their own citizens. For instance, at times the US has restricted trade with certain nations in the name of **human rights** (rights every living human possesses, such as life and liberty). As mentioned before, the US has not traded with Cuba for more than 40 years on the grounds that Fidel Castro's regime is a communist government guilty of oppressive policies and human rights violations. In addition, some countries might practice abusive policies towards minorities or women. Others might use child labor (requiring children to work) or pay their workers almost nothing in order to maximize profits. Still others might force political prisoners to provide slave labor. While some applaud US efforts to limit trade in the name of human rights, others are critical and point out inconsistencies in US policy. Cuba, for instance, is ostracized for alleged human rights violations. China, however, which commonly imprisons people for their political, social and/or religious beliefs, continues to trade regularly with the United States. Most agree that such contradictions are because of political factors. Cuban immigrants who fled the Castro regime are a formidable political force in the state of Florida. Because of its population, Florida has a large number of seats in Congress and a large number of votes in the Electoral College. For this reason, no politician wants to alienate the Cuban-American community by acting to re-establish trade with Cuba while Castro is still alive (the 2000 presidential election between Al Gore and George W. Bush was decided by who won in Florida). At the same time, due to its size and military strength, China is a country with whom the US seeks to maintain good relations. As you can see, economic, political and national security concerns greatly affect US foreign policy decisions. Still, the US has done much to promote human rights, and a number of nations have made greater efforts to respect such rights as a result of pressure from the US and other nations.

Berlin Airlift

In addition to human rights, the US has also led the world in offering foreign aid and humanitarian relief to developing nations and countries in need. Helping foreign peoples to recover from natural disasters, aiding refugees of war (people left homeless or forced to flee their homeland due to armed conflict), providing financial/military assistance to aid UN humanitarian efforts and donating money and manpower to battle diseases which affect the international community are all ways in which the US has contributed to offering humanitarian relief. One organization that the US has traditionally worked closely with is the **"International Red Cross."** In reality, there is no organization that is officially named the "International Red Cross." Rather, the term refers to an international association of distinct organizations, each devoted to providing humanitarian relief. The *American Red Cross* is affiliated with this organization through what is called the *International Red Cross and Red Crescent Movement*. Another arm of the "International Red Cross" is the *International Committee of the Red Cross* which is based in Geneva, Switzerland. Under international law, it has the authority to protect the lives and dignity of victims of armed conflicts as it provides humanitarian aid. The International Red Cross is perhaps best known for its efforts to tend to the needs of those in war torn countries who have been left homeless or victimized by the violence and destruction of armed conflicts.

Chapter 7

Practice 7.2 US Foreign Policy

1. Which of the following is ultimately MOST responsible for US foreign policy?

    A. the secretary of state

    B. the president of the United States

    C. a foreign ambassador of the United States

    D. the United States Senate

2. Advances in communications technology and travel that serve to connect economies worldwide and make them more interdependent than ever before are known as what?

    A. conditions of free trade

    B. favorable balance of trade

    C. factors of economic globalization

    D. international exchange rate

3. Which of the following is an example of *diplomacy*?

    A. A president sits down with his cabinet to discuss how to address an international crisis.

    B. A president meets with several world leaders in Geneva to discuss how they might decrease the risk of war and boost economic stability.

    C. A president asks for sanctions designed to hurt another nation's economy in hopes of making it respect the human rights of its citizens.

    D. The US sanctions military action against a nation that has attacked it.

4. Why is it usually in the best interest of the United States to help developing nations and do all that it can to ensure economic stability?

7.3 THE WAR ON TERROR AND THE THREAT OF NUCLEAR PROLIFERATION

911 Attacks

Osama bin Laden

Current foreign policy issues that are worth special focus are the *War on Terror* and *nuclear proliferation*. The **War on Terror** is the United States' aggressive policy to pursue terrorists and combat terrorism with military force while implementing stronger national security measures at home. It began in 2001, following the terrorist attacks that killed thousands of US citizens in New York, Washington, DC and Pennsylvania. In response to these attacks, President George W. Bush set about building an international coalition of nations to fight against terrorism. In October 2001, this US-led coalition launched *Operation Enduring Freedom*, a military action designed to bring down the terrorist-supporting government in Afghanistan and track down **Al-Qaeda** leader, **Osama bin Laden**. (Al-Qaeda is a radical Islamic terrorist network. It was first noticed worldwide following its attacks on US embassies in Africa in the 1990s and is most noted for carrying out the 9/11 terrorist attacks against the United States.)

WAR IN IRAQ

As part of his strategy in the War on Terror, Bush felt that the US could not simply sit back and defend itself against future attacks. He believed that the US needed to strike first against terrorists and states sponsoring terrorism. In 2003, this policy resulted in the US leading an international coalition of forces in an invasion of Iraq. The US-led coalition launched the **War in Iraq** based on intelligence in both the US and Great Britain suggesting that Iraqi leader, Saddam Hussein, had ties to Al-Qaeda and that he possessed *weapons of mass destruction* (weapons designed to kill massive numbers of people — both civilians and military personnel — such as nuclear and/or chemical weapons). Because Saddam had a history of using chemical weapons against an ethnic group called

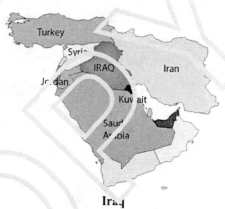

Iraq

the Kurds and because he refused to comply with UN sanctions designed to determine whether or not he had such weapons, the president, most members of Congress and several other world leaders believed the intelligence was credible. Although the US did not have the support of the UN, it did have support from a number of its allies. Together, military forces from several of these nations invaded Iraq and, in just 21 days, brought down the government of Saddam Hussein.

Chapter 7

Saddam Hussein

For all of the excitement over Saddam's fall from power, however, major problems followed in Iraq. Most notable, the alleged "weapons of mass destruction" were never found. Some believe that these weapons were never there to begin with. Others argue that they were moved out of Iraq prior to the invasion. The Bush administration came under harsh criticism because it was on the basis that such weapons existed and were in Saddam's possession that Congress had supported the war effort. The president's harshest critics accused him of lying. Others defended the president, stating that he simply acted on the information he had, and that Saddam's unwillingness to let the UN inspectors do their job made it necessary to assume that Iraq had weapons it was trying to hide. In addition, many people question whether Saddam's government ever had connections to Al-Qaeda. These critics claim that the war has been a diversion from the true terrorist enemies that the US should be focused on (i.e. enemies in Afghanistan). Proponents of the war assert that Saddam did have ties to terrorism, and, even if there were no weapons of mass destruction, both the people of Iraq and the world are better off for removing such a ruthless dictator from power and promoting democracy in the Middle East. Eventually, Saddam Hussein was convicted by an Iraqi court of "crimes against humanity," and executed in December 2006.

Successes in Iraq include the formation of a new democratic government, a new constitution, building projects and greater opportunities for women. However, terrorist insurgents and religious factions within the country have also served to increase violence and threaten the survival of the new government. As the death toll of US soldiers rises and the end of violence seems far off, many US citizens question whether or not the war in Iraq remains worth waging. In 2006, Congress appointed the *Iraq Study Group* to assess the situation in Iraq and make recommendations. Its findings describe the situation in Iraq as "bad" and in desperate need of a "new approach." The Group also suggested a gradual withdrawal of troops from Iraq, the possible redeployment of some of these troops to help stabilize Afghanistan and diplomatic negotiations with Syria and Iran which border Iraq. Because Syria has been accused of funneling support to terrorist insurgents, and Iran is believed to be encouraging religious violence to promote its own interest, President Bush refuses to negotiate with either nation until they cease such activities. Despite the Iraq Study Group's report, Bush and his supporters claim that it is essential for US forces to remain until Iraq's government is stable enough to ward off the threat of Islamic radicals; otherwise, Iraq could become a haven for terrorists. Critics, however, say that US actions in Iraq have actually increased terrorism already and that it is time to get out and focus attention elsewhere in the War on Terror. The war became the key issue of the 2006 midterm elections in which the Democrats recaptured control of the House and Senate for the first time in over a decade. In January 2007, President Bush addressed the nation on national television and announced a "new plan" that involves increasing the number of US forces in Iraq in hopes of speeding up the process by which the Iraqis can eventually handle things themselves. The newly Democratic controlled Congress, however, advocates a quicker withdrawal of US troops and vows to fight the president's plan. President Bush entered 2007 with the lowest approval rating of his presidency; in large part, most believe, due to his handling of the War in Iraq.

The United States and World Affairs

NORTH KOREA, IRAN AND NUCLEAR WEAPONS

Among the United States' chief concerns currently is that of **nuclear proliferation** (the spread of nuclear weapons to nations that don't already have them). Until recently, there have been eight nations which are known or believed to have nuclear weapons: the US, Russia, China, France, Great Britain, India, Pakistan and Israel. In 2006, North Korea (a nation hostile towards the US) joined this list when evidence suggested that it had successfully tested nuclear weapons as well. It also caused grave concern by test launching missiles that could potentially be armed with nuclear warheads and used to strike Hawaii or Japan. Meanwhile, Iran is openly pursuing the kind of uranium enrichment that could lead to such technology as well. Iran's history of antagonism towards the United States and its open call for Israel's destruction make Iran's nuclear program a matter of great concern to the United States and the rest of the world. The US is currently working with other nations to attempt to put pressure on both North Korea and Iran to get them to halt their nuclear programs. Both nations, however, remain defiant, insist they have the right to nuclear development and threaten to retaliate against the US and/or any other nation that attempts to stop them.

North Korean Leader Kim Jong-Il

Iranian Leader Mahmoud Ahmadinejad

THE SPREAD OF DEMOCRACY

One of the arguments used by US presidents to justify their foreign policy decisions has been the **spread of democracy**. The argument is that all people want to be free. Therefore, they long for democracy and a say in their own government. By establishing democracy in other nations, many believe the US ultimately promotes its own security while extending a basic human right to others. This philosophy has been used to intervene on behalf of protecting existing democracies, as well as to overthrow non-democratic governments. World War II, Korea, Vietnam and, most recently the War in Iraq, are all conflicts in which presidents have claimed that it is in the nation's interest to protect and/or help build democratic governments. While this is arguably a very noble cause, it also makes the US the target of international criticism as well. For example, while some Iraqis celebrate the fact that they are finally free to vote and elect their own parliament, others accuse the US of trying to impose its own form of government on a foreign people. Such critics, both at home and abroad, claim that the US is guilty of interfering with other countries' **national sovereignty** (right to govern themselves the way they see fit) and right to **self-determination** (make their own decisions) when it "imposes" democracy on other nations and or tries to control the actions of countries whose governments don't operate on the same principles as the United States. Others point out contradictions. As mentioned earlier, the US can sometimes be selective in which democracies it chooses to support. For instance, in one nation the US might choose to support a democratic government in the name of providing freedom for the people of that country. However, in another nation, the US may not be prepared to offer its support because a democratic government means that the people will likely elect leaders not friendly to the United States.

World War II

MacArthur in Korea

Soldier in Iraq (US Army)

120

Chapter 7

At times, because of the financial aid and military strength that the US can offer, the nation is seen as a "savior" and a valuable ally to nations in need of help and/or protection. At other times, the US is viewed as a bully, flexing its economic and military muscle to get what it wants at the expense of other nations. Regardless of how warranted its praises and/or criticisms are, the US has been and will continue to be a major player on the world stage.

Practice 7.3 The War on Terror and the Threat of Nuclear Proliferation

1. What was the initial justification for the US invasion of Iraq, what have been some of the criticisms of the war and what are the arguments for and against keeping US forces in that country?

2. What is the *War on Terror* and why was it launched?

3. Which of the following BEST describes how the rest of the world views the United States?

   A. Few nations worry about the US because they have their own interests to focus on.

   B. Most nations view the US as weak, both militarily and economically.

   C. Most nations appreciate the US because they admire its ability to remain isolated and stay out of foreign conflicts.

   D. Some nations view the US as an "international bully," while others value it as an important ally.

CHAPTER 7 REVIEW

Key Terms and Concepts

international community

representative democracy

presidential system

parliamentary system

authoritarian government

totalitarian government

absolute monarchy

limited/constitutional monarchy

dictatorship

oligarchy

theocracy

federation

confederation

unitary government

cultural differences

United Nations

US foreign policy

War Powers Act

economic globalization

international trade

foreign trade

free trade

tariffs

NAFTA

developed countries

developing countries

foreign aid

World Bank

International Monetary Fund

national security

diplomacy

arms control

arms race

economic sanctions

embargo

military action

national defense

NATO

international coalitions

human rights

"International Red Cross"

War on Terror

Al-Qaeda

Osama bin Laden

War in Iraq

nuclear proliferation

spread of democracy

national sovereignty

self-determination

Multiple Choice and Short Answer

1. The United States, Canada, Mexico, Russia, Iran, China and Indonesia are all part of what?

   A. NATO

   B. NAFTA

   C. the international community

   D. League of Developing Nations

Chapter 7

2. Alfonzo's party has just won control of the nation's legislature. Because he is the leader of his party, Alfonzo will undoubtedly be elected as the head of this legislative body and, as a result, will become the nation's leader in the eyes of other countries. Alfonzo's government operates on what kind of system?

   A. limited monarchy

   B. parliamentary democracy

   C. oligarchial representation

   D. presidential democracy

3. Which of the following actions would one expect to find in a *federation*?

   A. A state continues to object to national policies that conflict with its interests, so the national government abolishes the state legislature and removes the governor, replacing them with its own leaders.

   B. A law passed by the national legislature has no effect because several states rule it is unconstitutional and refuse to abide by it.

   C. The national government rules that the maximum speed limit nationwide is 75 mph. However, it allows each state to mandate what areas require lower speed limits and to implement many of its own traffic laws.

   D. The national government grants partial sovereignty to one region of the country, but makes it clear that, if that region fails to go along with national policies, the government will revoke this privilege and reinstitute direct rule by the national government.

4. Barbara is running for president of the United States. As part of her campaign, she advocates several ideas she has about how to negotiate a lasting peace in the Middle East. Omar, a successful businessman and immigrant from Jordan (a Middle Eastern nation), says that her ideas will never work because she is approaching the existing dispute from a Western, white, Christian perspective, rather than from a Middle Eastern, Arab, Muslim perspective. If Omar is correct, then Barbara's chief problem is best described as what?

   A. failure to understand cultural differences

   B. religious bias

   C. disregard for diplomacy

   D. lack of a real value system

5. Decisions by the US to remove tariffs, sign an arms control agreement, promote development of a Central American country, launch a military operation and/or enter an alliance with another nation, are all examples of what?

   A. diplomacy

   B. foreign aid

   C. foreign policy

   D. humanitarian relief

The United States and World Affairs

6. In which of the following situations would the US most likely skip diplomacy and take military action against another country?

   A. The US discovers that one of its allies is violating international agreements by testing nuclear weapons.

   B. An important trading partner is suspected of violating the human rights of its citizens.

   C. The US is concerned that war might erupt between two of its trading partners over a disputed strip of land between the two nations.

   D. A foreign terrorist group which is sponsored and protected by a sovereign nation kills hundreds of US citizens. The group threatens to kill more US citizens if the United States does not listen to and honor its demands.

7. Which of the following **best** represents an *economic sanction*?

   A. a tariff to promote products made in the US

   B. an embargo to prevent trade with a totalitarian government

   C. a decision by the government that it cannot afford to increase funding to developing nations

   D. free trade

8. A US president meets with his top advisors because he has just learned that a small nation in Asia has acquired nuclear weapons technology. Even more concerning, this nation has traditionally been hostile towards the US and has openly advocated the killing of US civilians. Which of the following would the president most likely be the **least** concerned about under these circumstances?

   A. the threat of terrorism

   B. nuclear proliferation

   C. the national sovereignty of other nations

   D. weapons of mass destruction

9. What are some of the basic US arguments for "spreading democracy" to other nations? What are some of the criticisms the US has received from the international community as a result of such ideas?

10. How might political, cultural and economic differences sometimes make diplomacy difficult?

Chapter 8
Geography and Government

This chapter addresses the following expectation from **Core Learning Goal 3 Geography**

Expectation 3.1	The student will demonstrate an understanding of geographic concepts and processes to examine the role of culture, technology and the environment in the location and distribution of human activities throughout history. *Indicators 3.1.1, 3.1.2, 3.1.3*

Geography and *demographics* greatly influence government policies. **Geography** refers to the earth's surface, climate, countries, peoples, industries, natural resources, etc. **Demographics** has to do with the characteristics of human populations within a geographic area (race, age, migration patterns, standard of living, average education, etc.). Demographics can be analyzed internationally, nationally, by states, regionally or on a local level. In this chapter, we will examine how geography and demographic factors affect government decisions.

8.1 POLITICAL ISSUES AFFECTING GOVERNMENT DECISIONS

In order to secure political support in different regions of the United States, within a state or in local areas, politicians must recognize and address regional concerns. In the rural South, citizens tend to be more conservative in their political views, while in the Northeast and large urban areas, they often tend to be more liberal/progressive. In the Southwest, immigration has long been a major concern. In the North and Upper Midwest, government policies that affect the welfare of industrial workers are an important issue. Midwestern and southern farmers are concerned about agricultural policies. Even within regions there are different interests. African-Americans and middle-class whites often have different perspectives and priorities. Latino migrant workers sometimes have different concerns than the US farmers who employ them. Northern business owners might have different attitudes about tariffs and free trade than northern industrial workers. Such various interests have great impact on political decisions as leaders attempt to address the concerns of their respective *constituencies* (the citizens they represent: i.e., the president represents a national constituency, a Senator represents a statewide constituency and a city councilman represents a local constituency).

REAPPORTIONMENT AND REDISTRICTING

Since US federal, state and local governments operate as representative democracies, leaders are answerable to the constituency that elects them and which they represent. As a result, reapportionment often influences government policies. *Apportionment* refers to determining representation in a political body. For instance, in the US House of Representatives and in at least one house of most state legislatures, apportionment is determined by population. The greater a geographic region's population, the greater that region's representation. The idea is to grant equal representation to each citizen regardless of where he/she lives. By comparison, the US Senate is an example of *malapportionment*. In other words, while it grants each state equal representation (2 senators each), it does not offer individual citizens equal representation. Take Montana, for example. It has one of the nation's lowest populations. Yet, it has 2 senators, just like New York, which has one of the nation's highest populations. As a result, each citizen in Montana experiences greater representation in the Senate than each citizen in New York. **Reapportionment** is when demographic factors (i.e., population) in a certain geographic area have changed and representation must be redetermined. How does reapportionment affect government policies? For instance, as a state's population grows, it gains more representation in Congress. Conversely, if its population declines, the state's representation and influence in Congress decreases. As constituencies grow in size, the priorities and issues that are most important to them gain political importance. If more people move to the South, then the South's representation in Congress and the Electoral College grows. As a result, leaders are inclined to pay much closer attention to southern concerns and make them a higher priority in their decision making. If more minorities are ascending from the lower class to the upper and middle classes, then government leaders who represent this population are more likely to implement policies geared towards middle class concerns rather than lower class concerns. In short, changes in apportionment for a certain group or geographic area tends to either increase or decrease its political influence over policy decisions.

Whereas reapportionment refers to changes in the governmental representation afforded to states, districts, regions, etc., **redistricting** is the redrawing of previously existing voting districts. Redistricting usually occurs every ten years after the **US Census** (although recent court decisions could lead to redistricting occurring more often). The US Census is the nation's official population count that also records demographic factors, such as average income, how much of the population is white versus minority, where most people live, etc. It is taken during years ending in zero. Citizens within a given voting district elect representatives to Congress and the state legislature. Usually, the boundaries of voting districts are determined by the legislative branch of state government. However, the federal government has gotten involved from time to time. In 1965, Congress passed the *Voting Rights Act* which made it illegal for states to engage in redistricting designed to limit the political power of minorities. Later federal court decisions served to make *all* forms of racially based redistricting illegal (i.e., states cannot use redistricting as a form of affirmative action). Like reapportionment, redistricting often occurs when demographic factors change. For instance, if a state's population increases enough that it is entitled to more representation in Congress, then additional voting districts must be created. Conversely, if a state's population decreases and its number of seats in Congress declines, then voting districts must be eliminated and formerly separate constituencies combined.

At times, politicians try to redraw districts to manipulate the outcomes of elections. For instance, the majority party in the state legislature at the time of redistricting might draw districts so as to concentrate the opposing party's advantage in as few districts as possible. This limits the impact of the minority party's votes, thereby helping the majority party to maintain control of the political process. Such a strategy is called *gerrymandering*. The term comes from a district drawn by Massachusetts Governor Elbridge Gerry in the early 1800s. Because the district was obviously drawn to disadvantage Gerry's opponents and was shaped like a salamander, the term "gerrymander" came to mean the act of drawing districts to maintain a political advantage. As mentioned before, this kind of redistricting has been declared illegal when it is done to either disadvantage or favor a particular race. Gerrymandering solely for the purpose of helping one political party over another, however, is not technically illegal (although some have claimed it is unethical).

THE BETTMANN ARCHIVE

Gerrymandering

VOTING PATTERNS

People in the same geographic areas and/or within the same demographic categories (gender, race, socioeconomic status, etc.) often vote similarly because they share the same concerns and priorities. For example, senior citizens usually care deeply about issues like Social Security and health care; parents are concerned about education; minorities care about affirmative action; union workers want job security and are concerned with labor issues; evangelical Christians often place social issues like abortion at the top of their priority list; those living in rural areas and small towns tend to have more conservative/traditional views than those living in large urban areas; and so on, and so on. In addition, middle class and upper class citizens tend to vote more consistently than lower income individuals; whites and older citizens tend to vote more often than minorities and young adults; and women generally vote Democratic proportionally higher than males.

Geographically, the United States has come to be divided into what political analysts and politicians often refer to as "*blue states*" and "*red states*." "Red states" are states where the majority tends to be more conservative and therefore usually votes for candidates who have conservative to moderate views. In presidential elections, "red states" often vote Republican. "Blue states," on the other hand, are states in which the majority of citizens tend to vote for candidates who are liberal to moderate. These states often vote Democratic.

Such voting trends are often referred to as **voting patterns**. Politicians study such patterns when forming campaign strategies. For instance, a more liberal candidate might realize that he/she has very little chance of winning conservative votes in a rural area, but a good chance of winning moderate votes in an urban area. By the same token, a conservative Republican running for president might realize that, by concentrating on one or two "blue states" that are more moderate, he/she might secure enough electoral votes to win, even if all the other "blue states" vote against him/her. By studying voting patterns, candidates learn where they should concentrate most of their efforts and what issues they should embrace or stay clear of if they hope to win votes.

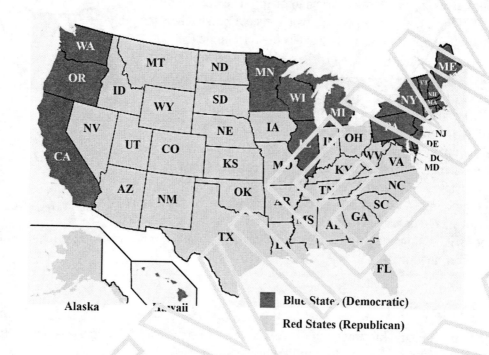

Blue States (Democratic)

Red States (Republican)

Practice 8.1 Political Issues Affecting Government Decisions

1. When demographic/geographic factors in a particular area have changed, and representation must be reassessed, it is referred to as what?

   A. malapportionment

   B. reapportionment

   C. redistricting

   D. gerrymandering

2. When voting districts are redrawn it is called what?

   A. reapportionment

   B. redistricting

   C. constituency

   D. gerrymandering

3. When voting districts are redrawn in such a way as to try and manipulate an election's outcome it is called what?

   A. malapportionment

   B. malapportioned redistricting

   C. voter fraud

   D. gerrymandering

4. Which of the following BEST describes a "blue state?"

   A. It is a state that tends to vote for Democratic candidates.

   B. It is a state that tends to vote for conservatives.

   C. It is a state that tends to vote for Republican candidates.

   D. It is a state whose senator represents a national rather than merely a statewide constituency.

5. Why is it useful for political candidates to be aware of voting patterns?

8.2 ENVIRONMENTAL ISSUES AND LAND USE

In recent years, US citizens have become increasingly concerned about the environment. As a result, the national, state and local governments have begun to seriously consider the environmental effects of public policy decisions. As mentioned before, the EPA (Environmental Protection Agency) is a federal agency devoted to making sure that industries abide by federal legislation designed to protect and conserve the environment. Meanwhile, the US **Department of the Interior** is responsible for the management and conservation of federally owned lands (i.e, national forests, etc.). Nationally, environmental concerns range from global warming and a possible "greenhouse effect" caused by man made pollution (review chapter 3, section 3.1), to attempts to preserve certain species of wildlife and clean up polluted areas. Conflicts often arise because what is sometimes viewed as best for the

environment also turns out to be costly from an economic standpoint. For instance, legislation limiting where oil companies may drill in the United States means that the US must continue to import large amounts of oil from other nations. It also limits oil supplies and keeps the price consumers pay for gas higher than if drilling was unrestricted. By the same token, forcing companies to adhere to specific environmental standards often means that businesses have to spend money to modify their operations that they otherwise would have spent on production or to hire more workers. As a result, unemployment is higher than if such standards did not exist while less production and/or increased expenses mean higher prices for consumers. Environmentalists claim that the benefits of environmental legislation are well worth the costs. Others, however, question some of the scientific evidence these environmentalist rely on and argue that the government sometimes goes "too far" and unnecessarily hinders US economic development and production.

In an effort to limit adverse impact on the environment, federal law requires federal agencies to submit an **Environmental Impact Statement (EIS)** prior to government activities that could significantly affect the environment (i.e., building airports, interstate highways, etc.). The EIS must state the purpose and need of the proposed action and describe the anticipated environmental effects. The document must also list any possible alternatives to whatever action the government is proposing.

STATE AND LOCAL ISSUES

The state of Maryland and local communities are also concerned with environmental issues. The state of Maryland has both the Department of the Environment and the Department of Natural Resources to address matters of environmental concern and ensure the protection of Maryland's natural resources (review chapter 3, section 3.3).

LAND

Land use is one of the major issues facing the state of Maryland and local governments. The Department of Natural Resources has launched a number of programs designed to acquire land for conservation and recreational use. The department works in conjunction with both the US Department of the Interior and local governments to establish and restore parks and recreation facilities, make sure that local **zoning ordinances** (regulations dictating how land may/may not be used and/or developed) do not conflict with environmental policies, ensure that development does not interfere with conservation objectives and help develop areas of the state in an environmentally responsible fashion. In 1967, the **Maryland Environmental Trust** was formed for the purpose of conserving Maryland's environment.

Rural Maryland

One program that is especially important is **Maryland's Rural Legacy**. This program conserves and protects Maryland's forests as well as agricultural and environmental resources for future generations. It is especially concerned with preventing the destructive effects of **urban sprawl**. *Urban sprawl* refers to the largely uncontrolled growth and development of land that accompanies the expansion of metropolitan areas. While growth is often positive, if left unchecked, it can have adverse effects on the environment. For instance, the growth of neighborhoods and cities often means that trees are cut down, forests are cleared, the natural habitats of animals are disturbed, water supplies are possibly polluted and so forth. Programs like Maryland's Rural Legacy are meant to ensure that development occurs with the least amount of harm to the environment as possible.

WATER

Chesapeake Bay Crabs

As a coastal state, Maryland has a great interest in maintaining clean and usable water resources. The **Chesapeake Bay** is especially important. It is the largest US *estuary* (a semi-enclosed coastal body of water with rivers and streams flowing into it and which is directly connected to the ocean) and home to a variety of wildlife. The bodies of water that feed and drain into the Bay comprise the state's **watershed**. The state of Maryland and communities which reside in this region of the state actively attempt to enact policies designed to protect and conserve Maryland's waters. The **Clean Water Action Plan** is a program launched by the Department of Natural Resources for the expressed purpose of maintaining "fishable, swimmable and safe waters..." as it seeks to enforce standards put in place by the federal Clean Water Act. In 1984, Maryland's General Assembly passed the **Critical Area Act**, which designated the Chesapeake Bay and its surrounding watershed as a "critical area" and established guidelines governing local land use and development for the purpose of protecting the environment and preserving wildlife. Finally, under the supervision of the Department of the Environment, Maryland also has the **Maryland Beaches Program**, which aims to ensure that Maryland's citizens and tourists enjoy clean and safe beaches.

AIR

The Department of the Environment is also determined to make sure Maryland has clean air. It monitors pollutants and enforces legislation like the federal Clean Air Act and **Maryland's Healthy Air Act**. As mentioned in chapter 3, section 3.3, the Healthy Air Act is one of the strictest power plant admission laws on the East Coast.

Practice 8.2 Environmental Issues and Land Use

1. The US Department of the Interior is responsible for which of the following?

    A. maintaining global warming

    B. making sure local zoning ordinances abide by EPA regulations

    C. enforcing the Critical Area Act

    D. conservation and protection of federally owned lands

2. What is *urban sprawl* and what are some of the adverse effects it can have on the environment?

8.3 GEOGRAPHICAL INTERESTS AND GOVERNMENT POLICIES

Government policies can revolve around any number of geographical interests. **International interests** are those which concern more than one country. Sometimes they involve the entire international community, such as international attempts to limit the spread of nuclear weapons or ensure that international laws are upheld. At other times, they only involve portions of it, such as when the US signed NAFTA with Canada and Mexico. **National interests** are interests that concern an entire nation. In the United States, national defense, maintaining adequate transportation systems (i.e., airline travel, interstate highways, etc.), the country's economy, the national standard of living, etc. are all national interests. There are also **state interests**. Public education, the use and conservation of natural resources and the environment within the state, state transportation, adequate representation in the national government, economic development, etc. are just a few examples of state interests. Finally there are **regional interests** that concern people in certain parts of the world, country or state.

Interstate Highway

Public Education

Geography and Government

DEFINING REGIONS

A **region** is a general geographic area. It may be small, such as one geographic portion of a state, or big, covering large portions of an entire country or several countries. Areas are defined as regions due to some kind of common trait amongst the people, culture, society, land, etc. Criteria for defining regions include: economic development, geographic location, common natural resources, ethnicity of the population, religion, climate, etc.

There are no set rules for how we define regions. *International regions* might be defined culturally, politically and/or by location in the world. For instance, the Middle East, Southeast Asia, western Europe, Scandinavia and Central America are all examples of international regions that consist of more than one country but share certain commonalities that link them together. Within the United States, there are numerous *national regions*. Currently, their are four major US geographic regions that are officially recognized by the US Census Bureau. The **Northeast** consists of the New England states, New York, New Jersey, Pennsylvania and Delaware. The **South** stretches from Virginia down to Florida and westward through Texas. Some also consider Maryland and West Virginia to be part of the South as well, while others classify these two states as part of the Northeast. The **Midwest** ranges from the state of Ohio in the east all the way to the Dakotas, Nebraska and Kansas in the west. The territory from Colorado to California, plus Hawaii and Alaska, is considered the **Western** United States. Each of these regions is united by either common climates, economies, natural resources, terrain, cultures or, at the very least, geographic location.

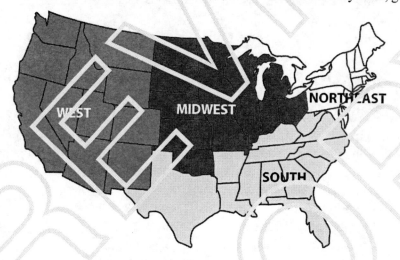

THE NEW ENGLAND AND MID-ATLANTIC STATES

New England

Within these larger regions are a number of "subregions." **New England** covers the northeast corner of the United States and consists of Maine, Massachusetts, New Hampshire, Vermont, Rhode Island and Connecticut. Its climate can vary, with winters being harsher and summers cooler in the upper half of the region than in the lower. Its rocky soil and climate prevents it from being among the nation's strongest agricultural regions; however, it does produce tobacco and dairy products and is famous for its maple syrup. Its economy relies a great deal on industrial exports both to other parts of the US and abroad, and it is known for its insurance and financial management industries. New England is also home to three of the most densely populated

132

Chapter 8

states in the nation (Massachusetts, Connecticut and Rhode Island) with its largest city being Boston, Massachusetts. Meanwhile, it also has two of the country's poorest cities: Providence, Rhode Island and Hartford, Connecticut.

The **Mid-Atlantic** region lies between New England and the South. It includes New York, New Jersey, Delaware, Pennsylvania, Maryland and Virginia (although Maryland and Virginia are often considered part of the South). The region boasts several large cities: New York (the nation's largest), Philadelphia and Baltimore. As a result, the region depends heavily on business and commerce and is home to a great deal of cultural diversity.

Mid-Atlantic Region

THE "BELTS"

Some areas in the United States are referred to as *"Belts."* The **Rust Belt** covers part of the northern Midwest and Mid-Atlantic regions. It is so named because of its traditional reliance on factories and industrial production as the foundation of its economy. Detroit, Cleveland and Pittsburgh are cities often associated with the Rust Belt. Because of its strong ties to industry, labor unions have long been a political and economic force in this region. Unfortunately, in recent decades, increased free trade with other nations and technological advancements have hurt a number of Rust Belt industries and left many workers unemployed and lacking the skills they need to compete in a changing economy. As a result, the area has experienced difficult economic times compared to other parts of the nation, causing many to leave the region.

By contrast, the **Sun Belt** is the fastest growing part of the country. This region stretches across the south from the Carolinas to the lower two-thirds of California. It is characterized by warmer climates, booming industries and growing cities. Areas like Research Triangle Park in North Carolina and Silicon Valley in California have become technology and research centers for not only the United States, but the world as well. Meanwhile, Charlotte, North Carolina is now the nation's second most important banking center, second only to New York. Lower costs of living and increased economic opportunities have led to many US citizens *migrating* (moving) from other parts of the US to the South. The population of this region has also grown tremendously due to the large number of *immigrants* who enter the United States each year across its southern border and settle in Sun Belt states. In 2007, Atlanta, Georgia was named the fastest growing city, not only in the Sun Belt, but in the United States as well.

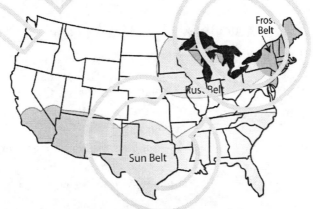

There are also other "belts." The *Bible Belt* refers to most of the US South and lower Midwest where evangelical Christianity (Christianity which is Protestant and believes strongly that the Bible is the word of God) greatly influences the culture. The *Grain Belt* stretches across the northern Midwest and is known for agricultural products like grain, wheat and soybean. Similarly, the *Corn Belt* is that portion of the Midwest

Geography and Government

where corn is the main cash crop. The *Frost Belt* is the area surrounding the Great Lakes known for heavy snowfall; the *Rice Belt* covers parts of Arkansas and the Gulf Coast where rice is produced; and the *Black Belt* refers to counties across the US South that have a high percentage of African-American inhabitants.

ROCKY MOUNTAINS AND PACIFIC NORTHWEST

Rocky Mountain Region

Pacific Northwest

The **Rocky Mountain** region runs from northern Arizona and New Mexico, through Colorado, Nevada, Utah, Wyoming, Idaho and western Montana. The common links are the Rocky Mountain range, climate, geography and a common time zone. The region tends to be politically conservative and, for that reason, often votes Republican. As home to the country's most impressive mountain range, Yellowstone National Park, the Grand Canyon and some of the country's largest Native American reservations, this region is concerned with environmental protection and the conservation of anything linked to the area's rich history and Native American heritage.

The **Pacific Northwest** consists of northern California, Oregon, Washington state and Alaska. Due in part to expanding technology industries, this region, like the Sun Belt, is growing. Except for sparsely populated Alaska and parts of northern California, this region tends to be more liberal and often votes Democratic at election time. Like the Mountain region, this area is also concerned with environmental issues due to its abundant forests and Alaskan oil reserves.

States will often work together to address regional concerns. For instance, Arkansas and Tennessee cooperated to build a bridge connecting their states across the Mississippi River. Georgia, Alabama and Florida have worked together because each state depends on water supplies from the Chattahoochee River. Meanwhile, both Virginia and Maryland are concerned with conserving wildlife and clean water in the Chesapeake Bay. As a result, these states often cooperate to achieve common goals.

REGIONS WITHIN MARYLAND

Within Maryland, there are distinct regions as well. For instance, the territory east of Chesapeake Bay is known as Maryland's **Eastern Shore**. The area comprises over a third of the state's territory, but only a small percentage of its population. The region is known for vegetables, grain, chicken farming, seafood and tourism. As mentioned earlier, the Chesapeake Bay area is an important part of Maryland and is known for its wildlife and seafood such as blue crab, oysters and striped bass.

Heading west, there is the **Piedmont Plateau**. The word *piedmont* means "foot of the mountain" and, as you might expect, is located between the Eastern Shore and the mountains that run through the western part of the state. The region is known for its dairy farming and has traditionally produced tobacco as well (although

134

government programs in recent years have sought to decrease the state's dependence on this controversial crop). The Piedmont is also home to the state's *fall line*. Here, the land changes from the flatter terrain of the east to the steeper terrain of the mountains. As a result, there are a number of waterfalls and rivers running downhill that make the area a great source of hydroelectricity (electric power produced using running water).

Finally, there is **Western Maryland**, sometimes referred to as the *mining region*, because of the rich deposits of coal and even gold that once defined the region. This is the mountainous region of Maryland that is less populated and sees lots of snowfall in the winter time. While the coal mining industry still exists in western Maryland, it is not as economically important to the state as it used to be due to the state's focus on technology, shipping and growing business areas like Baltimore.

By far, the largest portion of Maryland's population lives in the **Baltimore-Washington Metropolitan Area**. This area includes Baltimore, which is the state's largest and most populous city, as well as much of central Maryland. The city currently boasts an African-American majority with an increasing Latino population as well. Politically, Baltimore has been considered a stronghold for Democrats for well over a century. As the number of industrial jobs has declined and other parts of the nation and state have grown, Baltimore's population has decreased rapidly in recent years. In addition, statistics rank Baltimore among the nation's worst cities for violent crime and among those with the fastest drop in overall

Baltimore

population. On the positive side, however, Baltimore has also become a leading financial center and, thanks to Johns Hopkins University and Hospital is one of the nation's top areas for health services and bio-technology. Its close proximity to Washington, DC, makes the area home to a number of federal agencies and government offices as well.

THE EFFECTS OF GEOGRAPHICAL PATTERNS AND TRENDS ON THE ENVIRONMENT, SOCIETY AND GOVERNMENT DECISIONS

One key to understanding geographic trends and patterns is to study **population**. *Population* simply refers to the people who live in a region. It can be studied in terms of the number of people who make up a certain population, or in terms of cultural or socioeconomic factors. One obvious trend is that the US population is growing. In 2006 it surpassed the 300 million mark and all indications are that it will only continue to grow. Studies show, however, that this growth is not evenly distributed throughout the country. Census numbers show that people are leaving other regions to move to the

South and West. When the population of a country/region starts to leave one area to move to another area in large numbers, it is called a *population shift*. These shifts can occur for a number of reasons, such as greater economic opportunities, more affordable cost of living, availability of land, chance to live in a warmer climate, etc.

Geography and Government

Another key trend that is taking place in US society is the increasing **minority population**. These are citizens and/or residents who are not white. In recent years, the US Census has reported that the gap between the number of US citizens who are white and those that are not is consistently shrinking, with Latinos surpassing African-Americans as the most numerous minority group.

The US population is also aging. This is because better education about health, modern medical technology and, in many cases, healthier lifestyles, have led to longer lifespans. As a result, the average age of US citizens is increasing.

THE IMPACT OF TRENDS

Such trends have great impact on society, the environment and government decisions. For instance, as certain areas of the nation or state grow, the government is more inclined to focus attention and money on developing such areas. New roads are needed, public services are required for the increasing number of neighborhoods and homes that are being built, greater infrastructure to support the growth of booming cities must be provided, etc. In addition, in our democratic system based on representation, as areas grow in population, their political influence increases. Sun Belt states that are gaining in population also gain representatives in Congress and counties that grow the fastest gain influence in the General Assembly. As a result, when public policy decisions are made by these bodies, these areas have the advantage of having their interests strongly represented. Conversely, if a region's population is declining, then that area stands to lose political influence unless it can reverse the population shift.

Geographic patterns and trends affect policy decisions in a number of ways. **Government funding** (how the government chooses to spend money and what it chooses to spend it on) is inevitably influenced by what areas are growing and who makes up the population. As mentioned above, areas that are growing are more likely to get government funding for development and needed services, both because there is a need and because they are well represented in the government bodies that make such decisions. As areas grow in population, their need for government services and funding grow as well. Meanwhile, large/growing communities within the population also have great influence on government decisions. For instance, as the average lifespan of citizens continues to get longer and people get older, issues like Social Security and health care will become increasingly important and political leaders will likely do more to fund and/or provide for such programs/services. As the minority population increases, society experiences greater *multiculturalism* (presence of many different cultural backgrounds) and leaders become more sensitive to issues important to minorities. More funding might be provided for programs designed to reach minorities in the inner cities, bilingual education might be implemented in schools where there is a high Latino population and officials are often more inclined to support affirmative action policies. Multiculturalism also means that more minorities are elected to public office as well.

136

Chapter 8

In places where people are leaving cities and other geographic areas to move elsewhere, leaders may implement policies designed to reverse this process. For instance, many cities have poured large amounts of money into renovating downtown areas so as to encourage people to move from the suburbs back to the city. Some governments offer tax breaks to businesses that are willing to locate in their area, thereby creating jobs and encouraging the area's growth and economic development. At times, the government might examine geographic trends when deciding how to allocate *grants*. Grants are funds given by the federal government to states or local governments to assist programs designed to help lower income families, train unskilled workers for better jobs, improve public education, etc.

Population shifts also have an **environmental impact**. While development can be exciting and economically beneficial to regions, it also places a lot of strain on the environment. Natural resources are disturbed and, in some cases, destroyed as land is developed for new cities, neighborhoods, homes and industries. While development is often good and, in a growing population necessary, most leaders and citizens agree that it is important for society to balance economic development with protecting the environment and conservation.

MARYLAND AND "SMART GROWTH"

In the late '90s, Maryland's General Assembly passed the **Smart Growth Priority Funding Areas Act**. This law serves to channel state funds to develop future growth and economic development in "priority areas." The act also gives a certain amount of authority to local governments to designate certain areas as "smart growth areas" that are entitled to priority funding.

Practice 8.3 Geographical Interests and Government Policies

1. Recent statistics show that a country's armed forces are operating at level below the number of troops needed to provide an adequate defense. As a result, the government is concerned and wants to come up with a strategy for correcting this problem. The government is addressing which of the following?

   A. an international interest

   B. a national interest

   C. a local interest

   D. a regional interest

Geography and Government

2. Which of the following statements is true?

   A. The Rust Belt is the fastest growing region in the United States because of its thriving manufacturing industries.

   B. Part of the Sun Belt also comprises a large portion of the Bible Belt.

   C. Because of their common interests in environmental issues, the Mountain region and the Pacific Northwest tend to vote similarly at election time.

   D. Baltimore's rapidly growing African-American and Latino population has made it one of the fastest growing cities in the United States.

3. What are some of the characteristics that define a region and what are the four major geographic regions in the United States?

4. How do population patterns affect government funding decisions? Give examples.

CHAPTER 8 REVIEW

Key Terms and Concepts

geography
demographics
reapportionment
redistricting
US Census
gerrymandering
voting patterns
US Department of the Interior
Environmental Impact Statement
zoning ordinances
Maryland Environmental Trust
Maryland's Rural Legacy
urban sprawl
Chesapeake Bay
watershed
Clean Water Action Plan
Critical Area Act
Maryland Beaches Program
Maryland's Healthy Air Act
international interests
national interests
state interests

regional interests
region
Northeast
South
Midwest
western US
New England
Mid-Atlantic
Rust Belt
Sun Belt
Rocky Mountain region
Pacific Northwest
Eastern Shore
Piedmont Plateau
Western Maryland/mining region
Baltimore-Maryland Metropolitan Area
population
minority population
government funding
environmental impact of population shifts
Smart Growth Priority Funding Areas Act

Multiple Choice and Short Answer

1. The most recent census count shows that state X has experienced an increase in population of more than 30% over the last decade. Which of the following statements is **most likely** true?

    A. State X has benefitted from malapportionment

    B. State X has already experienced redistricting.

    C. State X needs reapportionment.

    D. State X is located in the Rust Belt.

2. Douglas and Maria are both representatives in the state legislature. Based on the findings of the most recent US Census, they devise a plan for redrawing voting districts that will most likely enable their party to maintain a political advantage for years to come. Their hope of drawing district lines so as to benefit their own party can **best** be described as what?

    A. reapportionment

    B. voting patterns

    C. demographics

    D. gerrymandering

3. Which of the following statements is **most likely** true?

    A. A Republican candidate for president would do well in a "red state."

    B. A liberal politician would likely lose in a "blue state."

    C. Oregon is a state that most Republicans would expect to win in a presidential election.

    D. A close study of voting patterns would probably lead a Democratic candidate to concede that he/she cannot win in Baltimore.

4. Which of the following would likely have the **least** adverse effect on the environment?

    A. urban sprawl

    B. mass migration to a previously sparsely populated area.

    C. increased economic development

    D. Maryland's Rural Legacy program

5. Which of the following is a strategy a politician might use to win votes in Baltimore?

    A. a pledge to promote affirmative action and racial equality

    B. a call for a return to "traditional," evangelical Christian values

    C. a promise to end bilingualism and deport immigrants who are in the country illegally

    D. praising the Sun Belt for its growth and announcing a plan to double government funding for the region.

6. What can be expected based on the news story below?

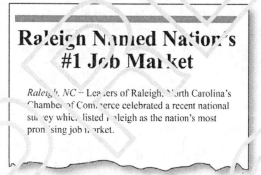

Raleigh Named Nation's #1 Job Market

Raleigh, NC – Leaders of Raleigh, North Carolina's Chamber of Commerce celebrated a recent national survey which listed Raleigh as the nation's most promising job market.

    A. population shift to the Frost Belt

    B. increased economic development in North Carolina

    C. decreased reliance on government services for Raleigh

    D. limited changes to Raleigh's environment

140

7. Everwon, Maryland is a bustling city. Its population is 60% white, 25% African-American, 10% Latino; and the remaining 5% consists of Asians, Native Americans and a small Arab community. Because the city council and the mayor have done a great job of attracting new businesses, the city is growing rapidly and new people are moving in all the time from across the state and the nation. Which of the following is most likely **false**?

   A. Everwon is a city that exhibits multiculturalism.

   B. Minority concerns will impact decisions made by the city's government.

   C. Because of the growing population, urban sprawl is not a concern.

   D. The legislative district in which Everwon is located will likely gain more influence in the General Assembly.

8. What is the difference between red states and blue states?

9. What are some of the steps the state of Maryland has taken to address environmental issues within the state?

10. Describe the defining features of the various regions within Maryland. What are some of the challenges facing Baltimore and what are some of the positive things happening is this city?

Chapter 9
Government and Economics

This chapter addresses the following expectation(s) from **Core Learning Goal 4 Economics**

Expectation 4.1	The student will demonstrate an understanding of economic principles, institutions and processes required to formulate government policy. *Indicators 4.1.1, 4.1.2, 4.1.3, 4.1.4*

9.1 THE BASIC ECONOMIC QUESTIONS

There are **four basic economic questions** that must be answered in any economy:

- What will be produced?
- How will it be produced?
- For whom will it be produced?
- When will it be produced?

In addition, who owns the means of production, what motivates producers and government's role in the market also influence and define economies.

GOVERNMENT'S HAND IN THE PROCESS

The role the government plays in a nation's economic system can differ from country to country. In general, there are four types of economic systems, each defined largely by how active or inactive the government is in regulating the economy.

Chapter 9

TRADITIONAL ECONOMIES

Global Economy

Traditional economies have existed throughout history and are grounded in long standing traditions. Generally, what is produced in a traditional economy is whatever has been produced in the past. Laborers in traditional economies usually produce at a subsistence level, making just what they need to survive. As a result, hunting, fishing and small scale farming are common features in such a society. A small wealthy class (aristocracy) that hands down property and wealth from one generation to the next often owns or controls the factors of production (i.e., land). Because both their occupation and their social status are inherited from their parents, laborers have little opportunity for economic advancement. The upper classes benefit from this system because it protects their wealth and position. Productivity is motivated by both the need to survive and a sense of purpose. Since one's lot in life is predetermined, it is not one's duty to advance to a higher social status, but rather to become an expert in one's assigned role. For example, if you are a ditch digger by birth, then you should strive to be the best ditch digger around.

Traditional economies are not as common today because they usually grow unstable once citizens become aware of other kinds of economic systems. Lower economic classes tend to be either attracted to the opportunities of market systems or the equity of command systems. Meanwhile, the middle and upper classes often desire the opportunities for even greater wealth and success present in a market system. Many of the European societies of the 1600s and 1700s (i.e., France prior to the French Revolution) were examples of traditional economies.

MARKET ECONOMIES

Market Economy

Next is a **market economy**. In a market economy, producers and consumers determine what gets made and for whom. Property and factors of production (land, labor, capital, etc.) are privately owned, with the government owning only enough to carry out its limited and defined role. Producers decide what to produce and how much to charge based on what consumers demand and what prices consumers are willing to pay. The motivating factor for producers is profit (selling products for more money than they cost to produce) while laborers are motivated by the prospect of earning higher wages/salaries and/or personal advancement. In a market economy, producers are free to produce what they choose to produce and consumers are free to consume what they choose to consume. The two parties, producer and consumer, make these choices in a *market* where they engage in economic exchanges. An economic *exchange* is simply a trade of one thing for another. In a market economy, this exchange is most often a good, service or resource in return for money. Every time you buy something, you are choosing to make an economic exchange in a market.

143

Government and Economics

COMMAND ECONOMIES

A third type of economy is the **command economy**. Command economies are drastically different from market economies and stem greatly from the beliefs of German philosopher/historian, Karl Marx. In 1848, he and his colleague, Friedrich Engels, published *The Communist Manifesto*, a work that attacked capitalism as an unjust system that privileged the rich and exploited the poor working class. He advocated a revolution in which the working class would rise up and establish *socialism*. Under socialism, government controls all capital and owns all property. Marx believed that socialism would, in time, evolve into *communism*. Communism is socialism at its "ideal stage." It refers to a society in which everyone does their best to contribute to the common good. Under a perfect communist economic system, resources are owned by everyone, governments ultimately disappear, and people distribute income according to need rather than production. Marx believed that profit motive and other incentives would be unnecessary, because people would produce just as much through cooperation (working together towards a common goal). In reality, no country has ever achieved such a state of communism. Countries that are called "communist" (i.e., China, Cuba, North Korea) are labeled as such because they are ruled by a communist party. Such governments continue to use socialist policies to control the economy.

Karl Marx

Under command systems, the government owns the means of production and determines production levels. Private ownership of property is minimal. Distribution is based on equity. In other words, output and wealth are meant to be distributed equally among the citizenry (at least in theory). Such an approach is known as **income redistribution** because the government takes income from those who produce and redistribute it more evenly among society. Although laborers tend to remain employed, they may or may not have a say in what kind of job they hold and/or under what conditions they work. The incentives to produce are

Command Economy

expected to be a sense of duty to the country/community and/or a sense of personal pride. Historically, command economies have proven to be less efficient than market economies. Although they initially attract poorer individuals because of their emphasis on economic equality, in reality, command economies have been susceptible to corruption and greed just as much as market economies. In addition, while national loyalty and personal pride are noble principles, they consistently fail to provide as much motivation for productivity as the promise of financial profit and personal advancement. Finally, command economies, because they are centralized, tend to be slow to react to changes in demand. As a result, they often produce too much of something that is not desired and too little of something for which there is a market. For example, in the former Soviet Union, it was not uncommon to see people lined up around the block waiting to buy scarce products like a loaf of bread or a roll of toilet paper.

MIXED ECONOMIES

In reality, most nations are actually **mixed economies**. In other words, they have elements of more than one type of economic system. The US is a mixed economy in that it offers great freedom to economic actors (producers and consumers) while at the same time implementing enough government control to hopefully avoid economic catastrophes (i.e., depression, massive inflation, crucial shortages of needed goods, etc.). For instance, the US has laws forbidding the production and sale of illegal drugs, limits what medicines can and cannot be purchased and blocks the sale of products from Cuba due to an embargo. Local and state governments often regulate the sale of products like alcohol and tobacco and place restrictions on where certain types of businesses may operate. The government will sometimes use taxes and deficit spending to manipulate the economy as well. In addition, a guaranteed minimum wage, laws forbidding monopolies, subsidies to protect farmers and tariffs imposed to limit foreign competition are all examples of government interference in free market competition.

By comparison, many communist nations (i.e., China) are mixed economies as well because, while the government still exercises a great deal of control, certain degrees of capitalism are allowed. Thus, the major difference between mixed economies lies in whether they tend to be more like market economies or command economies in nature.

International Finance Center
Hong Kong, China

Practice 9.1   The Basic Economic Questions

1. What are the four types of economic systems?

    A. production, market, command, free

    B. market, traditional, mixed, command

    C. command, labor, capital, traditional

    D. free, command, communist, mixed

2. Which of the following MOST resembles a *traditional economic system*?

    A. Susan became a nurse because her mother and grandmother were nurses. Although she could have chosen any profession, she wanted to follow in their footsteps. One day, she plans on returning to medical school and becoming a surgeon.

    B. Arthur is a talented man. He is intelligent enough to do almost anything, but the government has assigned him to work in an automobile factory. He hates his job but has no choice since the government makes all economic decisions and stresses the importance of everyone working for the good of the country.

    C. Nathan is an excellent cobbler. Because his family has practiced this profession for generations, it is all he ever hoped or was expected to be. The shop he works out of is on land owned by a wealthy landlord and, although he takes great pride in his work, Nathan will likely never advance beyond where he currently is in life.

    D. Paula has pulled herself up by the bootstraps. Although she was born poor, she worked hard in school and earned a scholarship. She graduated with honors and now works for a large corporation. Taking advantage of the opportunities afforded her, she was able to buy her parents a new house and send her baby brother to college as well.

3. What are some reasons why command economies have traditionally been less effective than market economies?

9.2 GOVERNMENT POLICIES AND SOCIOECONOMIC GOALS

SCARCITY AND OPPORTUNITY COST

Scarcity is the lack of adequate resources to obtain all of one's wants and/or needs. Although there might be large demand for a resource, there is simply not an adequate amount of it. **Economics** is the study of how individuals, businesses and governments can most efficiently allocate limited resources. One resource that is almost always scarce is *money*. Just about all of us know the feeling of wanting to buy something only to realize that we don't have enough funds. Whether its lacking the $1.25 needed to purchase a candy bar at the local convenience store, only having enough cash to get into the movies but not enough to buy popcorn or being unable to get that slick sports car because you just can't afford the monthly payments, in each case, the problem is the same: scarcity of money.

National Defense Expense: F-22 Raptors

Governments also have to deal with scarcity. Although there may be many programs the government would like to implement and/or actions it would like to engage in, it does not have the resources to tackle everything. Therefore, for every economic decision the government makes, it must evaluate what it is giving up by *not* choosing to allocate its resources towards another option. What the government is giving up by not choosing the alternate option is called **opportunity cost**. For example, if the government has $1 billion and chooses to spend 70% of it on national defense, 20% of it on education, and 10% on social programs, then its opportunity costs are what it gives up by not spending more on any one of these programs. In other words, it gives up the additional educational programs that more than 20% funding would have purchased. It also gives up the additional social programs that could have been financed for more than 10%. Even in national defense, there is an opportunity cost. Although national defense was allocated most of the money, the government still gave up the additional weapons, training, equipment, etc. that could have been purchased had it been allocated more than 70%.

COMPETING SOCIOECONOMIC GOALS

There are many socioeconomic goals which the government hopes to achieve. They include: health care, affordable housing, child welfare and adequate education to name a few. However, each time resources and effort are made to achieve one set of goals, less resources are available to pursue other, equally important objectives. In fact, sometimes these goals and objectives compete directly with one another. **Economic freedom** (the freedom to pursue economic success without government interference) has long been considered by many to be the backbone of US freedom and democracy. However, economic freedom is often at odds with economic **equity** and **security**. In other words, while economic freedom presents citizens with

146

the opportunity for success, it also leaves open the possibility of failure. As a result, society often becomes divided between the "haves" and the "have nots," rather than seeing a somewhat equal and "fair" distribution of income. In the past, total economic freedom has sometimes led to monopolies, exploitation of workers, unsafe working conditions, environmental damage, etc. On the other hand, government regulations limit economic freedom. Since it is generally in the best interest of government to both protect economic freedom and provide **economic stability** (consistent economic conditions that support the needs of citizens, thereby increasing a sense of economic security), the goals of economic freedom and equity/security often pull against one another. In general, those who value the freedom to pursue as much material wealth as possible, start their own businesses, fulfill an economic vision, etc. tend to favor policies that offer more freedom and less guarantee of success and equity. On the other hand, those who value the security of knowing they have a job, adequate health care, safe retirement benefits and a consistent income, tend to favor a more active government that ensures these things at the expense of some degree of freedom.

While **economic growth** has always been a goal of the US government, **environmental protection** has gained importance more recently. Originally championed by President Theodore Roosevelt at the turn of the twentieth century, environmental causes became a national concern during the late 1960s and 1970s. Today, few government policies are implemented without first considering their effects on the environment. Once again, however, there is conflict. Economic development and environmental protection are often at odds. As the government imposes regulations designed to protect the environment and conserve natural resources, it often prevents industries from building where they want to build, accessing resources that would increase production and lower prices and/or carrying out operations in the most efficient and cost effective manner. As a result, there is less **productivity**. Productivity refers to the amount of goods that a business or economy produces in a given amount of time. In general, the greater

the productivity, the healthier the economy and the more economic growth occurs. However, when government regulations decrease and productivity is encouraged, industries often employ methods and practices that are considered harmful to the environment. Once again, you can see the tension that sometimes exists between existing goals.

Practice 9.2 Government Policies and Socioeconomic Goals

1. Not having enough money to finance all of the social programs a government wants to reflects which of the following problems?

   A. scarcity of money

   B. scarcity of social programs

   C. lack of opportunity

   D. inadequate opportunity costs

2. Additional government regulations restricting the amount of gases a factory may omit into the atmosphere are MOST likely to have which of the following effects?

   A. increased damage to the environment

   B. less efficient productivity

   C. prevent future scarcity

   D. eliminate opportunity costs

3. Give two or three examples of competing socioeconomic goals and explain how pursuing one sometimes contradicts with the pursuit of others.

9.3 REGULATORY AGENCIES AND FISCAL / MONETARY POLICIES

GOVERNMENT REGULATORY AGENCIES

In an attempt to regulate the economy enough to protect public welfare, the federal government has established several agencies and regulatory commissions. Some of them and their duties are listed below.

- **Environmental Protection Agency (EPA)** – makes sure that laws regulating pollution, the use of certain chemicals/pesticides, and waste disposal are properly adhered to.

- **Federal Trade Commission (FTC)** – protects consumers by making sure companies do not engage in false advertising and that they disclose crucial information (i.e., health concerns or issues regarding safety). The FTC also makes sure that businesses do not violate antitrust laws.

- **National Transportation Safety Board (NTSB)** – responsible for investigating accidents involving airplanes and other forms of mass transit. It also investigates hazardous waste spills involving modes of transportation.

- **Federal Communications Commission (FCC)** – enforces federal regulations and issues licenses regarding modes of communication such as television and radio broadcasts. It regulates all interstate telecommunications as well as international communications in which at least one of the communicating parties is in the US.

- **Food & Drug Administration (FDA)** – responsible for regulating and approving all foods, drugs, medical equipment, dietary supplements and other products that could impact the health of citizens.

- **Consumer Product Safety Commission (CPSC)** – regulates the sale and manufacture of consumer products to make sure that they do not pose an unreasonable risk of injury to the public.

- **Federal Aviation Administration (FAA)** – regulates and oversees US civil air travel and transportation. It helps protect the public and ensure safe air travel through measures like mandatory rest periods for pilots.

- **Occupational Safety and Health Administration (OSHA)** – part of the Department of Labor, this agency works to prevent work-related injuries and illnesses by making sure employers abide by laws regarding workplace safety.

State agencies and local commissions/boards, like the ones we have discussed in earlier chapters, also serve to regulate the economy to a certain degree by placing limits on where businesses can build, how they operate and to what degree they are permitted to tamper with the natural environment.

THE BUSINESS CYCLE AND ECONOMIC INDICATORS

The US economy is similar to a roller coaster. Sometimes it makes its way uphill on a slow, steady rise. Then, just after it reaches the peak, it comes racing back down! Such economic ups and downs are called the **business cycle**. The steady rise up is called *expansion*, because the economy is growing. Many times it leads to a *recovery* because this growth often occurs after a less prosperous period. An expansion/recovery is sparked by something that happens to jump-start the economy. Government spending programs, tax breaks, increased investments and/or even a war that increases demands for production (i.e., WWII) can all lead to recovery. Whatever the reason, the economy improves as companies produce more goods, employment increases and people are able to buy more. As the "roller coaster" inches its way to the top, the expansion reaches its *peak*, in which production is high, unemployment low and wages increase.

A Breadline in New York City during the Great Depression

The peak period only lasts for a time, however, before the economy starts to come down. This period is known as *contraction* and is characterized by a fall in production, rising interest rates declining profits, and a slowdown in capital investments. Demand falls as consumers stop buying goods. As businesses sell less, they make less. As a result, they stop hiring and even lay off employees, thereby raising unemployment. If this trend lasts for 6 to 8 months, the economy experiences a **recession**. A *recession* is often defined as a decline in the nation's gross domestic product (GDP) for at least six months (we will discuss GDP more shortly). Recessions tend to be characterized by less production and high unemployment. Eventually, the economy hits its low point, its *trough*. The trough period is a time of high unemployment, low economic production, and falling stock prices. If it continues to worsen and last a long time, the nation may even slip into a *depression* (prolonged/severe recession).

GDP, CPI, AND THE NATIONAL DEBT

Economists use several **economic indicators** (facts/data that help show the present and/or future health of the economy) to track business cycles and measure how well the economy is doing. One means is by calculating the nation's **gross domestic product (GDP)**. The GDP is the total value of all final goods and services produced in an economy. Another economic indicator is the **consumer price index (CPI)**. This index measures inflation as it tracks monthly changes in the costs of goods and services that are typically purchased by consumers. The **unemployment rate** is also a common indicator used to measure the economy. It measures the percentage of those in a given society that are willing and able to work but who are currently without jobs. The higher the rate of employment, the higher the rate of production and consumption tends to be, thereby making for a healthier economy. **Full employment** is often defined as when all those who can and will work are employed. However, some economists refer to extremely low rates of unemployment (i.e.

under 5%) as "full employment" as well. While full employment is usually desirable, some government regulations actually serve to prevent rather than encourage it from occurring. Take, for example, a minimum wage. While workers often appreciate the government guaranteeing a minimum pay rate, the fact that employers have to pay a certain wage often prevents them from hiring more employees because they can't afford it. Thus, a minimum wage hinders full employment. Finally, economists look at the **national debt** (amount of money owed by the federal government). How much money the government owes affects fiscal policy which inevitably affects the economy and the business cycle. Economists study the GDP, CPI, unemployment rate and national debt in order to predict economic trends and propose solutions to economic problems.

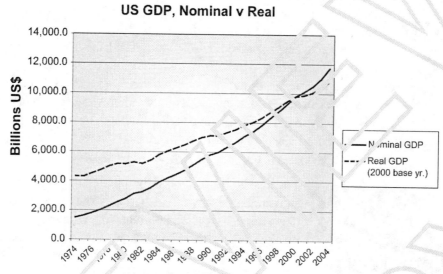

US GDP, Nominal v Real

FISCAL AND MONETARY POLICIES

FISCAL POLICY

Fiscal policy refers to the government's strategy for using public spending and taxation to influence the nation's economy. Both the executive and legislative branches of government play key roles in setting fiscal policy as they propose, debate, accept and/or reject different spending plans and tax legislation.

The first key component of fiscal policy is taxation. **Taxes** are money that citizens and businesses must pay to federal, state and local governments. They are sometimes collected as *income taxes*, which are taxes one must pay based on how much money he/she makes; *sales taxes*, which are taxes based on a percentage of what individuals spend on consumer goods; *excise taxes*, which are taxes on special products (i.e., tobacco or alcohol); *corporate taxes* on business profits, *Social Security taxes*, which take a percentage of one's income and apply it to Social Security; *tariffs*, which are taxes on imports and ultimately affect the price of goods made in both the US and in other countries; and so on. As the government decreases taxes, producers have more money to spend on labor, capital, etc. and households have more money to spend. This usually results in economic growth because companies tend to produce more and people buy more things. However, if not careful, it can also lead to severe **inflation** (rise in prices). Raising taxes, on the other hand, has the opposite effect. When people have to pay higher taxes, they have less money to spend on other things. As a result, producers cannot sell as much at higher prices. Therefore, they have to charge less, thereby lowering prices to attract consumers. That's why governments will sometimes raise taxes to deal with rising prices.

However, when the government raises taxes, production also slows and unemployment tends to rise because consumers don't demand products as much as they use to and producers cannot make as much for the products they sell. As you can see, fiscal policy has a great effect on a nation's economy.

US Budget Surplus or Deficit as a Percentage of GDP; 1945-2002

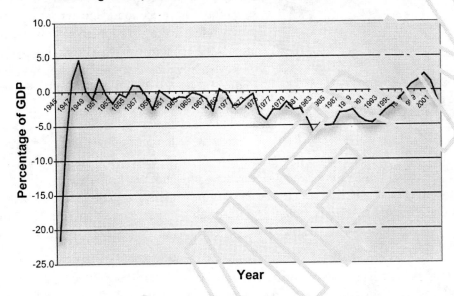

The money which the government takes in (mostly through taxes) is referred to as *government revenue*. How and what this revenue is spent on is referred to as *government spending*. The government's spending decisions comprise the second half of fiscal policy. By spending more of its revenue, the government pumps money into the economy and promotes growth. However, if a government wants to maintain a balanced budget, increased spending usually means having to raise taxes. Often, a government cuts taxes and increases spending at the *same time* to try to bolster the economy. When this happens, it usually results in **deficit spending** (spending more money than the government has in revenue) and an increase in the national debt. On the other hand, a government might also reduce government spending. Reduced spending means less money pumped into the economy because those who normally benefit from government spending have less money to spend in the market place. To review then, fiscal policy refers to the government's plan for taxation and government spending, both of which have significant impact on the economy because they affect how much money people and businesses have to spend in the market. when governments raise taxes, production slows and consumers spend less, but the government has more money to spend. Conversely, tax cuts stimulate the economy but leave the government with less money and possibly having to rely on deficit spending.

Government and Economics

MONETARY POLICY

Fiscal policy is often described as the government's "long-term approach" to improving the economy due to the fact that it takes a while for tax policies and government spending to have economic impact. By contrast, **monetary policy** refers to the government's "short-term approach" to impact the economy quickly by changing the nation's money supply. Monetary policy is controlled by the **Federal Reserve**. The "Fed," as it is sometimes called, is the nation's central bank and operates independently of any branch of federal government. Its role is crucial because the amount of money that is in circulation in the nation's economy greatly impacts things like production, consumption, prices, employment, borrowing, spending, etc. The Federal Reserve implements monetary policy in three primary ways. First, it controls the money supply by either raising or lowering the **reserve requirement** (amount of cash banks are required to keep on hand rather than loan). A *"tight money" policy* (high reserve requirement) limits the money supply, whereas an *"easy money" policy* (low reserve requirement) increases it because more people can borrow and spend money.

Ben Bernanke,
Chairman of the
Federal Reserve

Consider this simplified example. Say that 100 people want to buy a house. They all go to the bank to take out a loan for the purchase. The Federal Reserve, however, has just instituted a "tight money" policy. This means that the bank has to keep more money on hand and has less money to lend. As a result, the bank does not have the resources to grant all 100 households a loan. It can only loan money to 60 households. What consequences does this have? In addition to disappointing the 40 households that couldn't get a loan, it also means that 40 houses will not be bought that otherwise would have been. This means less money for the developer, fewer construction workers hired, less contractors employed, less demand for house inspectors, and less income for real estate agents. These people, in turn, will now have less income to spend in the market place, which means less money for store owners, fewer cars sold by auto dealers, fewer customers at restaurants and so on. On the other hand, if the Federal Reserve institutes an "easy money" policy, then the bank loans more money, more homes are bought, incomes increase, more money is spent, production tends to rise, etc.

The second way the Federal Reserve impacts the nation's money supply is through the *discount rate*. The **discount rate** is the interest rate that banks and other financial institutions pay the Fed in order to borrow money. In other words, the Federal Reserve acts like a "bank for banks." Banks and other financial institutions can borrow money from the Fed, and then — just like a household or business that borrows from the bank — pay it back with interest. An **interest rate** is a percentage that a lender charges a borrower in exchange for a loan. The higher the discount rate charged by the Fed, the higher the interest rate charged by banks. Higher interest rates encourage people to save, rather than borrow and spend, because they would rather *earn* high interest on money that they are saving than have to *pay* high interest on money that they themselves are borrowing. As a result, the money supply decreases as more money sits in savings and less is spent in the economy. Conversely, a lower discount rate allows banks to charge lower interest. This results in more loans and spending, causing the money supply to go up.

152

Chapter 9

Finally, the Fed uses **open market operations** (the sale or purchase of US treasury bonds) to control the flow of money. These bonds are a means of loaning money to the government. Those who purchase bonds are paid interest in exchange for the government's use of their money. Eventually, they are able to cash in the bond for the amount that they loaned plus any interest earned. When the Fed *sells* securities (bonds), it lowers the money supply and serves to fight inflation. How so? Understand that bonds are a form of saving for investors. They buy the bond to gain interest and then get their money back at a later time. Money that is saved (i.e., invested in bonds) is money that is not spent in the market. Therefore, the more securities sold, the more the money supply decreases. In addition, when the Fed sells securities, bank reserves of money decrease as households and businesses purchase bonds. This causes a rise in the discount rate as banks have to borrow more from the Federal Reserve to keep the required reserve on hand. This, in turn, raises interest rates and leads to less spending and less money in circulation. However, when the Fed *buys* securities, interest rates drop, spending increases and more money is pumped into the economy. Can you see now how important the Federal Reserve is?

Open Market Operations	
Federal Reserve Action	**Effect**
Sell Bonds	1. The nation's money supply decreases because more people invest in bonds than spend money in the market. 2. Since more people invest in bonds than put savings in banks and/or pay interest to banks on new loans, the discount rate increases because banks borrow more from the Fed and interest rates rise. This encourages saving rather than borrowing and spending.
Buy Bonds	1. This puts money back in the hands of the people who bought bonds. 2. This raises the money supply as people now have money they earned on bonds to spend in the market.

153

Government and Economics

Practice 9.3: Regulatory Agencies and Fiscal / Monetary Policies

1. The way the government conducts spending and taxation is called what?

   A. monetary policy

   B. economic policy

   C. free enterprise policy

   D. fiscal policy

2. The way the government chooses to control the money supply is called what?

   A. monetary policy

   B. open market operation

   C. reserve requirement and discount rate

   D. fiscal policy

3. What is the discount rate and how does it affect the money supply?

4. What is meant by "open market operations" and how does the Federal Reserve use it to control the money supply?

CHAPTER 9 REVIEW

Key Terms and Concepts

the four basic economic questions

traditional economy

market economy

command economy

equity

income redistribution

mixed economy

scarcity

economics

opportunity cost

economic freedom

security

economic stability

economic growth

environmental protection

productivity

Environmental Protection Agency (EPA)

Federal Trade Commission (FTC)

National Transportation Safety Board (NTSB)

Federal Communications Commission (FCC)

Food and Drug Administration (FDA)

Consumer Product Safety Commission (CPSC)

Federal Aviation Administration (FAA)

Occupational Safety and Health Act (OSHA)

business cycle

economic indicators

GDP

unemployment rate

full employment

national debt

fiscal policy

inflation

taxes

deficit spending

monetary policy

Federal Reserve

reserve requirement

discount rate

interest rate

open market operations

Copyright © American Book Company. DO NOT DUPLICATE. 1-888-264-5877.

Chapter 9

Multiple Choice and Short Answers

1. Economic system based on equity and in which the government decides what gets made and sets prices is called what?

   A. market system

   B. traditional economy

   C. political economy

   D. command economy

2. A small country in the Western Hemisphere is ruled by a communist government. The government, therefore, practices strict control over the economy. However, in reality, the government does allow some capitalism to exist because it finds that it helps bring much needed money into the country. This nation's economic system can **most accurately** be labeled as which of the following?

   A. command economy

   B. capitalistic economy

   C. mixed economy

   D. market economy

3. The ups and downs that the nation's economy goes through is officially referred to as what?

   A. a roller coaster

   B. expansion

   C. the business cycle

   D. economic madness

4. GDP, CPI, unemployment rate and the national debt are all what?

   A. signs that the economy is peaking

   B. signs that the economy is in contraction

   C. economic indicators used to determine the state and direction of the economy

   D. the results of economic expansion

5. The new president proposes an economic plan to Congress. In it, he calls for lower taxes and recommends several programs that he would like the government to spend money on. The president's proposal reflects what?

   A. his monetary policy

   B. his fiscal policy

   C. his desire to reduce inflation

   D. his ability to control the Federal Reserve

Government and Economics

6. The Federal Reserve comes to the conclusion that more money must be pumped into the economy in an effort to stimulate economic growth. Which of the following actions could the "Fed" take that would result in increasing the money supply?

    A. raise the discount rate

    B. raise the reserve requirement

    C. sell securities (bonds)

    D. buy securities (bonds)

7. Congress is about to pass a bill that will increase federal spending on social programs. The funds that they will allocate could have been spent on health care or job training. In the end, both houses decided to split the money 50/50, spending half on government funded healthcare programs and half on grants designed to train US workers for the changing job market. Which of the following is **not** an *opportunity cost* of Congress' decision?

    A. the additional job training that could have occurred with more funding

    B. the additional healthcare benefits that could have been provided with more funding

    C. the benefits that could have been gained by funding other social programs

    D. the monetary policy Congress could have established if it had more money to spend

8. What is the message of the above cartoon?

    A. The Federal Reserve has too much power.

    B. The Federal Reserve should do something to stimulate the economy.

    C. US citizens should buy more bonds.

    D. The US Fiscal policy is working better than its monetary policy.

9. What is the Federal Reserve? Describe how it uses the *discount rate* and the *reserve requirement* to manipulate the nation's money supply.

156

10. In what ways does the FDA and the CPSC prevent the US economy from operating as a purely free market economy?

11. Inflation is a rise in prices and tends to increase as more money is pumped into the economy. If inflation started to rise too high, what actions might the government take in terms of fiscal policy? What actions might it take in terms of monetary policy?

Chapter 10
Answering BCR and ECR Questions

This chapter addresses the following expectation(s) from **Core Learning Goal 1** Reading, Reviewing and Responding to Texts

Expectation 1.1	The student will use effective strategies before, during and after reading, reviewing and listening to self-selected and assigned materials.

As you no doubt noticed when you took the diagnostic test at the beginning of this book, some of the questions you will encounter on the Maryland government test are labeled as either BCR or ECR questions. **BCR** stands for *"Brief Constructed Response."* These are questions that require you to develop an idea or argue a point in just a few sentences. **ECR** stands for *"Extended Constructed Response."* ECR questions are asking you to develop your idea or defend your position including more information. In other words, BCR and ECR questions are similar except that ECR answers are expected to be longer. A BCR answer may only consist of three to five sentences. However, an ECR response may require more than one paragraph. The Maryland test typically consists of five to seven BCR questions, but usually no more than one or two ECR questions. The purpose of this brief chapter is to give you some helpful tips for effectively answering BCR and ECR questions.

CRITICAL THINKING

One of the most important things to remember about BCR and ECR questions is that they are intended to get you to *think critically*. In other words, these questions are not looking for "right" or "wrong" answers as much as they are meant to see how well you understand and can apply the things you've learned. In most BCR and ECR questions, you can score high marks regardless of the position you take or choice of answers you make *as long as* your arguments make sense and show a knowledge of the information covered in the course.

You Already Know How To Do This

The first thing to realize is that *you already know how to do this*. That is, you already know how to answer BCR and ECR questions. In fact, you do it everyday. Imagine you are with your friends and a discussion (or argument) breaks out about the best football team in the NFL, the best college basketball coach of all time, the greatest rock band in history, the best movie ever made, or the most talented contestant on this season's edition of *American Idol*. You have an opinion, right? So what do you do? You decide what point you want to make, then you state it up front:

"The Ravens are the best team in the NFL."

"Saving Private Ryan is the best movie ever made."

"Amanda is by far the most talented contestant on American Idol."

If you think it is necessary, you might even define certain terms or concepts more clearly to help the group truly appreciate your point:

"A football team has to do more than score a ton of points to be great."

"The best movie is one that touches you emotionally."

"Talent involves more than a great voice; it requires confidence and personality as well."

However, others in the group have different opinions, don't they? So what's your next step? You start giving reasons for your opinion that you feel will persuade the group:

"The Ravens are the best because of their strong defense."

"Saving Private Ryan makes you feel like you are right there fighting in the middle of World War II."

"Amanda has an amazing stage presence and sounds like a professional."

Now what? You begin to provide examples to back up your reasoning:

"Ray Lewis leads the league in tackles, and the Raven's defense always rises to the occasion inside the red zone."

"Even my great grandfather, who fought in World War II, said that he was moved to tears by Saving Private Ryan."

"When Amanda sang that Celine Dion song last night, she blew it out!"

Without being conscious of it, you have just done the same thing that you are asked to do with BCR and ECR questions. You went through a step-by-step process of building an argument based on information that you know. You:

- Decided what point you would make (Ravens are the best team)
- Stated the point up front (Made it clear to the group that you believe the Ravens are the best team)
- Defined any unclear terms or concepts (what defines a great team involves more than scoring points)
- Gave reasons for your opinion (Ravens are the best because of their defense)
- Backed up your reasons with examples (Ray Lewis leading the league in tackles and performance of the defense in the red zone)

Now let's take this same process and apply it to BCR and ECR questions about government.

BCR RESPONSES

In order to look at how we can effectively answer BCR questions, let's work with a sample question similar to the kind you will encounter on the Maryland test.

SAMPLE BCR:

The government established under the US Constitution is based on several key principles. Among these are federalism, separation of powers, limited government, and the idea that governments derive their power from the "consent of the governed."

- Which one of these principles do you think is the most important in the Constitution?
- Explain why you chose this particular principle.
- Include details and examples to support your answer.

Since the above question is BCR, we know that we are supposed to provide a brief response rather than an extended response. This means that we should provide an answer that includes enough information to answer the question fully, but we need not go into extra details. Therefore, our answer should be composed of just a few sentences and only one or two paragraphs.

STEPS TO ANSWERING BCR:

FIRST: *Decide what point you will make.* Like many of the ECR questions you will encounter, this question is asking you to *choose* something and then *give reasons for your decision.* Keep in mind, there is no wrong choice. You can choose any one of these principles and attain a high score for your answer *provided* you give good reasons for your choice. Now, consider each one of the principles listed:

1) federalism

2) separation of powers

3) limited government

4) consent of the governed

Since we know that any one of these answers is acceptable, decide which one you can <u>best</u> defend. Keep in mind that whoever grades your response is trying to find out how much you understand. Therefore, it is not as important that you choose the principle you feel is actually the most important, as it is that you choose the one you can *best defend* as the most important. For example, you might think that *separation of powers* is the most important because you know that it is not good for all the power to rest in one branch of government. However, you might also feel that you understand and can explain the impact and importance of *federalism* better than you understand and can explain *separation of powers*. For this reason, you should choose federalism since writing about it will better display how much you know and understand. Of course, if what you believe to be the most important principle is also the one you feel you understand the most and can do the best job defending, then that is even better. Regardless, don't forget that your score will be based on how well you display an *understanding* of the principle and its effects, not on what principle you choose.

SECOND: *State your point up front.* Since the "B" in BCR stands for "brief," the first sentence in your BCR response should get right to the point and clearly state your opinion. As an example, let's say you chose *federalism* as the principle you want to defend as being the most important in the sample BCR above. The first sentence of your response should include a phrase that makes this clear:

THIRD: *Define any terms or concepts.* Once you choose your point and make it clear to the reader, you next want to make sure you define the term or concept you are defending or focusing on. You want to do this for two main reasons: 1) It is important that the reader understand the term or concept in order to understand your argument. 2) It is important that you show the person grading your response that <u>you understand the term or concept</u>. Therefore, in the example we are working with, your opening sentence might read something like this:

> Federalism is the division of power between the federal and state governments and is the most important principle in the US Constitution.

Now your reader knows your main point (federalism is the most important principle) and understands what you mean by *federalism*. Just as importantly, the person grading your response is aware that you know what it means too.

FOURTH: *State reasons for your position.* Now that we know what your point is and we are clear on the meaning of the term or concept you are presenting, it is time for you to tell us WHY you believe your point is correct. You are arguing that federalism is the most important principle in the Constitution, now tell us why. Here, you are using what you know to convince the reader you are right. Say, for example, that you believe federalism is important because it allows states to deal with local and state concerns more effectively than the national government could and that the national government should not be bogged down in local matters. The next section of your response might read something like:

> *The United States is a large country with many different types of people, therefore federalism is important because it allows state governments to deal more effectively with local matters and keeps the federal government from getting bogged down.*

FIFTH: *Make sure you support your position with examples.* It is not enough just to state your reasons, you need to give examples that illustrate what you mean. In other words, you are giving readers something they can see or observe that demonstrates how your point is true. You are also making it clear to the person grading your response that you understand how your point relates to real life. Look at our response so far. Where might examples help illustrate our point? Since we are claiming that federalism is important because it allows states to deal with local issues more effectively and keeps the federal government from getting bogged down, then it would be helpful to apply some examples to illustrate how this is true. Our final response to the BCR example above, then, might look something like this:

> Federalism is the division of power between the federal and state governments and is the most important principle in the US Constitution. The United States is a large country with many different types of people; therefore federalism is important because it allows state governments to deal more effectively with local matters and keeps the federal government from getting bogged down. For instance, states can better deal with issues like education, traffic laws, how cities are established, and local land use because their elected officials come from among those affected by these issues. Meanwhile, the federal government is free to focus on broader issues like the nation's economy, national security, and relations with foreign countries, which ensure that these issues get the attention they require.

Notice the examples we added. Education, traffic laws, how cities are established and local land use are all *examples* of issues more effectively handled by state governments. Meanwhile, the freedom this gives to the federal government to focus on the economy, national defense, and relations with foreign countries is an *example* of how federalism keeps the national government from getting bogged down.

BOOM! There you go. You've just completed a brief constructed response.

QUESTIONS REQUIRING INTERPRETATIONS

BCR questions can take various forms on the test. Some will give you a list of things to choose from and ask you to pick and defend a position, like the example we just looked at. Others might involve some interpretation of a fact you are familiar with from your coursework. For instance, look at the following example

Read the quote below:

> "It is the duty of this government to uphold decency and morality, therefore certain words and subject matter should be prohibited from being said or discussed on public radio."
>
> – **Candidate for US Congress**

- Based on what you know about the Bill of Rights, explain why you think the view expressed in this statement is or is not constitutional.
- Include details and examples to support your answer.

This question is slightly different, isn't it? Still, you really already know how to do this; we're just adding one step at the beginning. Before we jump to deciding what point to defend, we have to make sure we understand the quote. What is the quote saying? It is saying that certain speech, in this case on the radio, should be censored. What is the question asking us to do? It is asking us to state whether or not the kind of censorship this person is advocating is constitutional based on the Bill of Rights. So really, all that was added was one step: *interpret the quote*. Now we follow the same process so that it looks like this:

1. Interpret the quote (it is advocating censorship of speech on public radio).

2. Decide what point you will make (i.e., This kind of censorship is constitutional.)

3. State your point up front.

4. Define terms or concepts.

5. State reasons for your position.

6. Support your decision with examples.

So you see, except for having to take a moment to interpret the quote, it is really the same kind of problem. Keep in mind, in this example you could choose either position and still score high. The key is defending your position with facts you learned in the course. You might be asked to interpret a quote, a political cartoon, a chart or table, some kind of hypothetical situation, or portions of a document like the US Constitution or the Maryland Declaration of Rights.

ECR RESPONSES

ECR (extended constructed response) answers basically follow the same process as BCR answers. The only difference is that ECR answers are meant to be longer. For this reason, you are expected to include more information, and/or make more than one argument. Let's take our *federalism* example again, only this time, let's make it an ECR question.

SAMPLE ECR:

US Capitol   **Maryland Capitol**

The government established unde the US Constitution is based on several key principles. Among these are federalism, separation of powers, limited government, and the idea that governments derive their power from the "consent of the governed."

- Which one of these principles is the most important in the Constitution and why?
- Explain what some of the disadvantages of the principle you chose are, and tell why you think it is still the most important principle despite its disadvantages.
- Include details and examples to support your answer.

The first part of the question is basically the same as our BCR example. You must choose one principle to argue as the most important, state it, give reasons, and support your reasons with examples, just as you did in the BCR. However, now you must also list some of the disadvantages of the principle you choose and tell <u>why</u> your choice is still the most important constitutional principle despite these disadvantages. To answer this question, we will use the same process, but we will use it to make more than one argument.

Our process, then, will look something like this:

First:	Decide what point you will make.
Second:	State your point up front.
Third:	Define the term or concept.
Fourth:	State your reasons for your position.
Fifth:	Make sure you supported your position with examples.

As you have probably already noticed, the first paragraph of our ECR response will more or less be the same as our BCR answer. We aren't finished yet, however. We still have to discuss the disadvantages and tell why we think federalism is still the most important principle. So, in a sense, we are simply repeating our process to make a second argument.

1. *Decide what point you will make.* (Federalism has disadvantages, however, it is still the most important principle in the Constitution.)

2. *State your point up front.*

3. *Define terms/concepts.*

4. *State reasons for your position.*

5. *Make sure you support your position with examples.*

The second part of our ECR answer, then, might look something like this:

> Federalism, however, does have disadvantages. Because power is divided, the government is sometimes slow to act since federal and state leaders often care about different things. State leaders may need additional federal money for healthcare programs, education, or to deal with natural disasters, only to run into resistance for national officials. Meanwhile, the federal government may want to see state leaders implement new environmental restrictions or support federal programs, only to be opposed by state officials because such measures are not popular in that particular state. As a result, decisions that could have quickly been instituted by one level of government sometimes get drawn out, if ever implemented at all, under federalism.
>
> Despite such disadvantages, however, federalism is still the most important principle in the Constitution because it prevents abuses of power and better ensures the rights of citizens. State governments cannot trample on the constitutional rights of citizens, nor can the federal government force its will on state governments which often speak more directly for local citizens. As a result, federalism allows matters to be solved taking into account local standards, thereby better maintaining peace and stability.

Notice how we developed our argument about the disadvantages of federalism and how federalism is still the most important principle. We stated our points up front in each paragraph. We gave reasons for our opinion (federalism can result in the government being slow to act / federalism prevents abuses of power). We used examples to back up our points (different interests of state and federal leaders / states cannot trample on constitutional rights, federal government cannot impose its will on states). Thus, our final ECR answer:

> Federalism is the division of power between the federal and state governments and is the most important principle in the US Constitution. The United States is a large country with many different types of people, therefore federalism is important because it allows state governments to deal more effectively with local matters and keeps the federal government from getting bogged down. For instance, states can better deal with issues like education, traffic laws, how cities are established, and local land use. Meanwhile, the federal government is free to focus on broader issues like the nation's economy, national security, and relations with foreign countries.
>
> Federalism, however, does have disadvantages. Because power is divided, the government is sometimes slow to act since federal and state leaders often care about different things. State leaders may need additional federal money for healthcare programs, education, or to deal with natural disasters, only to run into resistance. Meanwhile, the federal government may want to see state leaders implement new environmental restrictions or support federal programs, only to be opposed by state officials because such measures are not popular in that particular state. As a result, decisions that could have quickly been instituted by one level of government sometimes get drawn out, if ever implemented at all, under federalism.
>
> Despite such disadvantages, however, federalism is still the most important principle in the Constitution because it prevents abuses of power and better ensures the rights of citizens. State governments cannot trample on the constitutional rights of citizens, nor can the federal government force its will on state governments which often speak more directly for local citizens.. As a result, federalism allows matters to be solved taking into account local standards, thereby better maintaining peace and stability.

IN CONCLUSION

The important thing to remember is that, regardless of the form a particular BCR or ECR question takes, the critical thinking skills you need to use are basically the same. Be confident — you already know how to formulate the kinds of arguments necessary to score well on these types of questions. The key is making sure you know the information covered in the course well enough to be able to make good arguments based on facts about US and Maryland government.

ADDITIONAL PRACTICE

The following are some additional practice BCR and ECR questions, similar to the ones you will encounter on the Maryland test. Attempt to answer them using the tips discussed in this chapter, then discuss your answers with your teacher or test prep instructor.

1. **BCR:** Study the graph below:

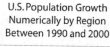

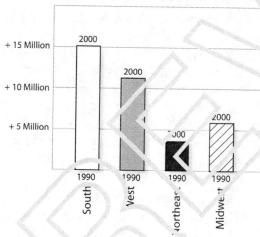

*   In what ways has the trend depicted in the graph most likely affected government decisions?
*   Why has this trend had such effect?
*   Include details and examples to support your answers.

2. **BCR:**
   - What point do you believe the cartoonist is trying to make?
   - Explain why you agree or disagree with the cartoonist's opinion.
   - Include details and examples to support your answers.

3. **BCR:** In 1789, Congress assembled and approved twelve new amendments for consideration by the states. Eventually, ten of these amendments were ratified and became the Bill of Rights.
   - What is the purpose of the Bill of Rights?
   - Which right guaranteed by these amendments do you consider to be the most important and why?
   - Include details and examples to support your answers.

4. **ECR:** Justices who serve on the United States Supreme Court are appointed by the president of the United States. Once they have been confirmed by the US Senate, they serve for life, until they retire, or until they are removed for some kind of wrongdoing.
   - Why are justices appointed rather than elected?
   - Describe the advantages and disadvantages of having justices appointed rather than elected to the Supreme Court, and explain why you agree or disagree with this process.
   - Include details and examples to support your answer.

5. **ECR:** A large supermarket chain wants to build a new store in a rural, but growing, area of Maryland. Some citizens and political leaders are excited about the possibility, while others are concerned and oppose the proposal.
   - Describe reasons why some citizens and leaders might approve of the new store and others oppose it.
   - What actions could citizens on both sides of the issue take to try and influence the zoning board's final decision?
   - Include details and examples to support your answer

Maryland High School Assessment in Government
Practice Test 1

The purpose of this practice test is to measure your progress in comprehending Maryland government. This practice test is based on the Maryland standards for School Improvement in Maryland using the Core Learning Goals and adheres to the sample question format provided by the Maryland Department of Education.

General Directions:

1   Read all directions carefully.

2   Read each question or sample. Then choose the best answer.

3   Choose only one answer for each question. If you change an answer, be sure to erase your original answer completely

1 The General Assembly of Maryland   1.1.1
has just passed a new law regarding
the purchase of handguns. However, because
he believes that certain parts of the law
violate the rights of citizens, the governor
vetoes the bill. What principle of
government does the governor's action
reflect?

A judicial review
B representative democracy
C popular sovereignty
D checks and balances

2 Which of the following would be part   4.1.4
of the government's fiscal policy?

F raising interest rates
G selling bonds
H lowering the reserve requirement
J cutting the number of federal entitlements

3 Which of the following is a   2.2.1
characteristic of an authoritarian
form of government?

A democratic elections
B limited government
C government based on consent of the governed
D restricted liberties

4 On election day, news media often use   1.1.4
exit polls to predict the winners
before all the votes have been counted. In
2000, George W. Bush's supporters
complained because media agencies
predicted that Al Gore had won in Florida
prior to all of the votes in the heavily
Republican panhandle (portion of Florida in
the central rather than eastern time zone)
being counted. Later, when Bush ended up
winning Florida by less that 1000 votes,
Gore's supporters were also upset at such
early predictions.

- Explain why both Bush's and Gore's
  supporters may have both been upset over
  early predictions of Gore's victory.

- Give reasons why you think news agencies
  should or should not predict winners of
  elections prior to the polls closing.

  Use details and examples to support your
  answers.

5 *Gideon v. Wainwright* served to do   1.2.4
which of the following?

A integrate schools
B protect civil rights in an educational setting
C protect due process rights of the poor
D establish that civil liberties are more restricted in schools than elsewhere

6 According to the chart below, which statement is true? 1.1.2

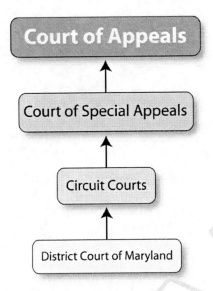

Court of Appeals

↑

Court of Special Appeals

↑

Circuit Courts

↑

District Court of Maryland

F The District Court of Maryland rarely has original jurisdiction over cases.

G The Court of Special Appeals usually has appellate jurisdiction over cases appealed from Circuit Court.

H The Maryland Court of Appeals has original jurisdiction over most cases.

J No case in Maryland is final until it is heard by every level of the courts.

7 Subsistence farming, children growing up to practice the same trade as their parents, wealth and power remaining in the hands of an aristocratic few, same products being produced over time. These characteristics describe a 4.1.1

A command economy.

B market economy.

C socialist state.

D traditional economy.

8 Which of the following actions is prohibited under the Americans with Disabilities Act? 1.2.2

F constructing a building which forces people in wheelchairs to use a separate entrance

G firing a disabled person for failing to perform up to company standards

H discriminating against qualified job candidates without disabilities in order to hire a predetermined number of disabled applicants.

I refusing to hire someone who's deaf for a job they are qualified for simply because they are disabled.

9 Before 9/11, most US citizens viewed illegal immigration as primarily a problem for states along the US-Mexico border. Now, however, many believe stricter immigration laws are needed to prevent potential terrorists from entering the country. This change in mindset serves to demonstrate what? 3.1.3

A Illegal immigration is not as big a threat as many fear.

B Illegal immigrants are viewed as terrorists.

C What was once a regional interest is now a national interest.

D That what was once a regional interest for southern states is now an international interest that involves another country.

10 Which one of the following least affects US foreign policy decisions? 2.1.2

F human rights

G national interests

H economic factors

J judicial review

 GO ON

Use the graph below to answer questions 11, 12, and 13.

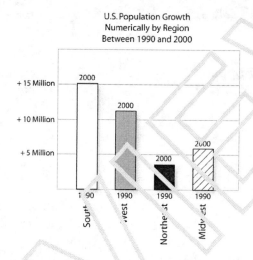

U.S. Population Growth
Numerically by Region
Between 1990 and 2000

11 Which region <u>probably</u> required the most drastic increase in government services between 1990 and 2000?   3.1.1

  A the South   **C** the Midwest
  B the Northeast   **D** the Western US

12 Which region <u>probably</u> benefited the least from reapportionment between 1990 and 2000?   3.1.1

  F the South   **H** the Midwest
  G the Northeast   **J** the Western US

13 Which region <u>most likely</u> saw its political influence in Washington, DC increase the most between 1990 and 2000?   3.1.1

  A the South   **C** the Western US
  B the Midwest   **D** the Northeast

14 Which of the following is designed to address a regional, rather than a national, interest?   3.1.3

  F the PATRIOT act
  G the EPA
  H the Smart Growth Priority Funding Areas Act
  J military spending

15 The purpose of the Bill of Rights is to   1.1.1

  A protect the rights of the government.
  B protect civil liberties.
  C restrict what citizens can do to each other.
  D establish a separation of powers in government.

16

BCR
- Explain the difference between a federation, a confederation and a unitary government.
- Explain why you think one of these forms of government is better than the others.
- Include details and examples to support your answers.

2.2.1

17 Why is the mass media sometimes referred to as the "fourth branch of government"?

1.1.4

A It is officially established under the First Amendment.

B The Constitution guarantees certain powers to the mass media.

C The mass media has tremendous impact on public opinion which affects government decisions.

D The media generally only concerns itself with political issues.

18 Together, the Supreme Court's ruling in *Tinker v. Des Moines* and *New Jersey v. TLO* established which of the following?

1.2.1

F The Bill of Rights does not apply in a public school setting.

G Free speech is guaranteed in schools to the same degree it is everywhere else.

H The Fourth Amendment does not apply in an educational setting.

J Students have rights but they are more restricted when at school.

19 Which of the following is an important element of democracy?

2.2.1

A censorship

B totalitarianism

C popular sovereignty

D theocracy

Use the following sample news article to answer questions 20 and 21.

City Council Says 'No' to Road, "Yes" to Fire Station

20 The news story depicts

4.1.2

F an opportunity cost.

G economic growth.

H environmental protection.

J productivity.

21 The news story depicts

4.1.2

A equity.

B scarcity.

C instability.

D productivity.

GO ON

Use the following political cartoon to answer question number 22.

22 The artist who drew this cartoon would most likely agree with which one of the following statements? 1.1.2

F Congress and the president usually cooperate.

G Congress' powers are rarely checked.

H The Supreme Court usually has no say in what becomes a law.

J The Supreme Court has a great deal of power over what laws actually stay in place.

23 Which of the following is a common weakness of command economies? 4.1.1

A equity

B under employment

C inefficient production

D abundant economic competition

24 Which of the following is an example of an entitlement? 1.1.3

F clean air

G health insurance through an employer

H food stamps from the government

J the right to vote

25 "Presumption of innocence" in a criminal trial means 1.2.5

A it is the responsibility of the defendant to prove he/she is innocent.

B it is the responsibility of the government to prove the defendant is guilty.

C it is up to the judge to determine what evidence is allowed at trial.

D the prosecutor must assume the defendant is innocent until he/she is convicted.

GO ON

26 A Maryland county is encouraged
that the area has grown considerably
over the last five years. However, while this
growth has helped economic development,
there is also fear that the rapid influx of new
residents and increase in the construction of
residential homes is occurring at a pace
damaging to the environment. The county is
facing the problem of

3.1.2

F   urban sprawl.
G   redistricting.
H   malapportionment.
J   under funding.

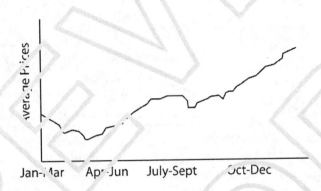

27 According to the above graph, the
economy has experienced which of
the following over the last year?

4.1.4

A   economic growth
B   inflation
C   no noticeable economic change
D   higher average incomes

28 Which agency would be __most likely__ to
investigate allegations that a factory
is releasing pollutants exceeding federal
limits into the atmosphere?

4.1.3

F   Federal Communications Commission
(FCC)
G   Maryland Department of Natural
Resources
H   Environmental Protection Agency
(EPA)
J   Consumer Product Safety Commission
(CPSC)

Use the following table to answer questions 29, 30 and 31.

United Nations	intended to provide a place where countries can negotiate rather than go to war; also acts to provide humanitarian relief to areas of the world experiencing economic woes and/or the distress of natural disasters
World Bank	provides finance and counsel to poorer countries attempting to improve their economic condition and encourages foreign businesses to invest in developing nations
International Monetary Fund (IMF)	oversees the international financial system by monitoring exchange rates, balances on payments between lender and debtor nations and offering financial and technical assistance
North Atlantic Treaty Organization (NATO)	agreement between the US and several western European nations to protect one another and acknowledge an attack against one nation in the alliance as an attack against all
International Red Cross	international association of distinct organizations, each devoted to providing humanitarian relief; has the authority to protect the lives and dignity of victims of armed conflicts as it provides humanitarian aid

29 According to the above chart, leaders of a developing nation hoping to encourage US businesses to invest in their country would most <u>likely</u> turn to what organization for assistance?   2.1.2

    A World Bank

    B United Nations

    C International Red Cross

    D IMF

30 According to the chart, which organization would be called on to provide food and medical help to civilians fleeing a bloody civil war in their home country?   2.1.2

    F World Bank

    G International Red Cross

    H IMF

    J NATO

31 According to the chart, which organization would be involved in diplomacy designed to avoid a war?   2.1.2

    A IMF   **C** United Nations

    B NATO   **D** World Bank

Session 2

32 The Magna Carta, signed in 1215, states:

1.1.1

> "No freeman shall be arrested or imprisoned or dispossessed or ... in any way harmed ... except by the lawful judgment of his peers or by the law of the land."

According to the excerpt above, the Magna Carta serves as a founding principle for which of the following liberties protected by the Bill of Rights?

- **F** separation of church and state
- **G** right to due process
- **H** protection from cruel and unusual punishment
- **J** protection from unreasonable searches and seizures

33 Which of the following represents an action taken by Maryland to ensure public safety?

1.2.3

- **A** restrictions on drivers under age 18
- **B** Clean Water Act of 1970
- **C** USDA regulations
- **D** environmental standards enforced by the EPA

34 The Clean Air Act of 1970 set national standards for guaranteeing cleaner air, while the Clean Water Act of 1972 was passed to help ensure cleaner water. Which of the following was a direct result of these laws?

1.1.3

- **F** The popularity of outdoor sports decreased.
- **G** Fewer people drove automobiles.
- **H** Industries modified the way they produced goods and disposed of waste.
- **J** Fossil fuel emissions and water pollutants were ultimately eliminated.

35 A politician running for president promises auto workers in Michigan that she will support tariffs on imported cars, while at the same time promising people in Colorado that she favors restrictions on air pollution, and assuring voters in the deep South that traditional family values based on biblical principles are important. This candidate is doing what to win votes?

3.1.3

- **A** appealing to regional interests
- **B** appealing to national interests
- **C** pandering to larger urban areas that have lots of electoral votes
- **D** relying on traditionally blue states for support rather than red states

Use the following political cartoon to answer question 36.

36 What is the above cartoon addressing? 4.1.4

F market economies

G social security

H inflation

J fiscal policy

37 Which of the following would <u>not</u> be an example of state action designed to maintain public order and safety? 1.2.3

A The governor declaring a state of emergency.

B The governor deploying the national guard to protect people from riots and looting following a natural disaster.

C The General Assembly passing laws to restrict the purchase of handguns.

D FEMA providing assistance to Maryland residents following a flood.

38 NAFTA caused controversy in the US because it 2.1.1

F restricted trade between nations in the Western Hemisphere.

G established free trade between North American countries.

H imposed an embargo against Cuba.

J limited economic globalization.

39 Which agency is responsible for radio broadcasts? 4.1.3

A Federal Aviation Administration (FAA)

B Consumer Product Safety Commission (CPSC)

C Federal Trade Commission (FTC)

D Federal Communications Commission (FCC)

178

GO ON

40 The news article below is an example of Congress using its powers under

1.1.1

Congress Authorizes Study of Possible Alternative Fuel Source

Washington, DC — Congressional leaders in both the House and the Senate today announced that they will support efforts to find alternative sources of fuel to help wean the United States off dependence on foreign oil...

F the elastic clause.

G the supremacy clause.

H the Tenth Amendment

J writ of habeas corpus.

41 Which of the following represents a form of "speech" that may be censored by the government?

1.1.3

A A group of students meeting for prayer outside a public school just before classes start.

B A magazine printing false stories that damage another person's reputation in order to sell more copies.

C A student wearing a red ribbon in support of AIDS research to school.

D A reporter breaking a story that reveals the lieutenant governor was involved in a crime.

42 Joshua is arrested for armed robbery and assault with a deadly weapon. If he is found "not guilty" in court, he cannot be charged again for the same crime because of constitutional guarantees against

1.2.4

F self-incrimination.

G double jeopardy

H eminent domain.

J writ of habeas corpus.

43 Because recent statistics show that people are leaving urban areas of the Northeast for the South, a number of northeastern states are asking the federal government for funds to help them rebuild and improve their inner cities in an effort to bring people back and attract business. Meanwhile, the growing southern states are asking for more money to finance desperately needed public services. What problem does this present for the federal government?

3.1.3

A how to decrease government revenue

B how to stop people from leaving cities

C how to stop people from migrating to the South

D how to balance the needs of different regions

44 A pharmaceutical company wants to market a new drug designed to prevent baldness. What agency will have to approve this drug before it can be sold to the public?

1.2.3

J Federal Communications Commission (FCC)

G Occupational Safety and Health Administration (OSHA)

H Environmental Protection Agency (EPA)

J Food and Drug Administration (FDA)

GO ON

Use the following political cartoon to answer question number 45.

45 The above cartoon is most likely making the point that   1.1.2

- **A** Miracles can happen.
- **B** Healthcare costs are becoming unaffordable.
- **C** People are living longer.
- **D** Social Security might not be around in years to come.

46 Which of the following is an economic problem state and federal governments must consistently deal with?   4.1.2

- **F** updating traditional economies
- **G** balancing competing socioeconomic goals
- **H** eliminating opportunity costs
- **J** mandating production

47 The governor has just announced the construction of a new building in Annapolis that will house a school devoted to educating Maryland's most gifted low-income students. As part of the building's construction, the state is sure to include plans for wheelchair ramps and elevators for those who cannot climb stairs. The state is making sure that it abides by what law?   1.1.3

- **A** Civil Rights Act of 1964
- **B** Higher Education Act of 1972
- **C** Real ID Act of 2005
- **D** Americans with Disabilities Act of 1990

48 Environmentalists in Maryland would <u>likely</u> be <u>most</u> upset by   3.1.2

- **F** passage of the Critical Areas Act.
- **G** legislation that promotes conservation.
- **H** urban sprawl.
- **J** stricter guidelines handed down by the US Department of the Interior.

Use the following graph to answer questions 49 and 50.

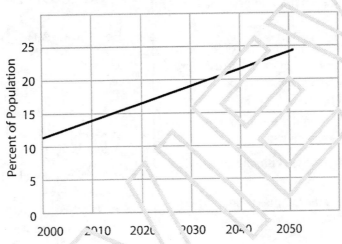

Estimated Hispanic Population Growth in US

49   3.1.1
BCR

- Describe two ways the trend depicted in the graph will most likely impact government policies.
- Include details and examples to support your answers.

50 According to the graph, the US   3.1.1
Latino population

F   has benefited from gerrymandering.
G   is a growing minority population.
H   is no longer a minority in the US.
J   has highly benefited from illegal immigration.

51 Which of the following was put in   2.1.1
place to protect Western Europe
from a communist invasion?

A   NAFTA
B   United Nations
C   NATO
D   OAS

52 Thomas Jefferson's belief that, while   1.1.2
the national government should
provide a structure for dealing with foreign
nations, the rights and powers of the states
should be protected and ensured, supports
the concept of

F   representative democracy.
G   popular sovereignty.
H   limited government.
J   federalism.

GO ON

53 David is suspected of participating in a terrorist plot. During the middle of the night, federal law enforcement agents come crashing through the door of his house without a warrant, arrest him and collect evidence that suggests he is a drug dealer.

1.2.4

ECR

- What constitutional arguments could David use to argue that the search and arrest were illegal and, therefore, the evidence not admissible at his trial?

- What arguments might the government make to show that the search was legal?

- Explain why you agree with one side rather than the other.

- Include details and examples to support your answers.

54

.2.2

> This law is important because it will give Native Americans control of those artifacts which so richly provide their community a link to its past."
>
> – federal official, 1990

The above quote is referring to the Native American Graves Protection and Repatriation Act. This law is a direct attempt to

F financially compensate Native Americans for past injustices.

G protect and show respect for Native American culture.

H improve the socioeconomic status of Native Americans.

I improve the educational opportunities afforded Native Americans.

US Approves $5 Billion in Foreign Aid to Developing Nations

55 Why would the US take the kind of action addressed in the above headline?

2.1.1

A Most developing nations are military powers.

B Developing nations tend to be strong democracies.

C It helps maintain economic and political stability.

D It discourages developing nations from taking military action against the US.

182

GO ON

Use the following political cartoon to answer question 57.

Mary Stoddard
© American Book Company

56 According to the above cartoon, political candidates often   1.1.4

   A depend heavily on campaign contributions.

   B are part of the mass media.

   C tend to oppose freedom of the press.

   D avoid saying things that might offend voters.

57 In 1999, eleven European countries adopted the euro as a common form of currency.   3.1.3

BCR

- Describe how this action likely impacted this region.

- Include details and examples to support your answer.

183

> ## Meredith Becomes First Black Admitted to Ole Miss After President Acts
>
> *Oxford, Miss* — James Meredith finally took his place as the first Negro admitted to the University of Mississippi, but not until after President Kennedy authorized federal marshals to ensure that the Supreme Court's order to integrate the university was carried out.

58 After reading the news story, it is apparent that President Kennedy's actions represent

    1.2.3

  F the process by which Civil Rights legislation becomes law

  G the role of the president to enforce federal laws.

  H the method the Supreme Court uses for enforcing its rulings.

  J the power of the states to overrule federal decisions.

STOP

184

Maryland High School Assessment in Government
Practice Test 2

The purpose of this practice test is to measure your progress in comprehending Maryland government. This practice test is based on the Standards for School Improvement in Maryland using the Core Learning Goals and adheres to the sample question format provided by the Maryland Department of Education.

General Directions:

1   Read all directions carefully.

2   Read each question or sample. Then choose the best answer.

3   Choose only one answer for each question. If you change an answer, be sure to erase your original answer completely.

Use the following sample headlines to answer question number 1.

> **Council Votes "No" on Issuing Permit to Liquor Store**

> **Conservationists Celebrate Opening of State Park**

> **Historic Society Petitions Zoning Board to Protect Landmarks**

> **State Threatens to Withhold Funding if Council Allows Bay Building Project**

1 The above news headlines all address the issue of   3.1.2

A environmental protection.

B gerrymandering.

C government entitlements.

D land use.

2 Efforts to clean and conserve the Chesapeake Bay would most benefit which Maryland region?   3.13

F Eastern Shore

G western Maryland

H Baltimore-Washington metropolitan area

J Piedmont plateau

186

GO ON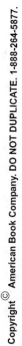

3 Recently, some members of Congress 1.1.1
have put forth the idea of passing a
ECR Constitutional amendment defining
marriage as solely a union between a man
and a woman. A number of these
representatives say that they feel an
amendment is necessary in order to prevent
the Supreme Court from striking down laws
upholding the traditional definition of
marriage.

- Discuss how the Supreme Court could go
  about nullifying laws passed by Congress
  regarding marriage and why it might do so.

- State how one might argue that this power
  possessed by the Court conflicts with the
  principles of popular sovereignty and
  representative democracy.

- Include examples and details to support your
  answer.

4 Which of the following best describes 1.1.4
the difference between an interest
group and a political party?

F Political parties are concerned with
who wins an election, while interest
groups only care about policy decisions.

G Political parties are official organizations, while members of interest groups
are independent of either major party.

H Political parties generally hire lobbyists, while interest groups don't.

J Political parties usually embrace a
number of issues, while interest groups
are generally concerned with one specific issue.

Labour Party Wins:
Taylor To Be
Prime Minister

5 This headline would most likely be 2.2.1
seen in a country with a government
based on

A   limited monarchy.

B   parliamentary democracy.

C   presidential democracy.

D   oligarchy

6 In 1984, Maryland's General 3.1.2
Assembly passed the Critical Area
Act. Under this act, the Chesapeake Bay has
been declared a "critical area" and is
protected by certain guidelines governing
local land use and development. The
purpose of this law can best be described as

F   attempting to stop industrial develop-
     ment in eastern Maryland.

G   attempting to promote new businesses
     in the Chesapeake Bay area.

H   attempting to protect national interests.

J   attempting to protect the environment
     and wildlife in and around the Chesa-
     peake Bay area.

7 Virginia and Maryland cooperating 3.1.3
to protect and conserve the
environment of the Chesapeake Bay is an
example of

A   states working as a confederation.

B   federalism at work.

C   zoning ordinances.

D   states working together to address
     regional interests.

GO ON

Use the following political cartoon to answer questions 8 and 9.

8 The cartoonist is most likely making which of the following statements?   4.1.4

   F US foreign policy is a failure.

   G Too many US jobs are being lost to other countries.

   H US workers need an increase in the minimum wage.

   J US foreign policy is creating jobs.

9 Which statement would most support the message portrayed in the cartoon?   4.1.4

   A Embargoes hurt the US.

   B The US needs to do more to help developing nations.

   C US businesses are finding it cheaper to conduct some of their operations in other countries.

   D Not enough is being done to spread wealth worldwide.

10 Which of the following is not a principle on which Maryland's state government is based?   1.1.2

   F confederation

   G popular sovereignty

   H limited government

   J representative democracy

11 Which of the following represents actions taken by executive order?   1.2.3

   A ratification of NAFTA

   B passage of the War Powers Act

   C Title IX in the early 70s

   D internment of Japanese Americans during WWII

188

GO ON

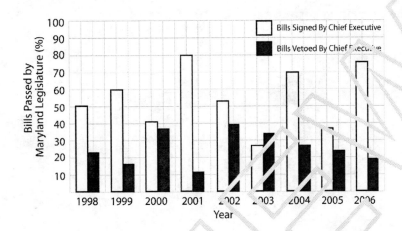

12 Which of the following statements is true based on the above graph ? 1.?.2

- **F** The ability of the legislative branch and the executive branch to work together has improved in the last eight years.
- **G** The ability of the legislative branch and the executive branch to work together has gotten worse in the last eight years.
- **H** The judicial branch has exercised its power to check the other branches of government less in the last eight years.
- **J** The legislative and executive branches of government's role have increased over the last eight years while the judicial branch has done little.

13 4.1.1

BCR

- Describe what is meant by a "mixed economy."

- Why do you think most economies are mixed economies?

- Include details and examples to support your answer.

14 According to President George W. Bush, the establishment of the Department of Homeland Security, winning the war in Iraq, the invasion of Afghanistan and the PATRIOT Act are all essential for what? 2.1.1

- **F** bringing down communist regimes
- **G** providing foreign aid
- **H** ensuring national security
- **J** establishing arms control

15 Joshua is arrested for armed robbery and assault with a deadly weapon. If some of the evidence to be used against Joshua was seized illegally by the police then 1.2.4

- **A** the grand jury will lack the authority to indict Joshua.
- **B** the case will be declared a mistrial.
- **C** that evidence will not be allowed at trial under the "exclusionary rule."
- **D** the evidence will still be allowed if the grand jury decides there was a crime.

Use the following map to answer questions 16, 17 and 18.

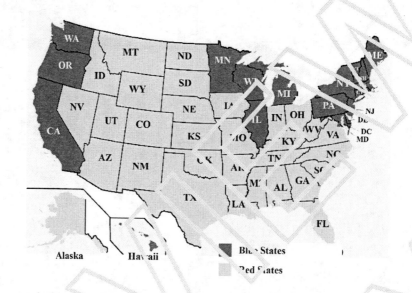

Alaska   Hawaii

■ Blue States

▨ Red States

16 According to the above map, in which state would a conservative Republican <u>most likely</u> stand the best chance of winning an election?   3.1.1

  F Illinois (IL)
  G Arizona (AZ)
  H Hawaii
  J New York (NY)

17 According to the map, in which state would a liberal Democrat <u>most likely</u> stand the best chance of winning an election?   3.1.1

  A Georgia (GA)
  B Wyoming (WY)
  C Maryland (MD)
  D Arizona (AZ)

18 According to the map, what region is <u>most likely</u> to vote predominantly Democratic in an election?   3.1.1

  F the South
  G the Rocky Mountains
  H the Pacific Northwest
  J the Bible Belt

19 The PATRIOT Act was passed after 9/11 and renewed in March 2006. It gives federal law enforcement agencies greater latitude to conduct investigations and gather evidence in order to prevent future terrorist attacks by lessening the restrictions on searches, etc.   2.4

ECR

 • What are some of the conflicts that exist between civil liberties and national security that surround the PATRIOT Act?

 • Argue for or against the PATRIOT Act in light of these conflicts.

 • Include details and examples to support your answer.

20 The Bill of Rights is <u>best</u> described as a part of the Constitution that is intended to   1.1.1

  F restrict government.
  G limit citizens.
  H enforce civic responsibility.
  J guarantee representative democracy.

GO ON

21 In a criminal case, the person charged with a crime is called the   1.2.5

A   plaintiff.
B   defendant.
C   prosecutor.
D   counsel.

22 Which of the following is responsible for enforcing laws?   1.1.2

F   governor
G   Supreme Court
H   Maryland Court of Appeals
J   Congress

23 Bill is an aggressive visionary who wants to pursue his idea for a new invention. Because he knows that developing his idea will require money, he wants to keep as much of his current salary as possible so that he can afford living expenses while working on his invention in his free time. As a result, Bill is very much against any tax increase. On the other hand, he wants to know that Social Security benefits will be there for him when he retires. Bill is experiencing what?   4.1.2

A   an opportunity cost
B   equity
C   conflict between competing socioeconomic goals
D   economic security

Use the following sample headline to answer question number 24.

Protesters Demand US Withdrawal from Middle East

London — Anti-war protesters assembled outside Parliament yesterday demanding that President Bush withdraw US forces from Iraq. Calling the US military presence and act of "criminal imperialism," leaders of the protest accused the US of forcing its "western ed will" on foreign peoples.

24 The above article most reflects which of the following?   1.1.1

F   the US' ability to spread democracy
G   criticisms of US foreign policy
H   dependence of developing nations on US military intervention
J   coalitions between foreign governments and the US

25 A Baltimore business is accused of discrimination against employees and job applicants over the age of 55. Such behavior is prohibited by which of the following laws?   1.2.2

A   Maryland Antidiscrimination Act
B   Equal Pay Act
C   Civil Rights Act
D   Americans with Disabilities Act

 GO ON

26 In 2000, Republican George W. Bush defeated Democrat Al Gore to win the **BCR** presidential election, despite the fact that more people actually voted for Gore.

1.1.2

- Describe how it was possible for Bush to win the election with fewer votes than Gore.

- Describe why you agree or disagree with our current system for electing presidents.

- Include details and examples to support your answers.

Wimark Industries wants to build a new plant in Back River, Maryland. Many residents and leaders are happy about the decision because it will create jobs and draw more people and businesses to the area. However, the city council has stipulated that Wimark will have to meet certain requirements to ensure that the area's air and water remain clean and that the wildlife remains relatively undisturbed. Wimark complains that the cost of meeting these standards will limit the number of employees it can afford to hire and will increase the costs of production.

27 Wimark and Back River are experiencing what?

4.1.2

A conflict between equity and security

B conflict between availability and scarcity

C conflict between economic growth and environmental protection

D conflict between a market and a command economy

Session 2

28 The leader of a left-wing political movement in the US delivers a speech over the radio on the Fourth of July and strongly criticizes the current president and his administration. During the speech he calls the president various names and, on a few occasions, uses profanity. Local officials arrest him and order him to pay a $100 fine. The young leader then challenges the arrest/fine in court as a violation of his First Amendment rights.

BCR

   1.1.1

- Explain why you believe this arrest is, or is not, constitutional.

- Include details and examples to support your answer.

29 Which case established the Supreme Court's power of "judicial review"?

   1.2.1

  A   *McCullough v. Maryland*

  B   *Gideon v. Wainwright*

  C   *Brown v. Board of Education*

  D   *Marbury v. Madison*

30 Ned is the head of an organization that wants to protect the endangered wooly-wooly bird. His group hires Joanne to meet with state legislators and Chris to meet with members of Congress. Together, they will try to convince lawmakers to pass legislation beneficial to the wooly-wooly bird. Which of the following statements is accurate?

   1.1.4

  F   Ned leads a political party, and Joanne and Chris are its candidates for legislative office.

  G   Ned leads an interest group, and Joanne and Chris are its lobbyists.

  H   Ned is a lobbyist who has hired Joanne and Chris to assist him.

  J   Ned leads a political party and Joanne and Chris are the party's lobbyists.

31 Which of the following represents a military alliance?

   2.1.1

  A   IMF

  B   NATO

  C   International Red Cross

  D   United Nations

Use the following graph to answer questions 32 and 33.

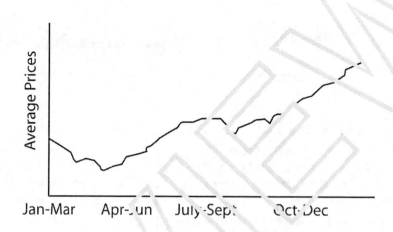

32 Which of the following can best be determined from the above graph?   4.1.4

F   Inflation has increased over the last year.

G   Prices have fallen over the last year.

H   The Federal Reserve will most likely lower interest rates if the current trend continues.

J   If the government raises taxes, the current trend will continue and increase.

33 Based on the information in the above graph, what action will the Federal Reserve likely take to reverse this trend?   4.1.4

A   raise the reserve requirement

B   lower the reserve requirement

C   buy bonds

D   raise taxes

34 If the government spends 60% of its budget on national defense, 30% on research and splits 10% between education grants and entitlements, then which of the following is an opportunity cost?   4.1.2

F   money spent on entitlements

G   money spent on education

H   the entitlements that could have been funded if less were spent on defense

J   national defense measures that could have been purchased for less than 60%

194

GO ON

Use the following political cartoon to answer question number 35.

35 What point is the above cartoon making?   1.1.2

A   White males climb the corporate ladder the fastest.

B   People with disabilities deserve equal opportunities.

C   People with disabilities are unqualified for many jobs.

D   People in wheelchairs don't deserve to climb the corporate ladder.

36   4.1.1

BCR

• Describe the difference between a command economy and a market economy.

• List some of the advantages and disadvantages of both and tell which one you think is better.

• Include details and examples to support your answer.

37 Which of the following is protected under the First Amendment's "right to free speech"?   1.1.3

F   students wearing plain red t-shirts in school to protest a war

G   a government official revealing top secret military information because he believes that the actions taken by the US military are uncalled for

H   someone calling in a bomb threat to a health club as a joke

J   a court official publishing information that was sealed by the court because she strongly believes the public has a right to know.

Use the following quotes to answer questions 38 and 39.

> "The executive power shall be vested in a President of the United States of America..."
>
> – Article 2, Section 1 of the US Constitution

> "...he (the president) shall take care that the laws be faithfully executed..."
>
> - Article 2 Section 3 of the US Constitution

38 Together, the above portions of the Constitution are used to justify   1.1.3

   F   presidential appointments

   G   treaties with foreign nations

   H   executive orders

   J   judicial hearings

39 The above portions of the Constitution have been used to justify   1.2.3

   A   the president's right to run for re-election.

   B   the president's authority to negotiate trade agreements.

   C   the president's authority to restrict civil liberties in times of crisis.

   D   the War Powers Act.

40 The Maryland Antidiscrimination Act bans employers from discriminating against employees on the basis of race, age, and/or sexual orientation. Which of the following would be a violation of this law?   1.1.3

   F   An employer tells a homosexual employee that he does not approve of his lifestyle.

   G   An African-American business owner refuses an invitation to his white employee's church because it is predominantly white.

   H   An owner refuses to offer the same benefits to her Latino workers that she does to white and African-American workers because she believes that they are more likely to leave after only a few months on the job.

   J   An employee organizes a walkout at work because he and other white employees are upset by their employer's affirmative action policy.

Use the following political cartoon to answer question number 41.

41 The cartoonist is <u>most</u> concerned with which of the following issues?

  1.1.2

 A salaries in the US

 B Congress' inability to pass a minimum wage increase

 C the failure of Social Security

 D state of the US economy

GO ON

Use the following political cartoon to answer question number 42

FORUM ON CHESAPEAKE BAY AREA DEVELOPMENT

I'M SORRY, BUT WE JUST DON'T SEE HOW YOUR PLAN HAS ANY ECONOMIC BENEFIT

ZONING BOARD

Mary Stoddard
© American Book Company

42 What point is the above cartoon making?

1.1.2

   F The environment often suffers due to economic development.

   G Urban sprawl is beneficial to the Chesapeake Bay.

   H Zoning boards rarely consider the economic effects of their decisions.

   J Economics should be the top consideration when planning how to use land around the Chesapeake Bay.

43 Which agency is responsible for making sure consumer products are safe?

4.1.3

   A Federal Communications Commission (FCC)

   B Occupational Safety and Health Administration (OSHA)

   C Consumer Product Safety Commission (CPSC)

   D Federal Product Safety Department (FPSD)

44

2.2.1

BCR
   • Explain the difference between a federation and a unitary government.

   • Explain why you think one of these forms of government is better than the other.

   • Include details and examples to support your answers.

 GO ON

45 Which of the following would most likely be addressed by the United Nations?   2.1.2

- **A** corporate disputes within a European nation
- **B** free trade between the US and Canada
- **C** the threat of nuclear proliferation
- **D** selection of the prime minister within a sovereign nation

46 As more and more citizens migrate to the South and West, these regions become more important in presidential elections because   3.1.1

- **F** they are where most of the people live.
- **G** they gain influence in the Senate.
- **H** they gain votes in the Electoral College.
- **J** they are more culturally diverse.

47 Which of the following is the responsibility of the Federal Communications Commission (FCC)?   1.3

- **A** enforce copyright laws
- **B** censor newspapers
- **C** license broadcasters
- **D** monitor air transportation

> "That all government of right originates from the People, is founded in compact only, and instituted solely for the good of the whole; and they have, at all times, the inalienable right to alter, reform or abolish their Form of Government in such manner as they may deem expedient."
>
> – Article 1, Maryland Declaration of Rights

48 Which of the following principles is proclaimed by Article 1 of the Maryland Declaration of Rights?   1.1.1

- **F** legal system guaranteeing due process
- **G** checks and balances between branches of government
- **H** government established according to consent of the governed
- **J** federalism

49 The National Transportation Safety Board (NTSB) would be most likely to investigate which of the following?   4.1.3

- **A** an airplane crash
- **B** an auto accident
- **C** a robbery on the subway
- **D** misconduct by the highway patrol

GO ON

Use the chart below to answer question number 50.

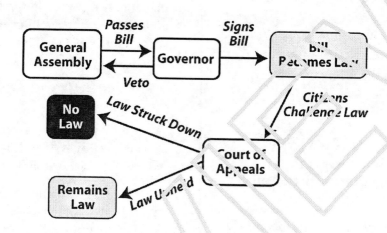

50 Which of the following conclusions can be drawn from this chart? 1.1.2

A   The governor may not serve more than two consecutive terms.

B   Checks and balances plays a key role in Maryland's state government.

C   The General Assembly must approve judicial appointments.

D   All laws must first be approved by the Maryland Court of Appeals before they may be enacted.

51 2.2.1

BCR

• What is meant by the terms "separation of powers" and "checks and balances"?

• How are these principles evident in Maryland's state government?

• Include details and examples to support your answers.

200

GO ON

| Civil Rights Advocates March on Selma | Voting Rights Act Becomes Law |
| Courts Uphold Busing | White Applicants Challenge University's Affirmative Action Policy |

Use the following sample newspaper headlines to answer question number 52.

52 The above headlines each describe events addressing   1.1.2

   F   racial discrimination.

   G   educational issues.

   H   voting rights of minorities.

   J   violations of Title IX.

53 Which one of the following would most immediately concern the Environmental Protection Agency (EPA)?   4.1.3

   A   mad cow disease

   B   an oil spill off the coast of California

   C   tornadoes in the Midwest

   D   commercial jetliner crash

Use the following political cartoon to answer question number 54.

54 What point is the above cartoon making about Social Security?

    F   It is a necessary part of the US economy.

    G   It has failed to fulfil its purpose.

    H   There may not be enough money to fund the program in the future

    J   Politicians cannot get elected without supporting Social Security.

GO ON

Use the following sample newspaper article to answer question numbers 55 and 56.

**Reeves Convicted;
Sentenced to
Twenty-five Years
for Robbery**

Baltimore — 37-year-old David Reeves was convicted yesterday of a string of armed robberies in the Baltimore area and sentenced to twenty-five years in prison...

Black Students Insist on Service at Segregated Lunch Counter

State Investigates Charges of Ageism Within Maryland Agency

Federal Government Apologizes for Japanese Internment

Higher Education Act Passed — Heralded by Feminists

55 The criminal case addressed in the news article was <u>most likely</u> tried first in the   1.1.2

   A   District Court of Maryland.
   B   Circuit Court of Maryland.
   C   Court of Special Appeals.
   D   federal court.

56 If the defendant convicted in the news story appeals, his case will <u>most likely</u> be heard next in what court?   1.1.2

   F   District Court of Maryland
   G   Circuit Court of Maryland
   H   Maryland Court of Special Appeals
   J   Maryland Court of Appeals

57 The above headlines all address the issue of   1.1.3

   A   civil rights
   B   the rights of ethnic minorities.
   C   affirmative action.
   D   segregation.

GO ON

58 **The cartoon is a statement on**

    F   the influence of interest groups.

    G   the powers of Congress.

    H   restrictions on Congress.

    J   judicial review.

STOP

Mayflower Compact, 19
McCain, John, 80
McCain-Feingold bill, 80
McCullough v. Maryland, 83
media bias, 78
Medicaid, 53
Medicare, 53
Medicare Prescription Drug, Improvement and
    Modernization Act, 53
Miranda Rights, 84
Miranda Rule, 84
Miranda v. Arizona, 84
misdemeanor, 96
mistrial, 98
mixed economies, 145
mixed economy, 144
monarchy, 108
    types of, 107
multinational conglomerate, 111
multi-party system, 72, 73

N

NAFTA (North American Free Trade Agreement), 112
National Association for the Advancement of Colored
    People (NAACP), 83
national convention, 75, 77
national debt, 150
national sovereignty, 120
National Transportation Safety Board (NTSB), 148
Native American
    discrimination, 59
    education, 60
    repatriation, 60
Native American Graves Protection and Repatriation Act
    (NAGPRA), 60
Native American Housing and Self-determination Act
    (NAHASDA), 60
NATO (North Atlantic Treaty Organization), 115
natural rights, 19
necessary and proper clause, 83
New Jersey Plan, 21
New Jersey v. TLO, 85
Nixon, Richard M., 87
No Child Left Behind Act, 60
nomination of candidates, 76
nuclear proliferation, 120
Nuclear Regulatory Commission, 66

O

oligarchy, 108
one-party system, 74
open market operations, 153
opportunity cost, 146
Organization of American States (OAS), 115

original jurisdiction, 44
Osama bin Laden, 113, 118
overseeing, 66
ozone, 54

P

Parliament, 18, 107
parliament, 18
parliamentary democracy, 107
PATRIOT Act, 88
peak (in expansion), 149
perjury, 98
Perot, Ross, 74
Persian Gulf War, 115
petit jury, 98
petition, 78
Piscataway tribe, 60
plaintiff, 96
plank (party platform), 75
platform, 75
plea bargaining, 97
Plessy v. Ferguson, 83
pocket veto, 33
political action committees (PACS), 75
political activism, 78
political campaign, 75
Political parties, 72, 73
preamble, 25
precedence, 30
preliminary hearing, 97
president
    bill, 32
    cabinet, 29
    powers of, 28
president pro tempore, 26
presidential election
    2000, 116
presumption of innocence, 98
primary elections, 76
Primary Seat Belt Law, 90
probable cause, 95, 97
propaganda, 76
proposal, 32
prosecutor, 97
prosperity, 149
public agenda, 78
public and speedy trial by jury, 35
public forum, 80
Public Works
    Board of, 42

R

radioactive waste, 54
Reagan, Ronald, 113

V

W

Product Order Form

Please fill this form out completely and fax it to 1-866-827-3240.

Purchase Order #: _____

Date: _____

Contact Person: _____

School Name (and District, if any): _____
_____

Billing Address:

Street Address: ☐ same as billing

_____

_____

Attn: _____

Attn: _____

_____

_____

_____

_____

Phone: _____

E-Mail: _____

Credit Card #: _____

Exp Date: _____

Authorized Signature: _____

Order Number	Product Title	Pricing* 10 books	Qty	Pricing 30 books	Qty	Total Cost
MD-M0407	Passing the Maryland Algebra/Data Analysis HSA	$169.90 (1 set of 10 books)		$329.70 (1 set of 30 books)		
MD-M0407	Passing the Maryland Biology HSA	$169.90 (1 set of 10 books)		$329.70 (1 set of 30 books)		
MD-M0407	Passing the Maryland English HSA	$169.90 (1 set of 10 books)		$329.70 (1 set of 30 books)		
MD-M0407	Passing the Maryland Government HSA	$169.90 (1 set of 10 books)		$329.70 (1 set of 30 books)		

10-1-08   *Minimum order is 1 set of 10 books of the same subject.

Subtotal	
Shipping & Handling 12%	
Total	

American Book Company ● PO Box 2638 ● Woodstock, GA 30188-1383
Toll Free: 1-888-264-5877 ● Fax: 1-866-827-3240 ● Web Site: www.americanbookcompany.com